# Effective

# Communication

## FOURTH EDITION

NICHOLAS HARVEY

Gill & Macmillan

Gill & Macmillan
Hume Avenue
Park West
Dublin 12
www.gillmacmillan.ie

© 2014 Nicholas Harvey
978 0 7171 5976 5
Print origination in Ireland by Carrigboy Typesetting Services

# Contents

# Preface

The fourth edition of *Effective Communication* is an update of the previous edition, taking into account the new FETAC Level 5 Communications module. It includes the latest developments in information and communications technology, a new chapter on legislation and an updated section on reading and summary-writing skills as required by the new module.

Some chapters and sections are specifically suited to FETAC assessment requirements, and others offer support, information, preparation for assessments, and/or material for class discussion. Points for discussion and activities are included in each chapter to help put some of the most essential skills into practice. This is to encourage active participation by students, and provides opportunities for expressing views and for developing speaking skills.

Further education attracts such a wide range of students of differing ages and abilities that tutors and class groups can decide for themselves how to proceed with discussions and activities in a way they feel is appropriate to their individual requirements, e.g. division into smaller groups, pairwork etc.

The book need not be read or studied in the order in which it is presented. It is possible to select and dip into chapters that are of particular interest or relevance.

Communication is not something we can become experts at in a year or two. It is a skill that can be refined over a lifetime and at the end we still won't have mastered it all. This book serves as an introduction to the main topics and themes. Oscar Wilde said, 'Nothing that is worth knowing can be taught.' Communication skills are best learned by doing, by practising and by experiencing. So take the ideas in this book and try them out by putting them into practice yourself.

The personal pronouns 'he', 'she', 'him' and 'her' are used randomly throughout the book.

# Acknowledgements

I would like to thank the following:

Jennifer Alford, Frances Gaynor, Anne Geraghty, Patrick Harvey, Niina Hepojoki, George Jacob and Thomas Riedmuller for their proofreading, useful tips and suggestions.

Staff and students at Sallynoggin College of Further Education and Kinsale College of Further Education for their support and encouragement.

Maria Raha for kind permission to reproduce her story, 'Angel'.

Marion O'Brien, Catherine Gough and Jen Patton at Gill & Macmillan for all their support and assistance.

# Part 1

## Introduction

# Chapter 1
## Introduction to Communication

## To Communicate is Human

Sometime between 50,000 and 30,000 years ago, two species of human, Cro-Magnon and Neanderthal, lived side by side in parts of Europe. According to fossil records, the Neanderthals died out around 30,000 years ago while the Cro-Magnon survived and evolved into Homo sapiens, modern humans. Some anthropologists believe that one of the reasons we survived was because of unique communication skills.

Humans are physically better equipped to communicate than most other species. We have a large brain, which can process and produce complicated language, and a tongue, jaw and throat which are shaped to produce a wider variety of sounds than other animals. We also have the urge to make contact with others. We are a social species. These abilities helped the Cro-Magnon communicate important and detailed information about survival that would have been shared with others, while the ill-equipped Neanderthals, keeping to themselves in small isolated groups, eventually became extinct. Put simply, we were better social networkers.

Fast forward to the twenty-first century and we find ourselves being bombarded by huge amounts of information coming at us via a vast array of technologies from all over the world.

The communications revolution has created an entirely new range of communication tools and techniques: the internet, email, social networking, mobile phones, texting, digital television etc. These are all changing the ways we communicate with one another and in turn we need to learn new skills to master them.

Fig. 1.1

Just as communication helped our species survive in the past, it seems it can still help us survive today's fast-paced technology-driven world. Information is a key to this survival. In order to have access to the latest information, be it about jobs, health, education, business, shopping, entertainment, or just social contact with others, we need to have good communication skills.

However, for all the marvels of technology that enable us to speak instantly to someone thousands of miles away, we are often still at a loss as to how to actually express ourselves. When it comes down to saying what we really want to say, we often find ourselves in a mess of muddled words and jumbled sentences. Words we use amongst our close friends won't necessarily impress a potential employer. We can't use words like 'cool' or 'crap' in an interview or a formal letter of complaint because we won't be taken seriously. The abbreviated language we use in emails and text messages is fine for informal situations, but we can't write 'I cn a1od an ntrvu @ ne time,' in a letter of application!

We can use the technologies available to us but we also need the skills to know what to say, how to say it and when it is appropriate to say it. The more ways we can communicate, the better equipped we are to deal with the modern world.

Communication and language are uniquely human traits. In a sense, learning how to communicate is about becoming more human. Some people have a natural flair for it and others don't. But no matter how good or bad we think we are as communicators, all communication skills can be learned and improved.

# What Is Communication?

The word 'communication' comes from the Latin word *communicare*, which means to share, impart or make common. How well we communicate is often determined by how easily we can share or impart information or find common ground with other people.

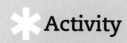

## Activity

What other words in English derive from the Latin *communicare*? Make a list and discuss the various meanings of each word. These might give us a fuller understanding of the meaning of the word 'communication'.

Communication is an active process that is forever changing. Language doesn't stay the same. It evolves and we don't use the same English today that Shakespeare did. Almost every time we speak we somehow put together a collection of words that we have never used before. When two people are put together, eventually they are going to start communicating with each other, and neither has any idea where they will end up. A frightening thought, perhaps, but an exciting one as well.

We can define communication as an exchange of messages between two people or two groups of people.

# Why Do We Communicate?

In their book *More than Words*, Richard Dimbleby and Graeme Burton list twelve needs and purposes of communication.

## Survival

We need to communicate to buy food and clothing; rent or buy accommodation; seek help from others if we are sick or in danger, all of which are necessary for survival.

## Co-operation

We communicate for the purpose of trade; to exchange ideas and information; for the enjoyment of interaction or just to get on with other people.

## Personal Needs

As humans we have a basic need for contact with others. Exchanging thoughts and feelings can help satisfy our personal needs.

## Relationships

Relationships are formed and sustained by communication. Problems that occur within relationships are often a result of a lack of communication. One of the best ways to sort out problems is by talking about them.

## Persuasion

In our everyday communication with others we may use persuasion more than we think. Whether we are trying to convince potential employers that we are the best person for the job, persuading a college teacher to give us a deadline extension or trying to borrow money we are using persuasion to get what we want.

## Power

We communicate for power by winning arguments and by impressing others with our knowledge and skill as communicators. More negatively, we can misuse it by making others feel inferior by putting them down.

## Societal Needs

Communication within and between all the different organisations in our society is crucial for it to function properly. Government departments, schools, colleges, hospitals and businesses would collapse without proper communication facilities to help run them.

## Economy

Buying and selling cannot take place without some form of communication between the buyer and the seller. Advertising also plays a role in this process.

## Information

Information is fundamental to human existence. It may be something as simple as reading a sell-by date on a food item or being told the time. Gossip is information, although it may not always be accurate! We send emails and letters to let friends and relatives know how we are and what we're doing. The media inform us about people and events in the world and advertising informs us about products. What we learn at school and college – education – is all information.

## Making Sense of the World

Children are naturally inquisitive. They often ask questions beginning with 'Why?' in order to make sense of the world around them. As adults we also ask similar questions when we need to understand something and to give events and situations meaning.

## Decision-making

When a couple talk about what to do on a date they are making a decision. When a company holds a board meeting to discuss the potential of a new product it is making decisions.

## Self-expression

When we are involved in the creative process, we communicate by tapping into the imagination and expressing ourselves in an artistic way:
1. Visual – painting, drawing, sculpture etc.
2. Writing – poetry, stories etc.
3. Music
4. Dance
5. Body adornment – make-up, jewellery etc.
6. Drama.

 **Activity**

Which of the twelve needs and purposes are being used in the following messages?

1. You only got a merit in Communications? I got a distinction.

2. Of course she should have left him years ago. That's what I always said.

3. Here, I've made you a nice cup of tea. Sit down there and relax.

4. She won't be left behind. She's got the brand new BTXL503.

5. You have the most beautiful eyes I've ever seen.

6. Please may I have a drink of water?

7. This is the third time you've been late for work this week.

8. How do you feel now?

9. 'Teachers to go on strike!'

10. Don't count your chickens before they hatch.

11. I will send you the goods as requested.

12. 'Strawberry Fields forever.'

13. No, let's not go to the cinema; let's just have a drink.

14. Someone left the milk out of the fridge again.

15. The telephone is ringing.

16. We'll make you an offer you can't refuse.

17. Can you spare some money for a sandwich?

## Discussion

In groups of four or five make a list of the specific communication skills you think you might need for your chosen vocation.

Now make a list of the communication skills you would like to improve for your own personal needs.

# ▶ How Do We Communicate?

Every time some form of communication occurs, there is a specific process that takes place. We can break this process down into its different parts so that we can see what exactly is happening and identify any problems that can occur. By doing this we can try to eliminate these problems and become better communicators. Keywords are in italics.

A *sender* (a person or persons) sends a *message* (information, thought, feeling etc.) to a *receiver* (another person or persons).

The message is encoded, *code* being the language used by the sender. It may refer to the actual language that we speak, e.g. English, Irish etc. or it can refer to verbal, e.g. spoken and written language, or nonverbal, e.g. body-language, facial expression, signals etc. It can also mean tone of voice.

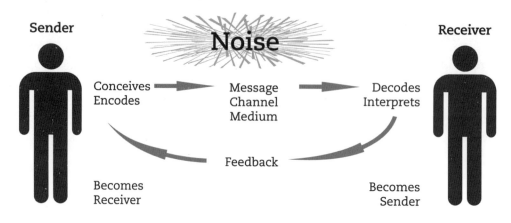

*Fig. 1.2 The communication process*

The *message* is transmitted by a *medium*, e.g. face-to-face, telephone, email, letter etc., and travels along a *channel*, e.g. telephone line, postal system etc.

The *receiver* receives the message and decodes it, i.e. makes sense of it. Some messages are literal. Others can contain implied meanings that may be misinterpreted. In this case the receiver may also have to *interpret* the message for other meanings. 'Do you want to come back to my place for coffee?' literally means an offer of coffee. What is its implied meaning?

The receiver gives *feedback* by sending another message back to the sender to reply or to acknowledge receipt of the first message. Feedback is vital in communication. Without it the sender has no idea if the message has been received, never mind if it has been met with agreement or not. Feedback can be either positive (supporting or agreeing with the message) or negative (criticising or disagreeing with the message).

Once feedback has been given, the process may continue with another message from sender to receiver, and so on, and the roles may swap so that the receiver becomes sender and sender becomes receiver.

*Noise* is any kind of interference that interrupts or prevents the successful transmission of the message. It can be:

▶ Physical – e.g. roadworks outside a building interrupting a conversation
▶ Emotional – e.g. mistrust between the sender and receiver interfering with the message

*Fig. 1.3 The language code!*

▶ Psychological – e.g. a receiver who is tired finding it difficult to take in a lengthy, complicated message

▶ Technological – e.g. fear of computers preventing some people using them to communicate.

The *context* is the situation in which the communication takes place. It usually refers to the time and place, but may also include the people involved. The context can influence the way we communicate. Communication in a work context is likely to be more formal than it would be in a nightclub.

Now we have looked at the process of communication, try to think of some of the pitfalls that could occur at each stage of the process. For example, at the encoding stage a sender might use an inappropriate level of vocabulary, which the receiver might not understand.

 ## Activity

### 1. One-way communication

A volunteer from the group will be the sender of a message and the rest will be the receivers. The sender stands at the back of the room, chooses one of the shapes in Appendix 1 of the book, and tries to describe it using words only. The receivers, who are not allowed to speak, will try to draw the shapes from the sender's description. The sender should not see what the receivers are drawing.

### 2. Two-way communication

Do the same activity as above, except this time the sender stands at the front of the room, facing the receivers, the receivers may speak and ask questions.

The purpose of this activity is to illustrate that in order for communication to be effective it has to be a two-way process. In the first part (one-way), there was incomplete communicating going on as no feedback was permitted. The two-way communication probably took longer, but the message will have been more accurately transmitted. Discuss any problems and difficulties experienced by both senders and receivers during this activity. A sender often makes the mistake of assuming the receiver knows more than he actually does. Communicators sometimes fail to realise that a sent and a received message are not always the same. This is one common cause of communication breakdown.

# The Media of Communication

We can put all types of communication into five media groups:

1. Written
2. Spoken
3. Visual
4. Technological
5. Mass Media.

## Discussion

Divide into groups of four or five. Each group should take one medium of communication and make a list of four or five examples of that medium. Then make a list of its advantages and disadvantages. Some examples may belong to more than one group. Television, for example, can make use of all five, but might best belong to Mass Media.

# Media Appropriateness

Some of the worst mistakes in communication are made as a result of using an inappropriate medium. There is no point in a company informing all its shareholders about a new business venture by telephone. It would be too time-consuming. A famous film star once finished his relationship with his girlfriend by sending her a fax. Is this an appropriate medium for this type of communication?

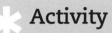

# Activity

What media of communication would you choose for the following and why?

1. Applying for a job
2. Firing someone from a job
3. Complaining about a holiday to a travel agent
4. Offering sympathy to the family (living abroad) of a friend who has died
5. Explaining a personal problem to your boss
6. Requesting information about different types of bank account
7. Asking customers to switch off mobile phones as they enter a theatre
8. Advertising a new leisure complex in a hotel
9. Asking for a bank loan
10. Informing a colleague that you resent his/her offensive behaviour
11. Telling the board of directors of a company your new marketing strategy
12. Informing your class teacher that you are sick on the day of an assignment deadline
13. Advertising a concert you've organised in your local community hall
14. Letting colleagues (ten or more) know about a meeting to be held the following week
15. Sending a list of costs and rates of the hotel you work in to a potential customer arriving in Ireland from Italy in two days
16. Asking someone out to dinner
17. Seeking a quote for paper and ink for your printers
18. A tutor giving students important information about an assignment – explanation, number of words required, deadline etc.
19. Complaining to a neighbour about persistent noise late at night
20. An electrician supplying a quote
21. Letting students in college know about the Christmas Social
22. Resigning from your job

23. Informing a client that their payment for goods received is overdue

24. Finding information on the latest cinema releases

25. Complaining to your boss about the extra hours that you've been asked to do

26. Finding out the latest football results

27. Relaying a detailed phone message to your employer.

# A Guide to Effective Communication

Here are some tips for improving communication skills in general.

## As Sender

### Conceive the message carefully

Decide what your communication objectives are. Do you want to inform, entertain, impress, persuade or get information? Aim for clarity and avoid vagueness, ambiguity and unnecessary jargon.

### Have Empathy

This means understanding where the receiver is coming from, her beliefs, feelings, values and interests. Put yourself in the receiver's shoes. She may not see things the way you do.

### Choose an Appropriate Code and Medium

Choose a code that the receiver understands and a tone that is appropriate. We wouldn't use the same tone talking to our employer as we would to a child. For medium, see activity above.

### Consider the Context (Time and Place)

An attempt to communicate with someone who is too busy to listen to us will inevitably fail. Reprimanding someone for a misdemeanour should take place somewhere private and not in a public place in front of others.

### Check for Feedback

As a sender it is vital to know that the message has been received and understood. Ask if it's OK.

## As Receiver

### Pay Attention

Many messages are lost due to poor listening or lack of concentration.

### Decode Correctly

Make sure you understand the message and if not, seek clarification. Be aware of implied meanings in messages.

Ask yourself these questions:

▶ Does this make sense?

▶ Does this person have an agenda?

▶ What do I think of this person?

### Give Feedback

Always let the sender know you've received and understood the message. A simple nod or 'Yes' is often enough to show the sender you've got the message.

## ✱ Activity

Think of two examples of communication you took part in during the past 24 hours. In each case write down the following:

1. The purpose of each communication

2. If you were the sender or receiver

3. If the message was well conceived

4. The choice of code, medium and channel

5. The context in which each took place

6. The feedback given

7. Whether there was any noise

8. Whether each communication was successful

9. Whether there was room for improvement.

# Chapter Review

1. What makes communication a uniquely human experience?
2. What are the chief purposes of communication?
3. Outline the main stages in the communication process.
4. Explain the importance of feedback.
5. Why is it important to choose the appropriate medium for communication?
6. Explain the following:
   - Code
   - Channel
   - Noise
   - Context.

# Discussion

1. When do we not communicate?
2. Are we better or worse communicators than our parents?
3. One of the biggest communication problems is that we don't communicate enough.
4. Discuss how a lack of communication might be harmful to the following:
   - Personal relationships/marriages
   - Between employers and employees
   - Amongst employees
   - In the home
   - Between a food company and the public
   - Between staff and students at school/college
   - Between the government and the public
   - Between a doctor and patient.
5. Is there ever a danger of too much communication?

# Chapter 2
## Perception and Culture

## ▶ Perception

Before children can speak or even understand words, they begin to make sense of the world around them by means of perception. They perceive the world through the fives senses of sight, hearing, smell, taste and touch. As adults we continue to make sense of the world by perception. We can say that perception is the way in which we select, organise and interpret information about the world around us.

Fig. 2.1 'The wife and the mother-in-law'
by W.E. Hill

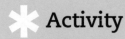 **Activity**

Look at the picture on page 15.

Describe what you see. Do you see a young woman or an old woman? There are two possible ways of seeing the picture. The chin of the young woman becomes the nose of an old woman.

## Sensory variation

The problem with perception is, first, that our senses are not 100 per cent reliable. Railway tracks appear to get narrower as they get further away; a straight stick appears to bend in water; an ambulance siren changes tone as it moves past us. Second, we all perceive things slightly differently from one another. Some people have better sight than others. A ferociously hot curry to one person may be mild to another. Deafening music to one person may be too quiet to another. This is called sensory variation.

 ## Discussion

Our perception influences how we communicate and if we perceive things differently from others, we may run into communication problems. Discuss how you think this might occur.

## Selection

We don't perceive everything that is going on around us, otherwise we would be bombarded by unnecessary information. So we only select what we need at a particular moment and the rest we filter out. Think of things you notice on the way to college. Now consider the amount of information you don't notice. What do you perceive where you are sitting right now? Why do we select some things and fail to notice others?

Once we've perceived and selected something, we organise it to make sense of it, matching it with what we already know, understand or believe. This depends on our experience of life. If, as a child, we had the experience of being bitten by a dog, the next time we see a dog we might perceive it as being a threat. If, however, our experience of dogs is that they are friendly animals, whenever we see one we will probably perceive it in a more positive way. Since we all have different experiences we won't always agree on what something *means*, and this can naturally lead to communication difficulties.

## Activity

Take two or three advertisements or photographs from a magazine or newspaper. Discuss what they mean to you.

## Discussion

It is possible to train the senses to become more effective. Visually impaired people may develop better hearing, smell and sense of touch than people who can see. Certain occupations need well-trained senses. Can you think of a few?

### People Perception

The most important type of perception for a course in communication is people perception.

## Discussion

We perceive people initially through their appearance: size, hair, clothes, skin, etc. What is the problem with this?

When we meet people initially, we perceive them based on their appearance and the role they are playing, and we match it to our own expectations and experience. We begin to weigh them up and make assumptions about them. We categorise them and put them in a 'box' based on our perception. Categorising is a useful tool as it enables us to label things and make sense of the world. Unfortunately, people are far more complex than things and we cannot use such a simple system of classification for perceiving them. The worst kind of categorising is stereotyping.

## ❱ Stereotyping

As a simple and convenient way of trying to understand the world, stereotyping can be useful. We stereotype objects, situations and people based on how we think they will live up to our expectations of them. Sometimes our expectations are accurate and sometimes they aren't. Stereotypes are generalisations, sometimes based on facts that are generally true about a group. They can also be based upon assumptions instead of facts.

# Discussion

Make a list of common stereotypes. They may be based on physical appearance, occupation, gender, age, nationality/ethnicity or religious beliefs. In groups of three or four, make a list of characteristics of one stereotype group. Which characteristics are based on fact and which are based on perception? Which are stereotypes? Share your results with the whole group.

## Iceberg Analogy

People perception is problematic because it is based on only a fraction of the whole person. Just as we can only see approximately 10 per cent of an iceberg, so when we initially perceive someone we only see 10 per cent of them.

Fig. 2.2

# ▶ Prejudice

Prejudice is our attitude towards a group or individual without having adequate knowledge of either and stemming from a stereotype, preconceived opinion or inaccurate perception. However, as the old saying goes: we can't judge a book by its cover.

Perception and communication are very much intertwined. On the one hand, perception influences how we communicate, for example, if we perceive someone as being authoritative and we admire them we'll probably communicate with them in a respectful way. If we perceive someone as being stupid or worthless we will probably communicate with them less than respectfully! On the other hand, communication influences our perception of others. The way someone talks, their accent, their articulation, their pitch and tone of voice can often shape our opinion and our perception of them.

 ## For Reflection

Next time you meet someone, pay attention to the way you perceive him. Do you perceive him as a potential friend or not, based on his appearance? Do you focus purely on his appearance or do you try to get to know the other 90 per cent? If you don't like his appearance, will this prevent you from trying to get to know him? Do you stereotype based on appearance/accent?

 ## Discussion

Describe an occasion when your initial perceptions of someone were totally wrong.

Fig. 2.3 People perception

What are your first impressions of the people in the photographs in Figure 2.3? Explain why.

# ❱ Culture

Culture is the set of beliefs, values, understandings, practices and ways of making sense of the world that are shared by a group of people. Culture is not static or fixed. It is constantly changing and evolving, adopting new practices and customs and losing old ones. The culture in which we are brought up determines our thinking, our behaviour, our perceptions and how we communicate.

## Discussion

Make a list of Irish cultural characteristics. How many of them are stereotypes? What other Irish stereotypes are there? How do non-Irish members of the class group perceive Irish cultural values and norms? In what ways do you think Irish culture has changed over the past twenty years?

## ✱ Activity

Individually, write down three ways you think you fit your cultural stereotype and three ways you don't. Discuss as a class group.

When we speak about Irish culture we often think of Celtic influences, because the Irish language is a Celtic language. However, Irish culture is a mixture of pre-Celtic, Celtic, Viking, Norman, English, Scottish and American cultural influences. Today, many people from all over Europe, Africa and Asia have come to live in Ireland, adding to the already interesting mixture. Ireland is a multicultural society, and this cultural diversity is a source of richness for society.

In such a culturally diverse world, we come into contact with people with hugely different experiences and backgrounds from our own in terms of their ethnic group, religious beliefs, skin colour, sexual orientation etc. To avoid misunderstandings we need to be aware of the differences in how they communicate.

## Discussion

In what ways do people from different cultural backgrounds communicate differently?

How we communicate with each other defines the culture to which we belong and in turn, our culture determines how we communicate. The language and expressions we use every day reveal our cultural origins, for example, 'I'm after eating my tea,' is English but is also a direct translation of an Irish idiom, and would not be found in other English-speaking countries. This is sometimes called Hiberno-English.

# Discussion

1. What other expressions and words are peculiar to Ireland? Would a visitor from another culture find it easy to understand these expressions even if she spoke English?

2. Proverbs, sayings and clichés illustrate how communication can define culture. Think of some Irish proverbs, sayings or clichés that underpin aspects of Irish culture. What do they say about the values and beliefs of Irish culture? For example, 'May you be in heaven half an hour before the devil knows you're dead,' shows the traditional Irish belief in heaven and the devil and perhaps the value of trickery. Non-Irish students in the class group could share their own proverbs.

# ▶ Social Communities

A minority culture can also exist within a larger dominant culture. Such groups of people are called social communities. Social communities may be defined by countries of origin, for example the Romanian community in Ireland, but also by their different ways of communicating and behaving.

# Discussion

1. Make a list of social communities that exist in Ireland today. They may be based on:
   ▶ Ethnicity
   ▶ Religious beliefs
   ▶ Skin colour
   ▶ Sexual orientation
   ▶ Social class
   ▶ Age
   ▶ Special needs
   ▶ Gender.

2. Consider your own identity. Write down a list of the social communities you belong to based on the above guidelines.

3. Have you ever experienced prejudice because of your particular culture or social community? Discuss your experience with your class group.

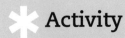

## Activity

Our language is full of words and phrases that can be hurtful and offensive to minority social communities. Make a list of these terms as they might apply to:

▶ Travellers
▶ Homosexuals
▶ Blacks
▶ Asians
▶ Elderly people
▶ Jews
▶ Muslims
▶ Protestants
▶ Catholics

Consider the origins and meanings of the words and phrases you associate with them.

Fig. 2.4

What is the purpose of the advertisement in Figure 2.4? Do you think it works? Why?

'Handicapped' is a term that was once used to describe people with special needs. It is now considered offensive because it refers to begging – 'cap in hand' – which is how many survived in former times.

## ▶ Xenophobia (pronounced 'zen')

Xenophobia is the fear and dislike of strangers. In primitive times this was useful because it lessened the likelihood of being captured or killed by rival tribes.

## ▶ Ethnocentrism

Ethnocentrism is the belief that our own culture or ethnic group is at the centre of the world, is normal or even superior and that others are strange or inferior.

# ▶ Race and Ethnicity

*Fig. 2.5 Chain prejudice*

The term 'race' has now become discredited as a word used to describe groups of people based on physical, biological or ideological differences. The acceptance of the term 'race' has been used to justify racism, in which one group believes it is superior to others and tries to dominate, suppress or even destroy them. The word 'ethnicity' has replaced 'race', so we talk about an ethnic group as being one that has a common identity based on a shared culture, history, ancestry and geographical origin.

# ▶ Sectarianism

Sectarianism is prejudice against people who belong to a different sect, or religious denomination. In Ireland this has particular resonance, because intolerance has for many years been displayed between some individuals belonging to the Roman Catholic Church and some from the Protestant Church. To many observers, it is ironic because both belong to the same Christian religion.

Sectarianism occurs in many parts of the world where groups with different religious beliefs live next to each other.

We can reduce ethnocentrism, racism and sectarianism by understanding that cultures vary in their beliefs, values and behaviour, and no one culture is the normal or right one. For example, we might find it strange that Jewish people don't eat pork or that Hindus don't eat beef. But the French might find it odd that we don't eat horse meat. Some might find it peculiar that there are people who don't eat any meat at all.

*Fig. 2.6 The Chuckle Brothers: successful intercultural communication. Two politicians from either side of the political and religious divide overcame their differences when forced to share power in the Northern Ireland Assembly. The Rev. Ian Paisley and Martin McGuinness were frequently seen laughing heartily together during their public appearances, which earned them the nickname 'The Chuckle Brothers'.*

# ▶ Gender

The words 'gender' and 'sex' are often used interchangeably, but whereas sex relates to biological differences, gender refers to what society considers to be appropriate masculine and feminine behaviour at a given time. For example, in Irish society it is generally considered inappropriate for businessmen to wear skirts. Different cultures would have different norms regarding gender behaviour. However, it is possible for a woman to exhibit behaviour and communication traits traditionally considered to be masculine, even though she belongs to the female sex, and vice versa.

# ▶ Sexism

Sexism is discrimination of a person on the grounds of his/her sex.

## Discussion

Discuss examples of communication that you consider to be racist, sectarian or sexist.

# Socialisation

Socialisation is the process by which we learn to fit in to our society and culture and the rules and expectations that govern each of those. We learn through relationships and experience how to behave appropriately in a variety of situations and communication is a vital part of that process.

Studies have shown that in Western society boys and girls are socialised differently in the games they play. Girls tend to play games that involve co-operation and talk such as house and school. Boys usually are more competitive and action-orientated and play at war and team sports.

These rules of play often continue later in life and women tend to communicate more expressively, talk about feelings and relationships and tend to see talking as vital in making and sustaining relationships. Men are usually more competitive in their communication, focusing on tasks and activities, preferring to do things with their friends and partners.

It must be stressed that the following differences between feminine and masculine communication traits don't apply solely to women and men respectively. Most people would have a mixture from each list and this is perfectly normal and sometimes preferable. Some men might even display more feminine ways of communication than women and some women may communicate more masculine traits than men. It is important here not to fall into the trap of stereotyping.

*Feminine communication in general:*

- Includes and shows interest in others
- Is co-operative
- Observes turn-taking in speech
- Is responsive to what others say
- Uses talk expressively – talk deals with feelings, personal ideas and problems, and is used to build relationships with others
- Seeks approval in an attempt to be liked by others
- Is better in private conversations and dialogue
- Asks questions to make connections, to lessen the potential for disagreement and to seek information that shows respect for another's knowledge.

*Masculine communication in general:*

- Is self-assertive and competitive
- Uses talk to establish identity, expertise and knowledge, to prove oneself, to seek status and maintain independence
- Uses talk to gain and hold attention, to take the talk stage from others, interrupt and reroute topics to keep the focus on oneself and one's ideas

- Uses talk instrumentally – talk accomplishes something such as solving a problem, giving advice, or taking a stand on issues
- Involves stories and jokes in an attempt to be the funniest, cleverest etc.
- Is better in public situations and monologue
- Doesn't like to ask questions as it shows a lack of self-sufficiency and independence and a loss of face
- Asks questions as a way of arguing.

(Adapted from Julia Wood *Communication in Our Lives*, p.91)

In positions of leadership, women tend to downplay their authority by seeking feedback, asking questions and expressing more doubt than men. They are unlikely to draw attention to their achievements or to their trappings of success as much as men. Compared to men, they will praise others more, apologise and accept blame more. As leaders, men generally downplay their faults and weaknesses, and see how another's position of power might affect their power.

Both feminine and masculine ways of communicating are equally valid, and neither is right or wrong. By being aware of these differences and by practising some of the styles of communication of the opposite gender we can avoid many misunderstandings.

We often experience pressure to conform to standards of masculinity and femininity, so that men are sometimes afraid of appearing effeminate and women of being 'butch'. However, the most effective communicators are equally comfortable using both ways of communicating.

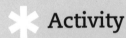

## Activity

Are the following typically masculine or feminine statements?

1. I'm sorry to hear about your illness. How are you feeling now?

2. So you lost your bet on the game. I won €70.

3. I'm going to apply for that managerial job. Do you think I have a chance?

4. Nice hat. Pity about the colour. Check mine out.

5. You've had your hair done. It's gorgeous!

6. I've been feeling very vulnerable lately.

7. I've always said that economic growth wouldn't last that long and I was right.

8. I like the shape of the windows – what do you think?

9. In my view, they're the best band around at the moment – no argument.

10. I'm sorry about the way I went on last night. I won't do it again.

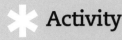

## Activity

In social and vocational situations observe a group of people having a conversation/discussion and note the gender differences in communication styles.

## For Reflection

Observe yourself in social and vocational situations and how you interact with different groups of people. Do you exhibit predominantly masculine or feminine ways of communication?

# ◗ Improving Intercultural Communication

Most of us spend most of the time with people from our own culture and social communities. We can communicate easily in these groups because we have shared understandings about appropriate language and behaviour. When we encounter people from other social and cultural groups we don't have the same guidelines. Researchers have come up with a process, which consists of five levels of response to cultural diversity. It can help develop an awareness of other cultures and minimise misunderstandings. It can take time to go from one stage to the next and some people will take to it more quickly and easily than others. Ultimately, it should reduce our ethnocentrism and improve our intercultural communication skills.

## 1. Resistance

This occurs when we regard other cultures' practices as being inferior to our own.  Level one is recognising our own ethnocentrism. We might believe our culture is the best, but that is merely an opinion, not a fact.

## 2. Tolerance

This is when we accept and tolerate differences of other groups, even though we might not understand or approve of them. We may still assume our ways are the standard and that others are somehow inferior. Level two is avoiding criticism of other cultures.

### 3. Understanding

At this stage we attempt to understand the values and beliefs of other cultures because we realise that there are various reasons why some social communities have different practices from our own.

### 4. Respect

At this level we begin to see others for what they are and appreciate their differences. If we show respect for people from other cultures, they will do the same to us.

### 5. Participation

The final level in this process is when we actively participate in some activity of another culture. We become 'multilingual' in that we can communicate with a variety of social communities without losing our own identity. Many immigrants in Ireland are already bilingual in that they can speak their own language but in order to fit in to the dominant culture they have learned English. At this stage we can focus on individual people, not cultures. Each culture is made up of individuals who all think and behave differently from one another. They won't all conform to stereotypes!

 **For Reflection**

Consider at which level you operate and try to progress to the next level.

By remaining stuck in our own culture's way of living we not only miss out on the richness of life but we also maintain a very narrow way of communicating. At some point we are going to meet people very different from ourselves and we need to be able to communicate with them comfortably and effectively.

Due to the power that language can have, some say it can be misused to legitimise dominant cultures and to label other cultures as inferior. Political correctness refers to language and behaviour that avoids causing offence to social communities and disadvantaged people. Whereas many of these terms succeed and are appropriate, many are over the top and even bizarre. Many people find 'male nurse' and 'lady doctor' offensive. In Ireland 'Travellers' has replaced 'itinerants' and 'tinkers'. Members of a group have a right to be called by a collective name with which they are comfortable.

# Discussion

What groups do you think the following terms apply to?

▶ African American
▶ Visually impaired
▶ Follicly challenged
▶ Socially misaligned
▶ Senior citizens
▶ Native American
▶ Flight attendants
▶ Vocally challenged
▶ Utensil sanitizer
▶ Non-human companions.

Can you explain the reason for the above words? Which do you find appropriate and which are over the top? What about the use of 'person' instead of 'man' as a suffix, e.g. chairperson, postperson, fireperson? Think of other examples and discuss whether you find them appropriate or not.

## Chapter Review

1. Explain how misperception can lead to communication problems.
2. Explain the role of sensory variation in the process of perception.
3. What does selection mean?
4. What is the significance of stereotyping in relation to perception?
5. What is culture? How does it affect the way we perceive and communicate?
6. Explain the concept of socialisation.
7. What is a social community?
8. What are the main differences between the way men and women communicate?
9. Explain the following:
   ▶ Cultural diversity
   ▶ Xenophobia
   ▶ Ethnocentrism
   ▶ Racism.
10. Outline the five stages for reducing ethnocentrism and improving intercultural skills.

# Part 2

## Listening and Speaking

### Some Examples

- Conversations
- Discussions
- Debates
- Interviews
- Meetings
- Classes
- Presentations
- Speeches
- Announcements

### Advantages

- Direct
- Personal
- Good for expression of feeling and tone
- Instant feedback
- Easier to convince/persuade
- All present can contribute
- Good for negotiations
- Inexpensive

### Disadvantages

- No written record
- Possibility of dispute
- Difficult to control
- Little time to prepare

# Chapter 3
## Listening Skills

'Most people do not listen with the intent to understand; they listen with the intent to reply.'

*Stephen R. Covey*

We should not underestimate the importance of listening as a communication skill. Most people listen to about 25 per cent capacity. In other words, they lose or misinterpret 75 per cent of the information they receive. Poor listening can result in anything from the loss of business or falling out with a friend or partner to industrial or international disputes.

# ✳ Activity

Look at the following statements and tick the boxes that apply to you.

| Statement | Usually | Sometimes | Seldom |
|---|:---:|:---:|:---:|
| 1 I keep eye contact with the speaker when I am listening. | ☐ | ☐ | ☐ |
| 2 When I am listening, I just listen to the facts. | ☐ | ☐ | ☐ |
| 3 I am easily distracted by other stimuli (e.g. mobile phone) when I am listening. | ☐ | ☐ | ☐ |
| 4 I interrupt the speaker. | ☐ | ☐ | ☐ |
| 5 When I am listening, I think about what I am going to say next. | ☐ | ☐ | ☐ |
| 6 I ask questions in order to gain clarification. | ☐ | ☐ | ☐ |
| 7 I stop listening when I am put off by the speaker's voice, accent or appearance. | ☐ | ☐ | ☐ |
| 8 I listen to part of the speaker's story and then I interrupt with my own story. | ☐ | ☐ | ☐ |
| 9 I listen out for the feelings behind the words. | ☐ | ☐ | ☐ |
| 10 I daydream easily when I am listening. | ☐ | ☐ | ☐ |
| 11 I just pretend I am listening. | ☐ | ☐ | ☐ |
| 12 I only listen to what interests me. | ☐ | ☐ | ☐ |
| 13 I listen to the full message before giving my response. | ☐ | ☐ | ☐ |

Which of the statements are positive listening habits and which are negative listening habits? Discuss.

Listening consists of three components:
1. Hearing – the ability to perceive sounds
2. Understanding – the ability to make sense of those sounds
3. Retaining – the ability to remember what has been heard.

# Listening and Hearing

Listening is a skill of perception that helps us make sense of the world. Like perception, we select what we want to listen to. From where you are sitting now, concentrate for a few moments on all of the sounds you can hear and make a note of them. How many of them were you actually aware of without concentrating on them? Probably very few. How many of them could you make sense of? All of them? This illustrates the difference between listening and

Fig. 3.1

hearing. We can *hear* many things going on around us but it is only when we *make sense* of them and *understand* them that we are *listening* to them. It isn't practical to listen to everything we can hear. It would also be exhausting. Listening is an active skill, which requires a certain amount of concentration, whereas hearing is passive. Effective listening isn't always easy, but it is a skill that can be learned.

# Types of Listening

### Informational Listening

This involves listening for information, for facts, times, names, places etc. It is the most common type of listening that we do most of the time.

### Critical Listening

Critical listening entails making judgements, evaluations and forming opinions about a speaker's ideas. A teacher evaluates a student's oral presentation by listening critically for signs of careful preparation, structure, accurate information and good expression.

### Relational Listening

Relational listening refers to the empathising we do when, for example, we are listening to a friend discuss his problems or worries. Relational listening often involves trying to understand another's feelings and interpreting signs that are hidden behind the information we hear.

### Listening for Pleasure

Listening for pleasure is what we do when we play a CD, go to a concert, poetry reading or comedy show. This normally doesn't need too much concentration unless we want to focus on specifics like a lyric or a drum beat in a song.

### Listening to Discriminate

This is what a mechanic does when fine-tuning an engine, detecting the subtle difference in sounds, or when parents decide if a child's crying is due to hunger, discomfort, a need for attention or a nappy change.

### Listening to Interpret

This means we can make sense of the words we hear and really understand what the speaker is saying. Interpreting also means we can summarise the message and rephrase it in another way.

## Activity

This is a good activity for breaking the ice when a class has first met. Students stand in a circle and the first one says his/her name and answers one of these questions:

▶ What was your favourite subject at school?
▶ Where would you like to go on your next holiday?
▶ What are your goals for the future?

He/she then throws a soft ball to another student who says his/her name and answers one of the three questions. Continue until everyone has introduced themselves and answered a question. Sit down again and try and write the names of all of your classmates and any other information they provided. How easy/difficult was it to focus/listen/remember names and information?

## ▶ Barriers to Listening

To try to improve our listening techniques, we must first isolate the problems that prevent us from listening. Here are some of the most common ones:

▶ Poor physical or mental state, e.g. hunger, cold, exhaustion, anxiety
▶ Lack of interest in the speaker or subject
▶ Prejudice about the speaker's appearance, accent, command of the language
▶ Prejudice about the subject, e.g. 'I disagree with her views so why should I bother paying attention?'
▶ Noise and distractions from the surrounding environment
▶ Daydreaming and thinking of things from the recent past or immediate future, e.g. 'She shouldn't have said that to me at break,' or 'I'm going to have the pasta for lunch.'
▶ Inability to understand what the speaker is saying

- The speaker's speed, e.g. too slow and we may get bored; too fast and we may not be able to follow what is being said
- The message is too complex or unclear
- Poor attention span. With increasing use of TV and the internet our attention spans are decreasing. While the average person can comfortably concentrate for up to 20 minutes, the average time spent by an internet user on a website is less than one minute. There are also particular times of the day when we may find it harder or easier to concentrate – some people are morning people, others are more alert at night
- Impatience.

## Activity

Look at the list below. Imagine you have to listen to each of the people on the list and try honestly to assess your listening ability using a scale of one (very poor) to ten (excellent) in each case:

- Your boss giving you instructions
- Someone you're trying to impress telling you about himself/herself
- A teacher you like (in class)
- A teacher you don't like (in class)
- A reprimanding parent
- A child telling you about his day at school
- A friend telling you about a personal problem
- A tourist asking for directions
- A very funny comedian
- Someone you are arguing with
- Someone complimenting you
- Someone explaining the current political/economic situation to you
- Someone giving you directions

Discuss the results. Why did you give greater scores to some than others?

## Activity

Brainstorm with your class and list several different conversation topics on the board/flipchart. Sit in groups of 7–10 people. Place an item such as a stick, box or ball in the centre of the circle. Participants can only speak when holding the item: everybody else must remain silent and listen. While holding the item, the student must talk on one of the conversation topics for one minute. Then they return the item to the centre of the circle. The next student may respond on the same topic or start a new conversation topic. Continue until everyone has spoken.

▶ What was it like to listen to the others without interrupting?
▶ What was it like to speak and be listened to?
▶ Was it easy to tune in or did you occasionally tune out?
▶  How much information do you remember?

## ▶ Selective Listening

We tend to pick and choose to whom and to what we want to listen. For the most part, we give our attention to people and subjects that we are interested in. Or we focus on individuals and things that can benefit us, and the rest we frequently ignore. However, when we're listening to important messages that need to be passed on to someone else, we have to select the important information and omit the rest.

## ▶ Active Listening

By giving the speaker verbal feedback (e.g. saying 'Yes' or 'Okay') or nonverbal feedback (e.g. making eye contact or saying 'Mmm', 'Uhuh') we are not only helping ourselves to focus and listen better, but we are also encouraging the speaker to speak better. This is active listening.

## ✳ Activity

Divide the class into pairs of A and B. A tells B what he did last weekend and B listens actively. Next A tells B what he will do next weekend and B gives no verbal or nonverbal feedback. Compare the different situations. Was it easier to speak to someone who is paying attention to you? Discuss how it feels to talk to someone who appears not to be listening. Did you struggle to keep talking? How does it feel to ignore someone who is speaking to you?

Finally, B tells A what she did last weekend and both A and B make constant eye contact. Discuss how this feels.

In normal interaction, who is it that makes more eye contact – the speaker or the listener?

# ◗ Paraphrasing

By repeating phrases back to the speaker we are showing him not only that he has been listened to but also understood. His feelings have been acknowledged. We do not have to agree with what he says, and this leaves us with the option of saying either yes or no to a request. This type of listening leaves us with the possibility of further communication and helps avoid conflict because it makes a distinction between acknowledgement and agreement.

## Sample paraphrase openings:

- ◗ 'So what you're saying is . . .'
- ◗ 'Am I right in assuming that you think/feel . . .'
- ◗ 'In other words . . .'

In each of these examples we are acknowledging what has been said, even though we might not agree with it. Such statements from the listener must be kept to a minimum. We should avoid taking over the conversation, but at the same time we want to keep it going. We also need to find the correct tone, using our own style, so that we do not sound insincere. Paraphrasing not only encourages the speaker but also helps the listener focus on the message, and the whole communication is improved.

## Asking questions is another way of actively listening:

- ◗ 'Do you mean to say . . .?'
- ◗ 'Can you elaborate on that . . .?'
- ◗ 'Would you like to explain that idea further . . .?'

## Other simple phrases we can use are:

- ◗ 'I hear you.'
- ◗ 'I understand what you're saying.'
- ◗ 'I see your point.'

# ◗ Interrupting

Interrupting a speaker is often considered bad manners and can cause conflict. It can indicate that we have not been listening, are not interested or believe what we have to say is more important. However, there are occasions when interrupting is just about the cut and thrust of conversation. During political debates on television or radio, we hear members of a panel say, 'If I can be allowed to finish . . .' We should always let someone finish her point before making our own contribution.

**Activities**

1. Divide the class into pairs of A and B. A gives B detailed directions on how to get from his house to college/work, including how to get to bus stops, stations etc. B paraphrases A's message. Swap roles and repeat the activity.

2. Write down a difficulty or problem you have experienced in the past week or two. In pairs, A describes her problem to B. B practises active listening by giving appropriate verbal and/or nonverbal feedback and then paraphrases A's information. Avoid giving advice or offering solutions, as this can mean you are not really listening. Swap roles and repeat the activity.

# ❱ Note-taking

When we are faced with an hour-long talk or lecture on a new subject, hearing shouldn't be a problem, but understanding may be a challenge and retaining information will be extremely difficult unless we take notes. Our memories are not capable of holding all the information given during the course of an hour, so a written record, to which we can refer later on, will help jog our memory.

Some suggestions:
- ❱ Always head the page with the date and subject
- ❱ Never try to copy entire sentences
- ❱ Listen for a few minutes and then summarise what has been said. Shorten everything – words by using abbreviations, sentences into keywords, phrases and headings
- ❱ Leave out examples, anecdotes and irrelevant information
- ❱ Stick to the facts.

These will be rough notes and they need to be read and rewritten later in the same day. If they are left too late the memory wears thin and they will make less sense than on the day they were taken. Note-taking challenges us to use both our listening and writing skills. As we listen we distil the information and jot down what immediately seems important and relevant.

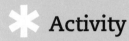

# Activity

In pairs, take it in turns to read each other a detailed message (see sample messages below). In each case the listener should listen carefully to all the relevant information, and then relay the message back to the speaker to check for accuracy.

As an alternative, try a game of Chinese Whispers. If possible, sit in a circle and relay a message around each member of the class, one at a time, quietly, so that no one else can hear. At the end the last person to hear the message should relay it to the whole class group, to compare it to the original message, and to see how much detail was lost in transmission.

## Sample Messages

1. Ms Williams, a company manager at Drumlinn Clothing Ltd, is returning from a trip to England on the 7.50 flight from Heathrow, which is due to arrive in Dublin airport at 8.45. She was due to give a report to staff at a meeting on the company's end of year progress, scheduled for 11.00. However, the flight has been delayed and will not arrive now until 10.30. It will take at least two hours for her to get to the Drumlinn Clothing office, so the meeting has been rescheduled for 13.00. She wants Sheila to pick her up at the airport.

2. Class starts at 9.30 each morning. You have a break of ten minutes at 11.15, and lunch is from 12.45 to 13.45. The secretary is in her office all day except during her lunch hour, which is 13.00–14.00. The principal is available from 10.00 till 11.00 each day and the Student Council meets on Tuesdays at 9.00 in the performance space. The computer room is open for students' use from 9.00 until 9.30 and during lunchtime, and the caretaker is around all day every day.

3. There was an interesting group doing the course in 2012. There were 12 students in total: 8 came straight from school, Angela and Dermot both had already completed degrees and Margaret and Alex had spent most of their adult lives working. There was also a good multicultural mix, with Christian and Helena from Germany, and Dan from the US. The age profile was also diverse, ranging from the eldest, Frank (52), and the youngest, Elaine (19).

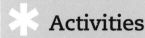

# Activities

1. Watch the TED Talk '5 Ways to Listen Better' by Julian Treasure and afterwards see how many points you can remember.

2. In pairs, write a message related to your own vocational area and read to other members of the class group for listening, retaining and relaying information.

3. Have someone in class read a passage from a book or a newspaper article. The rest of the students take notes from it, identifying the main topics and themes.

# ▶ Tips for Effective Listening

- ▶ Remove or resist distractions
- ▶ Make sure you can hear properly
- ▶ Concentrate
- ▶ Focus on areas of interest and ask yourself, 'What am I getting out of this message?'
- ▶ Concentrate on the content and not the delivery
- ▶ Be patient and hear the full message before judging
- ▶ Give feedback
- ▶ Ask questions
- ▶ Keep an open mind -- be objective
- ▶ Acknowledge the speaker and his/her emotional state
- ▶ Help to keep conversations going
- ▶ Thought is faster than speech so use the time to ask yourself internal questions and to challenge the message
- ▶ Observe body language and tone of speaker – there may be hidden messages!

Avoid:
- ▶ Fidgeting
- ▶ Frowning
- ▶ Looking at your watch.

It is also important not to be too exaggerated or artificial in our listening responses. Inane nodding, staring or grinning will put the speaker off so a balance should be found. The skills mentioned should be tried and practised and will depend on the speaker and the situation.

# Chapter Review

1. Give a brief explanation of the importance of listening.
2. What is the difference between hearing and listening?
3. List six barriers to effective listening.
4. Explain the meanings of active and selective listening.
5. How can paraphrasing help listening?
6. List six points for effective listening.
7. Name four things that can help us to take notes.

# Chapter 4
## Speaking Skills

'Mankind's greatest achievements have come about by talking, and its greatest failures by not talking.'

*Stephen Hawking*

Speaking, unless on the telephone, usually involves face-to-face interaction. It is the most direct, personal and open type of communication because it involves verbal, nonverbal and visual contact. We can hear the speaker's voice and its tone and see his facial expressions and body movements, giving a very complete, healthy and satisfying form of communication (see Chapter 8: Nonverbal Communication). It satisfies a basic human need for social contact with other people. Other benefits are the instant feedback from the receiver and the quick flow and exchange of thoughts, ideas and feelings. We can support what we say and can add expression and colour to our speech by using nonverbal signs. These nonverbal signs can reveal our emotions and personalities, which may be a good or a bad thing depending on what we want. Our accents can show our origins and our choice of words can reveal our level of education. So we cannot conceal ourselves easily in a face-to-face situation.

# ▶ The Voice

'It's the way you tell 'em!' This statement about telling jokes may seem trivial, but it rings true. Why is it that one person can tell a joke and it has the audience in fits of laughter, and then when we try to tell the same joke, word for word, it is met with an appalled silence? The reason probably lies in the way we use our voices. Many professionals take speech lessons to change the tone of their voice because they believe it will help their career. A powerful deep voice can sound more convincing when giving a speech at a business conference than one that is high-pitched or squeaky. The way we speak at an interview or during a speech can be more relevant to our success than what we actually say, so using the voice effectively is important in the study of speaking skills.

## Discussion

Consider what types of voice make people switch off. Which teachers did you enjoy listening to in school and which did you not enjoy listening to? Why?

Unlike writing, speech has a wonderful array of subtle variations that we use to alter the meaning of our messages. Of course these variations can lead to problems if we don't know how to use them properly but they enable us to liven up a word or phrase to give it depth, colour and meaning that is harder to recreate in writing. This is called paralanguage.

### Pitch and Tone

Younger people have higher-pitched voices than older people. Sometimes when we are nervous, our pitch becomes higher due to constriction of the throat. We can help reduce this by relaxing the muscles in the stomach, chest, shoulders and neck. A monotonous voice is one that speaks in monotone – one tone – and is boring to listen to. Inflection is the changing of the voice's pitch and this is something we do naturally in speech, often depending on our mood. The more we inflect, the more interesting we can sound.

### Volume

It is important that people can hear us when we speak. Some voices are naturally louder than others. A loud voice can be commanding and demands to be heard, but in some contexts a quiet, firm voice can be more effective than a loud one.

### Emphasis

We can illustrate the importance of specific words or phrases by placing emphasis upon them.

We do this by changing the pitch and volume. Which words would you emphasise in the following sentences?

1. The next train for Galway leaves at 11.45 from platform number three.
2. Don't you ever do that again!
3. Football is the most popular sport in the world today.
4. I will not tolerate this kind of behaviour.

## Pace/Speed

We tend to speed up if we are excited, nervous or angry and we slow down when relaxed and comfortable or if we want to give emphasis. If we talk too quickly we can lose our listeners; if we are too slow we may bore them.

## Articulation

When speaking we tend to contract words and sentences. 'What do you think?' becomes 'Whatcha think?' 'How are you?' becomes 'Howya?' 'Do not' becomes 'Don't' etc. It is easy to be lazy when speaking, especially in informal situations, and sometimes we just mumble and slur. We shouldn't be afraid to use our mouth, lips and tongue to full effect but without sounding forced or unnatural.

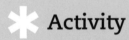 **Activity**

Try repeating some of these tongue twisters, focusing on articulation and pronunciation:

1. A big blue badly bleeding blister.
2. Rubber baby buggy bumpers.
3. A shifty snake selling snake skin slippers.
4. Eleven benevolent elephants.
5. Teaching ghosts to sing.
6. Selfish shellfish.
7. Really rural.
8. Unique New York.
9. The tip of the tongue, the lips, the teeth.
10. To titillate your tastebuds, we've got these tasty titbits.

# Activities

### 1. Give the voice expression

Sit in circles of five or six people. Take some of the phrases below. Each person says the phrase using a different expression from the previous speaker. Try to express some of the following: neutral, asking a question (pitch goes up at the end), bored, angry, excited, scared, surprised, shy, happy, sad, whispering, shouting, crying, laughing, rapping, Gregorian chant, opera, sarcastic, proud, tired, suspicious, seductive. Try out different accents too.

Suggested phrases:

- I want to go home
- It's my turn
- What are you doing tonight?
- We have to do an assignment
- The new computer's broken
- Hello, how are you?
- No one here gets out alive
- Drop it or else
- Just do as I say, will you?
- My helicopter is full of eels
- We've missed the bus
- This is getting ridiculous.

Alternatively, each student writes a line from a song/poem/film/play/book and it goes around the circle in the same way.

### 2. Newscaster

Read aloud a short newspaper article and try to make it sound as interesting as you can. Depending on the nature of the news item you will have to adopt an appropriate tone of voice, e.g. serious, tragic, funny, quirky etc.

Newsreaders and comedians are helpful to listen to as they use vocal techniques to keep their audience's attention.

### 3. Choose one of the following passages and read it aloud, using appropriate voice expression:

Sorry? You're sorry? Is that all you can say? I've been waiting here for 45 minutes in the freezing rain and all you can say is sorry. Why didn't you call me? You've got a mobile, haven't you? Or did you forget that too? You know, sometimes I wonder why I bother with you at all.

Now there is a breakfast cereal to really get you going – 'Eat and Go'! If you're feeling slow and sluggish in the morning, flush away those early dreary blues with 'Eat and Go'! Full of natural goodness, iron and vitamins, 'Eat and Go' is made from organic oats and wheat, grown especially on our own farms and scientifically tested in our laboratories. Get yourself up and out with 'Eat and Go'!

An evil has been unleashed upon the world, an evil older than history. In a race against time, a struggle against the odds, a battle with forces too great for mere mortals, only one man knows how to stop the destruction of the entire planet. Arnold Schickelgruber is John Steel. Power beyond imagination, terror beyond belief. A film that will chill you to the bone.

Once upon a time, in a land far, far away, there lived a princess who was the most beautiful princess in all the land. She lived with her evil stepmother and two ugly sisters in a great big castle. One day, news went out across the land that a magnificent ball was to be given by the handsome Prince Charming to find a suitable princess for him to marry . . .

# ▶ Language of Speech

The language of speech is very different from that of writing. It is far less formal and structured and grammar and punctuation often seem non-existent. We do, however, punctuate our speech with fillers such as 'well', 'you know', 'like' and 'em'. We hesitate, stammer, stop, restart, repeat and use redundant words. If we wrote down, word for word, what we said, it would look very inelegant compared to the written word.

Not all speech needs to be so chaotic. It depends on the context in which we are speaking. A conversation between friends would be very different from a prepared speech to a company board of directors. A well-prepared speech can be very close in structure and use of language to the written word.

# ▶ Conversation

Whether formal or casual, conversation forms an important social function in our daily lives and yet many people still feel they lack the confidence to carry on a good conversation. Good conversation can establish and improve personal and professional relationships. Like all forms of communication, it should be a two-way process and not dominated by one speaker.

Fig. 4.1

There are a number of distinct stages in a conversation:

- Greetings
- Introductions
- Small talk
- Core conversation
- Summary of decisions
- Small talk/exit

At the outset, a smile, eye contact and a greeting opens the door for the conversation to start. After the introductions comes the small talk. Here it's not what is said that is important but what it implies, i.e. that both speakers are on friendly and equal terms. It could be a comment about:

- The weather
- The immediate vicinity, e.g. 'What an amazing view of the sea!'
- Something both speakers have knowledge of, e.g. 'That was a great game last night.'

Small talk can also include:

- Open questions, e.g. 'How far have you come today?'
- Neutral topics, e.g. 'Traffic's not too bad this morning.'

▶ Ice-breakers/humour. This is down to personal taste, but be careful: a joke that fails can be extremely embarrassing, especially if you're trying to make an impression on someone.

Such small talk should elicit agreement, so avoid anything too controversial or threatening.

Keeping a conversation going is often a challenge. Asking questions of the other speaker(s) is useful as well as speaking about your own topics, stories and interests. Respond and react by giving appropriate feedback.

# ✳ Activities

1. In the following conversation, fill in the blanks with appropriate feedback responses.

    A: I'm going to France for my next holiday.

    B: _____.

    A: Yes, I'm going with some friends to celebrate our graduation.

    B: _____. And what are you going to do there?

    A: We're going to go kayaking down a gorge.

    B: _____.

    A: Although I think I also want to spend some time just lying on a beach reading my book.

    B: _____.

2. In pairs conduct a role-play in which you meet a friend/acquaintance outside a cinema or waiting at a bus stop and arrange to meet up for lunch. Include greetings and small talk. Enact another role-play in which one person is the other's employer/teacher.

3. Each student writes down a statement about something he did recently. Students take it in turns to sit in a chair at the front of the classroom and read their statement. The rest of the group asks three or more questions about the statement and the student has to reply quickly to these questions.

4. Consider the following typical spoken routines and insert appropriate formal and informal words, phrases or sentences.

|  | Formal | Informal |
|---|---|---|
| Greeting | _____ | _____ |
| Leave-taking | _____ | _____ |
| Asking the time | _____ | _____ |
| Offering a drink | _____ | _____ |
| Asking directions | _____ | _____ |
| Asking someone to be quiet | _____ | _____ |

# ◗ Formal and Informal Speaking

*Informal speaking* with friends and family is usually easy. We aren't under pressure to 'perform'. They will understand if we make mistakes, though we may occasionally feel a little foolish. Small talk, chit-chat and conversation are informal speaking activities we engage in everyday.

*Formal speaking* is more difficult. It needs to be more structured and grammatically correct and usually requires some planning and preparation. We use it in work situations, at interviews, giving talks and holding debates. Even giving someone instructions or directions needs to be clearly structured to avoid misunderstandings, which may lead to mistakes.

The following speaking activities are not too difficult and can prepare us for speaking assignments.

## Narration

Tell a story to the class group. Here are some suggested topics:

1. The story of your day up to the present moment. Begin: 'I woke up this morning . . .'
2. The story of a film/television programme/book you enjoyed
3. Describe what you did at the weekend
4. Describe a memorable holiday you went on
5. A simple story (we all know fairy tales – better still, make one up!)
6. A narrative-style joke.

Try to make it personal, and include details to make it as interesting as possible. Use your voice effectively.

## Description

1. Spend three minutes preparing a one-minute talk describing an activity with which you are familiar. Topics could range from your own pastimes to your work, sport, preparing a meal etc. Your teacher could give assistance in preparation. Your talk should result in your audience knowing roughly how to do the activity themselves.

2. Think of an everyday object/mechanical device/mode of transport etc. Describe it to the class group without revealing what it is. They should be able to work it out if your description is good enough.

## Expressing Opinion

Many of us shy away from giving our opinion on some specific 'hot' topic. We may feel we cannot argue our point effectively enough to do so. Or we may simply not have any strong opinions about anything. Is this a good or a bad thing?

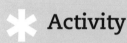

## Activity

Here is a list of topics you might use either for a class debate or for practising solo speaking. They may be adapted as required. Consider the following before speaking:

1. Decide if you want to do some research on the topic beforehand.

2. Decide how you will approach the subject, e.g. an argument for or against, an informative or a persuasive speech etc.

3. What tone of delivery will you use? Angry, passionate, calm, reasonable etc.

- 'If I ran the country . . .'
- What I like/dislike about college
- Asylum seekers
- The internet
- Mass media
- Young people drink too much
- Legalise cannabis
- The environment
- Global warming
- Vegetarianism
- Advertising
- Religion
- Racism
- Mobile phones
- Television
- Gay marriage
- Water fluoridation
- When the oil runs out.

Think up your own topics. There may be something specific to your own vocational area which you'd like to speak about.

# ▶ Intent and Consent

Sometimes if we need to have a discussion with someone it is helpful to:
- State our intent
- Ask for consent

By stating our intent, we are preparing the receiver for our discussion and if she is prepared she will be in a better position to partake in and contribute to it.

By asking for someone's consent to have a discussion, he is more likely to oblige than if we dump him straight into the middle of it. We are also showing him respect by allowing him to decline our request if he wants. We shouldn't assume a person wants to, or has time to, talk to us. Stating intent and asking consent invites co-operation and reduces the potential for misunderstandings.

Sometimes a simple phrase such as 'I need to talk to you, do you have a couple of minutes?' is a sufficient statement of intent and request for consent.

## Activities

Compare the following statements.

- ▶ 'My assignment is giving me a lot of trouble. For starters, I can't find any information on...'
- ▶ 'I would like to talk to you about my assignment. Have you got a few minutes?'
- ▶ 'This new job I have is really bothering me. You see, I have to stay behind an hour later everyday...'
- ▶ 'I'm not sure about my new job. Do you have a minute to talk about it?'

Which statement is likely to get a better response?

## Activities

Try the following role-plays. Each can be adapted to suit the group's vocational area.

- ▶ An employer has given an employee a job to do, for which the employee feels she is not qualified, and/or is not part of her normal duties. Employer and employee discuss the situation.
- ▶ A client is complaining about poor service/shoddy goods. Client and company/ organisation representative discuss the problem.
- ▶ An employee has been making comments that a colleague feels are sexually harassing/racist/discriminating. The two employees discuss the problem.
- ▶ Two colleagues were supposed to meet to discuss an important issue at work. One colleague didn't turn up. Next day, the other colleague confronts him.

# ▶ Negotiation Skills

Nelson Mandela once said, 'No problem is so intractable that it cannot be resolved through talk and negotiation rather than force and violence.' He went on to say that, in negotiations, neither side is right or wrong, but all sides need to compromise.

We might think that negotiation is about business, but it is any discussion between two people or groups of people when each wants something that the other might be unwilling to give. It is a process of finding compromise with each side gaining but also giving something.

Negotiation takes place when:

▶ An employee wants a wage increase
▶ A child wants to eat sweets and the parent wants her to eat vegetables
▶ A customer bargains for a better deal with a salesperson
▶ A couple has to decide who will drink and who will drive
▶ A band wants €10,000 to make a record and the record company offers €5,000.

Each side is usually out to get what it wants and this can result in distrust, suspicion, even anger and confrontation. We negotiate, because the alternative might be worse, e.g. a workers' strike, the break-up of a relationship, a court case, even war. These alternatives are often used as negotiating tactics, e.g. 'If you don't give me what I want, I'll sue you.'

## Guidelines for Negotiation

### Pre-negotiation

1. Know your opposition's situation, skills, assets, strengths, weaknesses etc.
2. Be clear about your goals:
   (a) What are your initial demands?
   (b) What would you settle for?
   (c) What's your bottom line?
   (d) What do you both agree on?
3. If possible, choose a neutral space within which the negotiations can take place, where neither side feels at an advantage or disadvantage.
4. Timing – if it's late in the day some people may be tired or irritable.

## Discussion

The negotiations for the 1921 Anglo-Irish treaty between Britain and Ireland led by Michael Collins were held in Downing Street. How do you think this affected the parties?

### During Negotiations

1. Aim for a win-win situation, where both sides leave reasonably satisfied.
2. Begin by asking for more than you think you will get.
3. Be prepared to compromise.
4. Never give ground without gaining something in return.
5. Don't put all your cards on the table at the outset; keep some in reserve.

### Communication in Negotiation

1. Be clear and use plain language.
2. Clarify any possible ambiguities.
3. Keep a record of all proceedings, especially any agreements.
4. Make sure both sides clearly understand the outcome.

### Non-verbal Signs

Be aware of nonverbal signs:

1. Direct eye contact shows a firm, positive attitude and willingness to communicate.
2. A warm facial expression shows interest and willingness to be persuaded.
3. A cold, steely-eyed, hard-faced expression can mean an inflexible attitude.

*Lack of confidence* is shown by:

1. Excessive smiling
2. Fidgeting
3. Hesitation
4. Speaking very quickly.

*Confidence* is shown by:

1. Direct eye contact
2. Upright posture
3. Leaning forward slightly
4. Speaking slowly and deliberately.

Negotiators should be flexible, firm, courteous, reasonable, persuasive, self-controlled, realistic and prepared to listen.

### Breakdown

If a deal cannot be reached, one side might walk out. If there is a walkout, contact should be made immediately afterwards to prevent the proceedings from turning sour and to arrange another meeting.

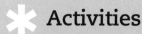

# Activities

1. Divide into groups of six. Conduct negotiations between management (three) and staff (three) of a company/organisation of your choice about proposed working hours and conditions over the Christmas period.

2. In groups of six, negotiate between those in favour of the construction of a wind farm in a local area and those against.

The following activities are for one-to-one negotiations:

3. Two people, A and B, are at a market and both see something they want to buy. A has enough money, B doesn't. B reminds A that she owes him money, the exact amount of the item for sale. They negotiate a deal.

4. You arrive at the station to catch the last train home, which is due to leave in five minutes. You suddenly realise you've lost your ticket and have no more money. Negotiate with the ticket collector to let you on to the train.

5. A rock star and her manager are arguing about how to leave the airport after a successful world tour. The fans are screaming outside and the manager wants them both to leave by a back exit but the star wants to meet the fans.

6. Granny is coming to stay. You have to give up your room but don't want to. Negotiate with your mother.

7. You want to buy a CD at a market stall, but it costs just a little bit more than the money you have on you. Negotiate with the stall holder.

8. The landlady wants to raise the rent. You cannot afford to pay what she is asking for. You'll only be there till the summer holidays and there are odd jobs you could do in the house. Negotiate a deal.

## Presenting a Point of View

To present a point of view or opinion effectively, it is important to back it up with good reasons. If you can list your reasons by numbering them, so much the better: others will take you more seriously. Another good technique is to give other points of view, comment on them and reach your own point of view, having explored the other ones. You can reach a better conclusion this way. This is useful in situations such as interviews, group discussions or when giving a presentation.

# Activities

Make a list of controversial discussion topics on the board. Divide into groups of 4–5 people. Each group chooses a topic to discuss for 20 minutes. Try to present your point of view as clearly and convincingly as possible and to back it up with reasons.

## Persuasion and Advocacy

Speaking to persuade or speaking in support of a cause needs certain skills in order to get the message across effectively. Here are a few guidelines:

▌ Present the facts about your subject. Use statistics and evidence to support your argument.

▌ Try and tailor it to your listeners' needs or interests. Try and connect with them. Is there any reason why they should listen to you/believe you?

▌ Structure your argument well. If you sound disorganised, it will be harder to convince your listener.

Here is a sequence of topics to follow:

1. Present information that grabs the listener's attention.
2. Explain why there is a need or a problem that needs solving.
3. Present your solution to the problem.
4. Visualise the future when the problem has been solved.
5. Suggest a course of action for the listener to take in order to reach the solution.

In this type of speaking you need to be both persuasive and informative. It might be a useful technique for an oral presentation.

# Activities

1. As a group, brainstorm the subject of climate change using the guidelines above. Students could volunteer to stand up and be the advocate for a more sustainable lifestyle.

2. Make a list of causes you feel strongly about and, in pairs, take it in turns to try and persuade each other to take up one of the causes. Alternatively try and persuade each other to take up a sport, hobby or activity you feel strongly about.

# Chapter Review

1. In what ways can we use our voices to improve our speaking skills?
2. What are the main differences between formal and informal speaking?
3. Explain the importance of intent and consent.
4. How do you effectively present a point of view?
5. What is advocacy and what are its key components?
6. What is negotiation?

# Chapter 5
## The Interview

> **In This Chapter**
> - Preparation
> - Structure
> - Formal or Informal
> - Types of Question

The purpose of an interview is to get information about someone by asking questions. There are many types of interview, which we may experience in our college, working and social lives, such as a counselling or medical interview, or a progress interview in which an employer or tutor will assess our work and performance. This section will focus on the employment interview.

The main reason for an employment interview is for the employer to assess the potential employee. It also provides the candidate with an opportunity to learn about both the position and the prospective employer and to see whether or not she might fit in.

What is important about an employment interview is that the employer gets to meet the potential employee face-to-face, to see and hear him first hand. It illustrates the benefits of this kind of communication over all others. A letter, a CV and a photograph can only impart so much information. The interview fills in the gaps that they have left.

An employment interview is not always simply a one-to-one question-and-answer session. Nowadays, candidates may have to do a psychometric test (a series of rapid written questions, which determine a candidate's personality and ability), a role-play and may even find themselves at a group interview with a panel of up to five interviewers and a number of other candidates. It is as well to find out beforehand what type of interview you will have.

# ▶ Preparation

## Pre-Interview

An interview for a job is likely to be a formal type of communication and, as such, we must be prepared for it. Here are some tips for interview preparation:

1. Be familiar with details in your CV and application letter.
2. Find out about the job/company/organisation, e.g. employer's name, number of employees, products and services offered.
3. Find out the job requirements (what qualifications are needed) and job specifications (what duties and responsibilities it entails).
4. Be aware of any recent developments in the job sector.
5. Prepare any relevant documents you might want to take with you.
6. Dress formally, avoiding bright colours, strong perfume or after-shave and excessive jewellery.
7. Be neat and tidy.
8. Prepare a list of your USPs (unique selling points), e.g. strengths, skills, experiences, qualifications, achievements, interests. These must be relevant to the job.
9. Think of ways to turn weaknesses into strengths.
10. Do a mock interview using the questions at the end of this section.

## At the Interview

1. Be on time! Aim to arrive 15 minutes before the time of the interview.
2. First impressions last, and it only takes 30 seconds to make your first impression. Try to appear friendly, polite and sincere.
3. Use appropriate nonverbal communication:
   - ▶ Shake hands firmly at the start and finish – the interviewer will usually offer her hand first.
   - ▶ Don't be afraid to smile.
   - ▶ Sit when asked. You may not be asked, so sit when it feels comfortable after the handshake, or just ask, 'May I sit down? Thank you.'
   - ▶ Keep a straight but not rigid posture and lean slightly forward.
   - ▶ Don't cross legs, fold arms, slouch or fidget.
   - ▶ Try to appear relaxed.
   - ▶ Maintain appropriate eye contact with the interviewer.
4. Speak formally, avoiding slang and fillers such as 'like', 'um', 'you know what I mean'.
5. Try to elaborate on 'Yes' and 'No' answers.
6. Give full answers, stick to the point and avoid waffle.
7. Be honest. If you don't know an answer say, 'I'm sorry, I don't know the answer to that.'
8. If you don't understand a question, ask to have it explained.

9. If you 'freeze', or your mind goes blank, just say, 'Sorry, could you repeat the question, please?'

10. If the interviewer discovers any mistakes you've made or weaknesses you have, don't deny them.

11. Try to turn any weaknesses into strengths, e.g. 'I've never done spreadsheets before, but I'm good at basic word-processing and I am quick to learn computer skills.'

12. Listen carefully to the questions and don't rush your answers. Take a second to pause and gather your thoughts.

13. Be positive and enthusiastic. You want this job, so try to show it!

14. Don't relax too much. Some interviewers use an over-friendly tactic to catch candidates off guard.

15. Don't become defensive or argumentative if questioning becomes too rigorous.

16. Don't be afraid to sell yourself. Be confident but not cocky.

17. Never criticise a previous employer. It shows a lack of loyalty.

18. Always be constructive in criticism, e.g. 'The course was excellent but it would have been better if we'd had more Communications classes.'

19. Have your own questions prepared in case you are asked if you have any.

20. At the end, thank the interviewer for seeing you and shake hands again, if offered.

21. The interview isn't over until you've left the room, so as you leave be polite, smile and don't slam the door.

## After the Interview

An assessment and analysis of your performance afterwards is useful as preparation for future interviews.

List the questions you were asked. Evaluate the following:

▶ Your appearance
▶ Your entrance
▶ Your NVC (nonverbal communication)
▶ Your good answers
▶ Your bad answers
▶ Your listening ability
▶ Your own questions
▶ Details you forgot
▶ Your exit.

An interview, no matter what type it is, should be structured in a particular way so as to create a positive communication climate. This is largely up to the interviewer since she is the one who is leading the way, so to speak. However, interviewers can get tired, bored and nervous during long days of interviewing, so if you can create a positive communication climate by smiling and appearing warm and enthusiastic, it can be beneficial.

# ❱ Structure

In very structured interviews there are often three stages: the opening stage, the main body and the closing stage.

## The Opening Stage

In the opening stage an effective climate is briefly created by means of small talk or some sort of preview of what will be discussed. For example:

❱ 'I see you come from Galway. Do you like living there?'

❱ 'Since the last time you were with us are there any changes that have occurred in your life?' (If being interviewed for a job in the same organisation/company.)

Fig. 5.1

❱ 'I see you went to Drumlinn College. Is Mr Maguire still teaching there?'

Jobs can be gained or lost based on the first three minutes of an interview.

## Main Body of Interview

This is where the main questions are asked and an interviewer often uses the funnel sequence of questioning, i.e. moving from broad topics to specific ones.

❱ Tell me about yourself.

❱ So, you're a good teamworker?

❱ Have you held any positions of responsibility?

❱ How would you deal with someone you didn't get on with?

❱ Tell me about a situation in which this happened.

## The Closing Stage

The closing stage is also brief. You could be asked if you have any questions, there may be a short summary of the content of the interview, statement of a follow-up, e.g. 'We'll let you know . . .' and a friendly parting.

If there is an interview panel, each interviewer may take a different stage, or different set of topics to ask, depending on the job. Be careful not to be lulled into a false sense of security if the first or second interviewer comes across as friendly. You may find the next one is more rigorous!

# ◗ Formal or Informal

In highly formal interviews, both parties remain in their social and professional roles. So in an employment interview, the interviewer is the potential employer and the interviewee the prospective employee. The interview will follow a standard format which the interviewer may have prepared and written out. Nonverbal signs from the interviewer, e.g. a firm handshake, formal dress, a formally decorated room and straight postures, all communicate a formal style.

Informal interviews tend to be more relaxed, are less likely to follow a rigid structure, and the roles of the participants will be less clearly defined. Informal surroundings, casual dress and more in the way of chat and smiling can signify an informal interview style, but are no less serious for that.

# ◗ Types of Question

## Open Questions

These allow the interviewee to expand and elaborate on certain topics. Examples:
◗ 'Tell me about yourself.'
◗ 'What sort of work experience do you have?'
The interviewee has the opportunity to steer the communication towards topics that will interest him or show him in a positive light.

## Closed Questions

These call for a specific response, usually either 'yes' or 'no', but try to elaborate on such answers.

◗ 'Did you enjoy your time at Drumlinn College?'
   'Yes, it was a great experience. I met some really interesting people and I learned a lot about . . .'

◗ 'How many modules did you take?'
   'I did eight modules in the first year, including Communications, Work Experience . . .'

They may be followed by open questions, e.g. 'What did you enjoy about it?'

## Probing Questions

A probing question is one that tries to get beneath the surface to gain more information from an interviewee on a topic.
Interviewer: What did you enjoy about college?
Interviewee: There was a good mixture of people there and it had a friendly atmosphere.
Interviewer: What do you mean by a good mixture of people?

Interviewee: There were people from different backgrounds, different nationalities, different ages and cultures.
Interviewer: Why do you think that is a good thing?
Interviewee: It helps to broaden your mind when you meet people from different walks of life. It makes it more interesting and stimulating. You begin to see that there is more to the world than simply your own way of looking at things.

## Hypothetical Questions

These kinds of questions give the candidate a hypothetical situation to see how he would deal with it. For example:

'Supposing you have a colleague who always arrives late and leaves early so that you are often left to cover for him/her. What would you do in this situation?'

## Mirror Questions

Mirror questions reflect or bounce off the previous response.
For example:
Interviewer: Tell me about yourself.
Interviewee: I'm very interested in working with other people.
Interviewer: So you enjoy being part of a team?
Interviewee: Yes. I was involved in the Student Council at college.
Interviewer: Then you're interested in organising things with a group?
Interviewee: Yes. I think working as part of a group improved my communication skills.

In this way, interviewees have a degree of power over the direction of the interview.

## Summary Questions

These generally cover topics that have already been discussed, or are intended to allow the interviewee to add anything of relevance that has been left out, e.g. 'Is there anything else you'd like to discuss?'

## Leading and Discriminatory Questions

The following two types of questions are undesirable in an interview:

### Leading Questions

These usually suggest a desired response and don't get an honest reply from the candidate. For example, 'You wouldn't mind travelling as part of this job, would you?'

### Discriminatory Questions

These are based on gender, marital status, race, religion and colour and are illegal as they may unfairly disadvantage the candidate. If asked such a question the interviewee may politely refuse to answer, e.g. 'I'm sorry. I would rather not answer that if you don't mind.'

# Typical Interview Questions

Here is a list of typical interview questions:

## General

- Tell me about yourself.
- What are your strong/weak points?
- What are your best qualities?
- What is your greatest achievement?
- What have you done that illustrates initiative?
- How do you cope with stress?
- Can you work under pressure?
- What do you do in your spare time?
- Do you read?
- Do you play any sports?

## Education

- What did you like about college?
- What did you dislike about college?
- Tell me about your course at college.
- Why did you go to college?
- How did you find the course?
- Why did you choose to study Permaculture?
- Are you satisfied with your results?
- Was there anyone you didn't get on with?
- Describe a problem you had to deal with at college.

## Current Application

- What experience do you have for this particular job?
- Give me some reasons why I should employ you.
- Why would you like to work for this company/organisation?
- What attracted you to this job?
- What could you bring to this company/organisation?
- What skills or qualities do you have that would be useful for this job?
- What do you know about this company?
- Do you have any creative ideas that could benefit the workplace?
- How did you find out about this position?
- What are you looking for in a job?
- Where would you see yourself in five years' time?
- What kind of salary do you expect? (See below for questions about salary.)

### Previous Experience

- Tell me about your last job.
- Tell me about your previous employment experience.
- Have you held any positions of responsibility?
- What have you learned from any positions of responsibility?
- Have you ever worked as part of a team?
- How well did you fit into the team?
- Did you have to work with anyone who let down the team?
- How would you cope with a colleague you might find difficult to work with?
- Describe a problem you had to deal with in your last job.
- What were your main responsibilities in your last job?
- Why did you leave your last job?
- What did you like/dislike about your last position?
- What skills did you learn in your last job?

### Do You Have Any Questions?

It is good to have prepared a question or two of your own as it shows you are interested in the job. Here are some suggestions:

- Do you provide training?
- Are there opportunities for promotion?
- What sort of hours would I be working?
- Do the employees get together socially?
- Do you have any plans to expand the company?
- Are there opportunities for working overtime?
- What qualities are you looking for in an employee?

Questions, either from the interviewer or interviewee, about salary always cause a little consternation. Many job advertisements include information about the salary, in which case there is no reason for the interviewee to ask, unless he feels the work is excessive for the amount being paid. An interviewee could ask, 'If offered this position, what would the rate of pay be?' Many people feel embarrassed asking this, so only ask if you feel comfortable doing so. It is useful to find out the rate of pay of the job for which you are applying.

# ✳ Activities

1.  In pairs, interview each other as if for a job. Don't prepare the exact questions you will ask each other. At an interview we don't know exactly what we will be asked, so keep it as authentic as possible. Use the list of questions on the previous pages as a guide.  If possible bring in your CVs so that questions might be relevant to the interviewee.

2.  For a more involved activity, put together an interview panel of three to five students. The panel should prepare what kinds of questions each member will ask, e.g. one can introduce, another can focus on education, another on work experience etc. Conduct a number of interviews with volunteers and the rest of the group can assess the performance of each candidate.

## Tips

▶ Prepare well beforehand.
▶ Dress appropriately.
▶ Arrive early.
▶ Check your nonverbal communication.
▶ Show interest and enthusiasm.
▶ Give full, complete answers.

## Chapter Review

1.  Outline the importance of nonverbal communication in an interview.
2.  List five important points to be aware of.
3.  List five things you should do to prepare for an interview.
4.  List five things you should not do during an interview.
5.  List five things to do after the interview. Why are these important?
6.  Explain the meaning of open and closed questions.
7.  What are leading and discriminatory questions and what is wrong with them?

# Chapter 6
## Groups and Meetings

We all belong to a variety of groups. From our families, through our colleagues at work or classmates at college, to our friends and members of clubs or societies, we are constantly involved with some form of group. Belonging to a group can have a positive effect on our wellbeing. We are, after all, highly social beings: regular interaction with others makes us feel socially 'connected' and this can contribute enormously in terms of life satisfaction. Being a member of a variety of groups helps us relate, interact and communicate with others and this interaction can improve our sense of social belonging as well as our self-confidence.

Interaction in a group is also a vital part of our working lives. Many employers look for people who can get along with their colleagues and work effectively as part of a group or team. If we can communicate well in group situations we will enhance our opportunities for employment and promotion.

# ▶ Reasons for Joining Groups

Although we can often find ourselves in groups we didn't choose to join, for example our ethnic group, our family and our school, there are specific reasons why we join groups.

1. Security – we feel safe in the company of others who have the same interests
2. Identity – being a member of a particular group gives us a sense of who we are
3. Common goal or cause
4. Social reasons
5. Information/education.

## Lessons from Flying Geese

**Fact 1:** As each goose flaps its wings it creates an uplift for the birds that follow. By flying in a V formation, the whole flock adds 71 per cent greater flying range than if each bird flew alone.

*Lesson:* People who share a common direction and sense of community can get where they are going quicker and more easily because they are travelling on the thrust of one another.

**Fact 2:** When a goose falls out of formation, it suddenly feels the drag and resistance of flying alone. It quickly moves back into formation to take advantage of the lifting power of the bird immediately in front of it.

*Lesson:* If we have as much sense as a goose, we stay in formation with those headed where we want to go. We are willing to accept their help and give our help to others.

**Fact 3:** When the lead goose tires, it rotates back into the formation and another goose flies to the point position.

*Lesson:* It pays to take turns doing the hard tasks and sharing leadership. As with geese, people are interdependent on each other's skills, capabilities and unique arrangements of gifts, talents or resources.

**Fact 4:** The geese flying in formation honk to encourage those up front to keep their speed.

*Lesson:* We need to make sure our honking is encouraging. In groups where there is encouragement, the production is much greater. The power of encouragement (to stand by one's heart or core values and encourage the heart and core of others) is the quality of honking we need.

**Fact 5:** When a goose gets sick, wounded or shot down, two geese drop out of formation and follow it down to help and protect it. They stay with it until it dies or is able to fly again. Then they launch out with another formation or catch up with the flock.

*Lesson:* If we have as much sense as geese, we will stand by each other in difficult times as well as when we are strong.

(Taken from a speech (based on the work of Milton Olson) by Angeles Arrien at the 1991 Organizational Development Network.)

# ▶ Group Influence

The groups to which we belong have a strong influence on how we think and behave. We are usually obliged to conform to the group's norms, i.e. patterns of thought and behaviour that are considered to be normal within a particular group. This may involve what we can and cannot speak about, the toleration of humour, an actual set of rules to which we must adhere or even wearing a specific type of clothing. These group norms are common to all members of the group, and help develop and build trust between members. Other groups who think and behave differently may be perceived as a challenge or threat. Our peer group often exerts peer pressure upon us to do things with which we may not always feel comfortable.

# ▶ Effective Group Communication

To make the most of our group situations we need to know how to interact with others successfully and how to make our groups effective in their tasks and to foster group cohesion. Dialogue and negotiation skills come into play in group situations, but there are a number of specific communication skills which can help us contribute towards the groups to which we belong and maximise our benefits from them:

▶ Acceptance of other members and their ideas
▶ Offering support and praise to group members for their contributions, e.g. 'Well done', 'That's a good idea'
▶ Taking turns so that everyone can contribute
▶ Listening to others
▶ Positive body language – facing and making eye contact with other members
▶ Keeping focused on the group's objectives
▶ Creating a relaxed atmosphere, using humour perhaps, without it becoming a distraction from the main purpose
▶ Showing agreement with other members
▶ Offering contributions, either by suggesting ideas or volunteering to take action
▶ Evaluating others' ideas positively, e.g. 'That's a good idea, but it might work better if we . . .'
▶ Inviting the views and opinions of others, e.g. 'What do you think?'
▶ Bringing ideas together, e.g. 'Are we all agreed on that?'
▶ Suggesting actions, e.g. 'Why don't we . . .?'

## Negative Group Communication

▶ Never contributing
▶ Speaking out of turn
▶ Being distracted from the group's objectives
▶ Insulting remarks about/to other members and their ideas
▶ Negative comments about the group's goals/purpose
▶ Regular disagreement with other members
▶ Behaviour that goes against what is acceptable to the group
▶ Self-centred communication
▶ Aggression
▶ Dominating behaviour.

Such negative attitudes and behaviour within a group can lead to problems such as a bad atmosphere, resentment or hostility between members. This in turn can result in a lack of progress and productivity.

# ▶ Synergy

Synergy, which comes from the Greek word 'sunergos', meaning working together, means that the combined effect of the whole of a group is more than the sum of its parts. In other words, a group works to its maximum effect if each member puts aside his/her individual interests in favour of the interests of the group. If we find our interests constantly clash with those of the group, maybe it's time for us to leave. If we don't actively contribute to the group, remain passive and silent, we become like a limb that has no purpose. The worst we can do is constantly be at odds with the group, in which case we may be asked to leave.

# ▶ Group Discussion

Discussion in groups usually focuses on one or several specific aims or goals. It is important to keep the purpose of the discussion in mind, to keep from straying from the group's task and avoid red herrings. Discussions often get bogged down when one or two members concentrate and dwell for too long on minor and unimportant details. Discussions should move forward in the direction of a satisfactory outcome. Contributions to the discussion should:

1. Be relevant to the task at hand
2. Focus on the goal
3. Be constructive
4. Move the discussion forward.

# Activity

Divide into groups of four or five. Each group is a band in search of a manager. There are five candidates for the job and each group has 15 minutes to select the one they think is best suited to the job.

The candidates are:

- Mick. Early twenties. Mediocre Leaving Cert results. Great charm and very popular. Could talk his way out of anything. Bit of a chancer. No musical talent of his own. Daytime job as salesperson. Never lets things get on top of him. Close friend of band since schooldays together.

- Alan. Late twenties. Boyfriend of band's lead singer. Accountant. Rather reserved – perhaps shy. Extremely efficient and clear-headed. Dresses conservatively. A perfectionist, he's interested in the business possibilities.

- Sheila. Mid twenties. Degree in theatre studies. Some experience working in an arts centre. Vivacious with a sympathetic personality. Level-headed and sensible, she relates easily to others. No particular knowledge of the music scene but she knows what she likes.

- Don. Mid thirties. Has extensive experience of DJ work and local radio. Encyclopaedic knowledge of music world. Thinks that at last he has spotted a winner. Tends to boss, and keen on doing things his way. Superficial jollity but quite a cold personality. Ambitious to make it, but time is running out.

- Lucilla. Has done a further education course in journalism and, at twenty, is looking for openings in the media. Very energetic and bright. Good organiser but makes no secret of the fact that she doesn't suffer fools gladly. Sarcastic and funny. Quick to learn. Comes from a wealthy background.

Give an honest assessment of your own and your group's performance by answering the following questions without consulting the rest of the group:

- Did the group reach a consensus, i.e. agreement?
- Did the group go about the task in an organised way or not? How?
- Did anyone take charge/dominate?
- Did everyone contribute to the discussion?
- Were your contributions positive or negative?
- Did you put your views across clearly?
- Did you listen to others' contributions?
- Did you enjoy working as part of a team?
- What improvements would you make next time?

Compare your answers with the other members of your group.

(From Stephen Daunt, *Communication Skills*)

# ▶ Meetings

Fig. 6.1

Meetings are crucial to the smooth running of most organisations. Important decisions are made at meetings at every level of social and working life. A large company might hold a meeting to decide on new product development; trade union meetings take place to discuss the welfare of the employees; a Student Council meeting might be held to arrange a social; even when a family sits down at home to make plans for a holiday it is a kind of meeting.

Many people dislike having to attend meetings, as they are often badly planned and poorly run. Meetings should be positive, constructive, stimulating and well organised. They can have many advantages. Within an organisation they can promote a sense of belonging, identity and involvement amongst members as each person is allowed to have an input. They can encourage a wide range of ideas and suggestions from the different participants. In short, they are democratic in that everyone can and should have an equal say.

## Purpose of Meetings

1. Problem-solving
2. Decision-making
3. Negotiation
4. Generating ideas
5. Giving and receiving information.

## Types of Meeting

1. *Formal* – held according to specific rules and procedures, perhaps contained within a constitution
2. *Informal* – no specific rules
3. *Ordinary general meeting* – regularly held monthly or weekly to conduct routine discussion or business
4. *Extraordinary* – held outside the regular times to deal with a specific issue, often a crisis
5. *Committee* – a sub-group of the parent organisation
6. *Public* – any member of the public may attend, held in a public place, often dealing with political or community issues
7. *Private* – only members of the organisation may attend
8. *Annual general meeting (AGM)*.

# ▶ Formal Roles

## Chairperson

'Through the chair,' often precedes comments made at meetings. This means the chairperson is the 'channel' through which all comments and discussion are directed. This ensures that a certain degree of order is maintained and that any potential conflict is avoided, as participants do not communicate directly with each other. The most important person at a meeting is the chairperson. A meeting's success or otherwise can depend on how effectively it is chaired.

Some organisations today use the term 'facilitator' instead of chairperson. 'To facilitate' literally means 'to make easy', so their job is to do whatever they can to make the group's task as easy as possible.

### An Effective Chairperson:

▶ Draws up the agenda with the secretary before the meeting
▶ Sticks to the agenda
▶ Keeps control without being dictatorial
▶ Encourages participation from everyone
▶ Is impartial
▶ Steers the discussion towards decision-making
▶ Seeks consensus on decisions, by a vote if necessary
▶ Sums up the main points, making sure everyone understands them.

A chairperson should also have excellent communication skills: listening to the members, keeping the discussion relevant, having qualities of tact, empathy, warmth, humour and good judgment and summarising the main points discussed.

### An Ineffective Chairperson:

▶ Dominates the proceedings

▶ Loses control

▶ Allows private conversations and interruptions among the participants.

## The Secretary

Before the meeting, the secretary:

▶ Sends out notice of the meeting

▶ Draws up the agenda with the chairperson

▶ Prepares any relevant documents, e.g. correspondence

▶ Prepares a suitable venue/room.

During the meeting, the secretary:

▶ Records attendance

▶ Reads minutes of the previous meeting

▶ Reads correspondence

▶ Gives a secretary's report if required

▶ Takes notes for the minutes

▶ Supports and assists the chairperson.

After the meeting, the secretary:

▶ Writes up the minutes

▶ Deals with correspondence

▶ Acts on the decisions that have been made.

## The Treasurer

The treasurer manages all finances and funds of the organisation and gives a treasurer's report if required, usually at an AGM.

# ▶ Documents for Meetings

## The Notice

Some meetings are held regularly on a specific day each month, and as members will be aware of this, no notice is required. However, if meetings are less regular the secretary should give notice, at least one week beforehand. It may be sent as a letter, memo, email or simply as a typed or handwritten notice on a notice board, although each member should also receive an individual copy.

### Sample Notice for Individual Member

Dear Member,
The next meeting of the Student Council will take place on Wednesday,
21 October at 1.15 in room 20.
Yours faithfully,
Caroline Stevens
Secretary

### Sample Notice for Notice Board

**Drumlinn College of Further Education**
**Student Council**

The next meeting of the Student Council will take place on Wednesday,
21 October at 1.15 in room 20.

Caroline Stevens
Secretary

## The Agenda

This is a list of all the items to be discussed at the meeting, letting participants know in advance so that they can prepare. The secretary and chairperson draw it up, though participants may request to have specific items included. It is often included with the notice.

## Sample Agenda

---

**Drumlinn College of Further Education**
**Student Council**

Agenda

1. Apologies for absence
2. Minutes of previous meeting
3. Matters arising from the minutes
4. Correspondence
5. Use of computer rooms
6. Next social
7. Any other business
8. Date of next meeting

---

Items 1 to 4, 7 and 8 above are almost always included. After the minutes are read (item 2) they should be approved (proposed and seconded) and accepted by the chairperson signing them. Item 3 is to allow members to discuss anything relating to the minutes, for example to find out what action was taken since the previous meeting. Item 4 consists of any letters, memos or emails that the secretary has sent and received since the previous meeting. In order to save time these won't actually be read out in full unless the secretary is requested to do so. Item 7 is often abbreviated to AOB and gives members the chance to bring up any other topics for brief discussion.

## Minutes

The minutes are a brief record of what was discussed and decided at a meeting. They are written up by the secretary and should be accurate and impartial. They should contain only the relevant points, but all motions and resolutions should be recorded word for word. They should be written in the past tense and record the name of the organisation, the date, time, venue and attendance.

### Types of Minutes:

- *Resolution Minutes* record only the decisions or resolutions. All discussion prior to this is omitted.
- *Narrative Minutes* record both discussion and resolutions. This requires good summarising skills, including only relevant discussion and leaving out unimportant details.
- *Action Minutes* record a brief summary of the meeting and a column listing the names or initials of those responsible for implementing decisions made. These columns are important for recording who is responsible for what.
  Sometimes the minutes will consist of a combination of all three.

## Sample Minutes

**Drumlinn College of Further Education**
**Student Council**

**Minutes of the meeting held on Wednesday, 21 October at 1.15 pm in room 20.**

Present:
John Crowe (Chairperson)
Caroline Stevens (Secretary)
Orla O'Connell (Treasurer)
Neville Harding (Staff)
Sinéad Lombard
Joseph Onyesoh
Patricia McCarthy
Fiona O'Brien
Caitriona Connolly
Toki Tanaka
Fred Kenny
Stephen D'Arcy
Apologies: Joe Hayes, Kevin O'Shea, Sabina Meyer.

### Minutes of previous meeting
The minutes of the meeting on Wednesday, 14 October were read, approved and signed.

### Matters arising
The chairperson reported that he had met with the Principal and that a quotation for new lockers had been sought and that the lockers would be purchased in the new year.

### Correspondence
The secretary read a letter from the Bayview Hotel offering student rates for the end-of-year social, and a letter from the Simon Community thanking the students for their fundraising activities. It was decided that a similar fundraiser will take place this year.

### Use of computer rooms
Patricia McCarthy expressed concern that students on her course did not have sufficient time in the computer rooms to work on assignments and that more hours should be made available to them by the computer department.

Toki Tanaka agreed and suggested that an extra hour each evening between 5 and 6 o'clock should be requested.

**Next social**

Sinéad Lombard reported that she had confirmed the booking of Frankie's Nightclub for the next social, and that it was free of charge. Ticket prices were agreed at €10, and Joseph Onyesoh volunteered to design and print tickets.

**AOB**

Stephen D'Arcy said that a number of his classmates had complained about the canteen facilities. He said that the sandwiches were unsatisfactory and that hot food would be welcomed. There was broad agreement with his comments and Fiona O'Brien suggested that a canteen committee consisting of students, teaching staff and canteen staff be set up to discuss improvements. Neville Harding said that he would raise the issue at the next staff meeting.

The meeting closed at 1.50 and the next meeting was set for 4 November.

The timing and environment of meetings can often be factors that determine their success or failure. Most people are at their best around mid-morning, and slightly tired immediately after lunch. Many people with families to feed may find the hours between 5 pm and 7 pm awkward. The size and arrangement of the meeting room is an important consideration and it is the secretary's job to ensure that it is suitable for the size of the group and that the layout will encourage, rather than inhibit, communication. Here are some possible seating arrangements:

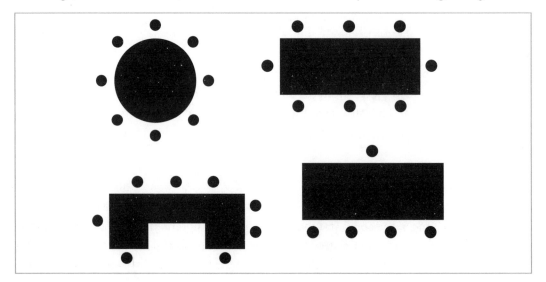

*Fig. 6.2 Different seating arrangements*

## Discussion

What are the advantages and disadvantages of these different seating arrangements?

# ▶ Communication at Meetings

As soon as everyone has arrived and is seated, the chairperson will open the meeting with, 'I will now call the meeting to order . . .' or a similar phrase. The chairperson has the ability to set the tone by being firm but friendly.  A word of greeting or welcome can often help in this regard. Once the routine items have been quickly dealt with, the first item should be introduced and the chairperson should address the whole group with a question like, 'What does anyone think about . . .' or 'Does anyone have any suggestions for . . .'

Discussion is often dominated by a small number of participants who may intimidate new or shy members, and the chairperson should encourage everyone to contribute. A direct question here is useful, for example, 'What is your view on this matter, Fiona?'

Be aware of nonverbal communication at meetings, such as eye contact, facial expression, posture and gestures, and avoid sending out ambiguous or negative signals. Try to use a tone of voice that is positive, decisive and firm and doesn't become angry or aggressive.

When speaking at a meeting we should begin by clearly signalling to the chairperson our intention to speak by raising our hand before the previous speaker has finished or by saying, 'Through the chair'. If we hesitate the moment may be lost as topics are moved along quite quickly by the chairperson. We can start our contribution with a simple question: 'May I just ask what the previous speaker meant by . . .' or a simple comment: 'Through the chair, I agree with the previous speaker . . .'  Only speak when it is relevant. We cannot know it is relevant unless we listen carefully to the discussion. As with other forms of communication we should be clear, concise and courteous.

The chairperson must determine that all aspects of a topic have been fully discussed before moving to a decision and that time is not wasted by spending too long on any one item.

# ▶ Conflict

Conflict can be useful at meetings as it stimulates ideas and discussion, ensures that all perspectives are examined and increases members' understanding of opposing viewpoints. Displaying effective and empathic listening techniques such as, 'I understand you feel strongly about this, but . . .' can help alleviate conflict. If a member becomes so unruly that the meeting cannot continue, a last resort may be to ask the member to leave or to abandon the meeting.

When there is no conflict at all, it could mean that not all aspects of a particular subject have been explored, and as a result there may be a lack of thorough analysis.

Two types of group conflict have been identified: *disruptive conflict* and *constructive conflict*. Disruptive conflict is when members are competitive, self-interested, adopt a win-lose approach, ignore opposing views, create an unhealthy communication climate which intimidates others, communicate defensively and resort to personal attacks. Constructive conflict occurs when participants are co-operative, focus on the interests of the group, adopt a win-win approach, listen to opposing views, create an open and positive atmosphere and communicate supportively. From the outset, it is again up to the chairperson to set the tone for the meeting and if conflict does occur he must remain impartial and calm.

# ▶ Decision-making

Group decision-making can range from informal agreements to formal voting. Once a discussion has taken place and the chairperson thinks it has been covered sufficiently, she may suggest an action to be taken and ask if everyone agrees. If no one objects, a decision has been made. If there is no overall agreement, a vote may be taken and the majority wins.

## Motion

A motion is a proposal to make a decision or take action about something. A motion must be proposed, seconded and start with the word 'that'. For example, 'I propose that the next social will take place in Coast Night Club.' It is then followed by a vote, and if passed, becomes a resolution.

## Consensus

Today more and more groups and organisations are using consensus as a means of decision-making because it can transform a gathering of diverse individuals into a strong and healthy group. In consensus, every group member's opinion is valid and is heard. It is different from majority rule by virtue of its more co-operative approach and the idea that decisions by vote might leave a minority feeling less committed to the decision and/or the group.

Groups that use consensus have similar roles but use different names, such as facilitator instead of chairperson and note-/minute-taker instead of secretary. A timekeeper is employed to ensure that the group sticks to the agenda and a 'vibes watcher' might be employed to observe nonverbal cues as to the general mood of participants. He will let the facilitator know if there are any signs of impending conflict or fatigue, for example.

### The Process of Consensus

An idea is discussed and the group arrives at a point where a decision is ready to be made. Someone will formulate a proposal, e.g. 'I propose that we use consensus as a decision-making tool.' The facilitator will ask, 'Do we have consensus?' (i.e. 'Are we all agreed?'). In making the decision, a participant can take one of three actions:

1. Give consent – agree to the decision, even if she has some reservations or disagreements with it.
2. Stand aside – when she cannot agree to support the decision but thinks it is fine for the rest of the group to support it. This action absolves the individual from any responsibility for the decision.
3. Block – this is when someone cannot support the decision and believes it would be bad for the whole group, so the decision cannot be made. It is a serious action and should not be taken lightly. It is said that you have a lifetime limit of three to four blocks.

Stand-asides and blocks are recorded in the minutes. If consensus is not reached, those who don't agree raise their concerns, which are discussed, and an amendment to the proposal is made. The cycle is repeated until consensus is achieved.

## Open Space Technology and World Café

Two cutting-edge methods of group facilitation, Open Space Technology and World Café, are being used more and more by organisations that adopt a less formal and hierarchical approach. Both are powerful tools for groups of any size wanting to explore specific important questions or issues.

**Open Space Technology** is a complicated-sounding term for a simple process and can seem a bit chaotic if you are a person who likes to be in control. It has four rules and one law. The four rules are:

1. Whoever come are the right people.
2. Whatever happens is the only thing that could have.
3. Whenever it starts is the right time.
4. When it's over, it's over.

The one law is the law of two feet: 'If you find yourself in a situation or discussion where you are neither learning nor contributing, feel free to use your feet to go to a more productive place.'

A facilitator explains the process at the start. The group sits in a circle, or concentric circles if there are too many people to fit in one circle. In the centre is a pile of A4 sheets and pens, and the title of the event, which is the question or issue being discussed, should be displayed on a wall or board so that everyone can see it. Also on the wall is an empty timetable, with session times on one axis and breakout spaces on the other, as in the table. Each of the blank spaces on the timetable should be A4 size.

|  | 1 Library | 2 Computer room | 3 Main office | 4 Table in hallway |
|---|---|---|---|---|
| 10 am–11 am |  |  |  |  |
| 11 am– 12 pm |  |  |  |  |
| 12 pm–1 pm |  |  |  |  |

Then the facilitator asks people to come up with ideas for discussion related to the main topic and people write these on the A4 sheets. Whoever writes a suggestion has to lead that particular discussion. The topics are then slotted into the timetable, and if there are too many, they can be combined into similar-themed topics.

When the timetable is full, participants look at it for a few minutes, and the facilitator announces the first session. Each breakout space should have lots of flip chart paper and pens.

At the end of the sessions, someone from each group gives feedback on their discussion to the whole group. The ideas can then be written/typed up and sent/emailed out to each participant later. This is a great way to draw people out who are passionate about a subject.

**World Café** was developed when someone realised that the best discussions at conferences took place during the tea break, so why not have one big tea break instead? Seven principles of World Café have been devised:

1.  Set the context. Prepare the event well:
    ▶ Topic for discussion
    ▶ Venue
    ▶ Invite participants
    ▶ Time
    ▶ Hoped-for outcomes.
2.  Prepare the venue. Make it comfortable, with enough chairs and tables (big enough to sit up to five people), a supply of flip chart paper, pens and plenty of tea, coffee and snacks.
3.  Carefully frame the question for discussion.
4.  Encourage everyone to contribute. The more people who discuss, the more ideas and the more collective intelligence is unlocked.
5.  Connect diverse perspectives. Every participant moves to another table every 15 minutes, bringing with them the ideas from their previous conversation. One

person at each table remains. This is the table host, who writes down the ideas of that table. This means that over the space of a couple of hours, everyone will get to meet almost everyone else. At each changeover, the table host shares the discussion from that table with the new group of participants.

6. Listen together and notice patterns. Listening is crucial for World Café, so:
    ▶ Listen to every speaker with the assumption that they have something important and wise to say.
    ▶ Listen with a willingness to be influenced.
    ▶ Listen with an open mind to a speaker even though he may have different perspectives and opinions from yours.
    ▶ When speaking, be clear and succinct – don't hog the discussion.
7. Share collective discoveries. Each table host can give feedback on his table's discussion points; the sheets of paper can be put up on the walls of the room for all to see; information can be typed up and emailed out to all participants.

## Other Meeting Terms

*Quorum* – the minimum number of members required to attend a meeting in order for it to be valid.

*Standing Orders* – the written rules, which an organisation uses to run its meetings.

*Point of Order* – when a member checks to see if the proper procedure is being followed.

*Amendment* – a proposal to change a motion.

 # Activities

*Warmer*

Divide into groups of between five and ten. One person starts by saying 'Brenda is going on holiday and in her suitcase she packs . . .' adding one item. The next person repeats this and adds another item and so on around the group. Anyone who changes the order of items or forgets any item is out. If this takes too long, just do two rounds.

*Preparation for Meeting*

The group should elect participants to the key roles required, decide on a topic for discussion (see suggestions below), make a list of items to be discussed at the meeting and draw up a notice and an agenda.

Suggested Scenarios:

1. Class meeting to discuss a forthcoming social event/trip.

2. Class meeting to discuss any issues or problems you are experiencing at college.

3. A residents' association meeting to discuss the problem of loud concerts being held at a venue in your community.

4. A residents' association meeting to discuss the problem of drugs and drug-dealing in the community.

5. A small rural community meeting to discuss how to incorporate a group of 30 immigrants who have recently arrived.

6. A small rural community meeting to discuss the establishment of a wind farm in the locality.

7. A union meeting to discuss pay and working conditions.

8. A meeting at work to discuss the promotion and sale of a new product.

9. A meeting at work to plan a social event.

10. A meeting of football supporters to plan a trip to the next World Cup.

Alternatively, make up your own scenario.

Hold the meeting in class and if possible record it on audio or video. Afterwards listen to or watch the recording. Each member writes up the minutes of the meeting, acting as secretary.

Take note of your own communication skills at the meeting. Could you improve them in any way?

This may take a number of class sessions.

## Tips for Effective Group Discussions and Meetings

- Listen to other members.
- Don't interrupt.
- Raise your hand to indicate that you wish to speak.
- Avoid sarcastic or offensive comments.
- Keep the discussion relevant.
- Keep comments clear and concise.
- Move the discussion towards a decision.
- Turn off mobile phones.

# Chapter Review

1. What are the advantages and disadvantages of group interaction?
2. List four ways of improving group communication.
3. What is synergy?
4. What are the purposes of meetings?
5. What are the duties and functions of a chairperson and a secretary?
6. Give explanations of notice, agenda and minutes.
7. Explain the two types of conflict.
8. What is consensus?
9. Outline the consensus decision-making process.

# Chapter 7
## Presentation Skills

There are a number of situations in which, at some stage in our lives, we may be asked to give a talk:

▶ Weddings and other celebrations
▶ Welcome/farewell occasions
▶ Acceptance speeches
▶ Presentation of a new idea or product
▶ Introducing a guest speaker or new colleague at work
▶ Giving instructions/speech to new colleagues, clients or students about our job
▶ Television or radio presentation.

These range from very brief, informal, chatty talks, which require little preparation, to extensive, detailed and formal presentations that need careful planning and organisation. The latter is what is normally required of students for the purpose of a communications course.

Fig. 7.1

# ❱ Fear of Public Speaking

Few of us like the idea of standing up and giving a talk in front of a group of people. This is known as communication apprehension or stage fright and it is perfectly normal. Most professional speakers, whether they are actors, politicians, media presenters or teachers, suffer from nerves at some stage during their careers, and they all know that the first time is the worst. For many students this will be the first time they have given a presentation, and many reluctant students learn that they are in fact better speakers than they initially thought and surprise themselves with their good results. Having completed the task, they gain confidence, knowing that they have cleared the first hurdle of public speaking.

An oral presentation is one form of speaking for which you can and must be well prepared. The better prepared you are the more confidence you have, and the more confident you are the better the presentation.

First, it is important to remember that everyone gets nervous when giving a talk, so you are not alone. Second, even though the attention is on you when you are speaking, you should focus on the subject matter, not on yourself. Concentrate on getting the message across. This can take some of the pressure off.

Here are some techniques for relaxing and reducing nerves before giving a speech.

❱ Progressive muscle relaxation: Find a quiet place to sit or lie down and start with the feet – flex the muscles in your feet, then relax them. Slowly work your way through each muscle group in your body, tensing and relaxing each group.

- Deep breathing: Breathe slowly into your stomach, feel it expand then move the breath into your midriff and feel your ribs expand and finally breathe into your chest and feel it and your shoulders expand. Hold your breath for several counts then exhale slowly through the mouth. Do this three times.
- Hydrate: 'Dry mouth' often occurs when we are nervous, so make sure to drink plenty of water beforehand, or suck a mint or lozenge.
- Coughing not only helps to clear the throat but also helps relax the diaphragm, which in turn can reduce anxiety.
- Pressure point: You need to locate a specific point on your inner wrist, 3–5 cm from your wrist crease. Use your thumb to repeatedly press firmly but gently on this pressure point for 1–3 minutes.
- Swinging the arms, rolling the head and shoulders and rubbing the earlobes may all help to reduce stress and anxiety before a presentation.
- Realise that you cannot give the perfect speech. You will tend to notice your mistakes more than the audience will, so don't be afraid of minor errors. Remember that the main thing is to get your message across.
- Conversation is full of minor errors and we tolerate those. A speech is like an extended conversation.

It is virtually impossible to eliminate nerves completely before public speaking and it is also undesirable. A little anxiety is good, as it sharpens the concentration, but using some or all of the techniques above can help reduce nerves.

 **Activity**

Make a list of the reasons why you become nervous at the idea of giving a presentation.

Here's what the experts would say are the causes of this type of anxiety:

- The fear of communicating with people you don't know
- A new or unusual situation
- Being the centre of attention, which makes you self-conscious and embarrassed if you appear to say something foolish
- Evaluation – when being watched by a tutor or a video camera, you feel you are being examined
- Past failures in similar situations
- A learned anxiety from seeing others who are nervous of giving a presentation.

# ▶ Extended Conversation

Most of us have no problem sitting with a group of friends and telling them what we did at the weekend. But moving from this situation to standing up in front of a group is quite a big shift. The main differences are:

▶ Everyone's attention is focused on you
▶ You are standing and they are sitting
▶ There is a greater expectation on you to 'perform'
▶ There is no turn-taking or instant feedback.

Another important difference between conversation and a speech is that a speech has been planned, prepared and organised.

Public speaking is a bit like an enlarged conversation, so we should try to speak as if in a conversation. A good speech does not need to be in overly formal language. Often an audience will respond better to an informal, personal style, which helps them to feel they are partaking in a conversation rather than being lectured to. Don't try to use language that wouldn't come naturally, but avoid using excessive slang as well. Most listeners will tolerate minor errors and stumbles, as they do in normal conversation.

# ▶ Preparation

An effective presentation is the result of careful planning, preparation and rehearsing. Without adequate preparation the presentation will be ineffective and you will disappoint both yourself and your audience. It is a good opportunity to try something new, even if it is a daunting task, and many students of communications surprise themselves at the excellent results they achieve in this skill.

## Choosing a Topic

If you have the option of choosing your own subject, then choose a topic that:

▶ You are interested in
▶ You know something about
▶ You can get information on.

If you are interested in the subject, it is more likely that you can make it interesting for others. You might choose some aspect of your course or a pastime/hobby.

Ask yourself:
- ❯ Is it suitable material for an oral presentation?
- ❯ Is it appropriate for the audience? Will they understand it/find it interesting?
- ❯ Is it appropriate for the occasion?
- ❯ Am I sufficiently interested in the topic?
- ❯ Where can I get information on it?
- ❯ Can I get some visual aids to make it more interesting?

## Brainstorming

When you have chosen your topic, begin by brainstorming all the relevant themes associated with it, and create a mind map on a page (see p.91). This will give you an idea of how large the subject matter is and you may need to narrow it down to one or two subtopics.

## Communication Objective

There are three main speaking purposes:
- ❯ Entertainment
- ❯ Information
- ❯ Persuasion

Decide what your objective is. Do you want the audience to take up tennis or join Amnesty International? Do you want to show them how to grow their own vegetables, or how to paint? Or do you want to have them rolling in the aisles? Perhaps you will use a combination of all three.

You should be able to summarise the main idea of the talk in one concise sentence. This may then be used as an opening statement and should be memorable even if the listeners don't remember the details of the speech.

## Audience

It is important to know who your audience is going to be. Are they already interested in the subject? Do they have any prior knowledge of the topic? Will they share your sense of humour? Are they captive, i.e. will they listen to your every word, or will it be a struggle to force them to pay attention? A good understanding of your audience beforehand will assist you in knowing what kind of talk you will give, and what sort of language and tone of voice you will use.

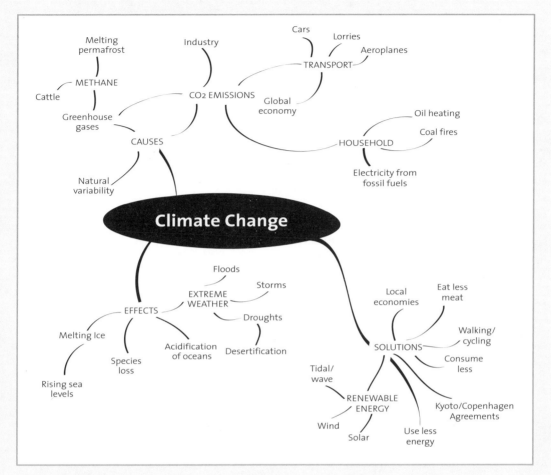

*Fig. 7.2 Mind map*

# ▶ Structure and Organisation

A well-organised speech can be a stimulating and inspiring piece of communication that will stay in our minds for some time afterwards. A disorganised presentation will be ineffective and even embarrassing. We have all experienced sitting in a class or listening to a speaker who rambles from one topic to the next, but do we remember what the main thrust of the speech was or any of the details? Probably not.

A well-organised speech works for the following reasons:

- ▶ It is easier to understand and digest
- ▶ It is easier to remember
- ▶ It has more impact and is more persuasive
- ▶ It increases the speaker's credibility.

## A Well-organised Speaker

▶ Uses short sentences which are easy to follow
▶ Introduces the listeners to forthcoming information, e.g. 'The results of global warming are twofold: . . .'
▶ Gives information in a clear and logical way, e.g. 'First . . . second . . .'
▶ Uses detailed statistical evidence to support information given
▶ Avoids vague and ambiguous information.

## Structure

There are three basic elements of an oral presentation:

1. Introduction – tell the audience what you are going to say.
2. Body – say it.
3. Conclusion – tell them what you've said.

## Introduction

The opening of your speech is vital in that it can win or lose the audience. First impressions last, so try to get the listeners' attention from the start and explain briefly what the talk will be about. The introduction should have three sections:

1. An opening statement that will get the audience's attention. Consider using one of the following:
   ▶ A controversial statement, e.g. 'The Irish are a nation of drunks and dreamers.'
   ▶ A quotation
   ▶ An interesting statistic
   ▶ A visual aid with impact
   ▶ A rhetorical question – one that doesn't need an answer, e.g. 'Have you ever wondered what it's like to swim in a crocodile-infested river?'
   ▶ A personal experience
   ▶ An anecdote
   ▶ Humour (but be wary of using a joke – it could ruin your talk!).

2. A statement of the main idea, which should give the audience a good understanding of what it will be about.
   ▶ Today I'm going to tell you about the causes and effects of global warming.
   ▶ This presentation is going to try to illustrate the dangers of alcohol abuse.
   ▶ Today I want to inform you about rock-climbing.
   ▶ This morning I'm going to show you how to grow your own tomatoes.

3. A rough outline of the main points to be covered. This gives the audience an idea of what it is you are going to say – a bit like a table of contents. An audience likes to know where it is being taken.

## Body of Presentation

In a five- to ten-minute speech, aim for three to four main points, selected from the mind map. They should be logically organised and they should flow smoothly from one topic to the next. It is important to try to link topics together, and signposts can be used for this purpose. These can be single words, phrases or whole sentences. It is crucial to let the audience know when you are moving on to a new point. If you jump from one topic to the next too abruptly, the audience may get confused and lose interest.

Typical signposts might include the following:

- First, second, third . . .
- Due to this, because of this, as a result of this, consequently . . .
- Therefore, and so . . .
- Finally . . .
- Now that we've seen how the internal combustion engine works . . .
- I've looked at the causes of insomnia, now let's have a look at the effects . . .

Nonverbal signposts can also be used:

- The fingers can indicate first, second and third points
- Silence or a pause can let the audience know that you are moving on to a new topic
- Visual aids can be used to introduce a new point
- Intonation is a good way of showing that you have reached the end of one section of your talk.

## Conclusion

An effective conclusion is vital so as to finish on a strong note that will leave a lasting impression on the audience. At all costs avoid trailing off limply at the end. A conclusion is often like the introduction in reverse. Use it to summarise the main points and to leave the audience with a final thought on the subject that they will hopefully remember. Don't be afraid to repeat information at the end of the talk. The audience cannot rewind to go back over the topics already stated, so it is useful to restate some of the key ones, especially the main idea. As with the introduction, it should be brief and no new themes should be introduced at this stage. Try to keep the ending positive and upbeat.

Typical concluding statements:

- I hope you now have a better grasp of . . .
- Let me leave you with one final thought . . .
- Today I've given you a brief outline about . . .
- I hope I have succeeded in informing you about . . .

## Timeline of Presentation

Break your talk into sections using the topics from your brainstorm. Along with the introduction and conclusion, it might look something like this:

- Introduction – 30 seconds
- Subtopic 1 – two minutes
- Subtopic 2 – three minutes
- Subtopic 3 – two minutes
- Conclusion – 30 seconds
- Total – eight minutes

Now it seems quite manageable, because you only have to talk for a couple of minutes on each subtopic.

Next you should write out your speech in full. This gives you the opportunity to go through each point carefully, and to make sure that it is properly structured. Give each topic a heading. Practise by reading through it a few times to get used to the flow of it. Select keywords and phrases and write these on **cue cards**, which will be your notes during the presentation. Write three or four points on each one, on one side only, and number each cue card so you don't get them mixed up.

# Delivery

## Nonverbal Communication

An audience responds to a speaker's body language. If your body language shows interest and enthusiasm for the subject, the audience will respond in the same way. If you show that you aren't interested or that you're bored, the audience will feel the same. There are a number of points to consider:

## The Voice

The voice is obviously crucial in an oral presentation. The following are the main points to consider:

1. *Volume:* You must be audible and loud enough so that the people at the back can hear. Practise projecting your voice to someone at the opposite end of a classroom.
2. *Tone and pitch:* You should aim to make it sound interesting by sounding interested. Otherwise, it may sound flat and monotonous. Inflection, changing the pitch of the voice so that is goes up and down, adds interest to a speech. We do this naturally when we speak about something that interests us. When we are nervous, unfortunately, we tend to remain at one level. Practise changing the pitch of your voice at different parts of your presentation.
3. *Emphasis:* Try to put stress on words that need emphasising.
4. *Pause:* Pausing is effective and useful to let the audience take in an important point, to signal a change of topic and to give yourself a break to check your notes. Don't be afraid to pause briefly every now and again.
5. *Speed:* We speed up when nervous. If you're too fast you may lose the audience; too slow and you'll bore them.

In all of the above, aim for variety as this will make it sound interesting and hold the audience's attention.

## Posture

Listeners pay more attention to a speaker who has a straight posture than someone with a crooked or slouched one. Stand with a comfortably straight spine and neck.

Avoid:

1. Shifting from one foot to the other
2. Putting your back or shoulder to audience
3. Folding arms
4. Hands in pockets
5. Hands behind back.

## Gestures

Appropriate and controlled hand gestures can help support a speech. Unanimated speakers can be boring to watch, but don't use exaggerated gestures that will distract the audience.

Avoid:

1. Wringing hands
2. Rattling keys/coins in pockets
3. Fiddling with hair, pens, glasses etc.

## Facial Expression

Introducing yourself with a smile can win over an audience from the start, and an occasional and appropriate smile during the talk can keep them on your side. The eyebrows are a very expressive part of the face and we can emphasise a point by raising them.

## Eye Contact

Ideally we should make eye contact at least once with everyone in the audience. But by staring at one person we can make him feel uncomfortable. By looking at the back wall, out of the window or at the floor, it appears that we are communicating with these things and not with the audience.

# ▶ Venue

You should find out about the venue beforehand. What sort of equipment is available? Is the room big or small? Will your voice reach those sitting at the back? Will there be a podium or somewhere to put your cue cards and/or visual aids? If you don't know the venue beforehand you might be surprised to find yourself somewhere totally unsuited to your needs.

# ▶ Support Material

A presentation that involves just speaking can be quite dull, so support material can help to make it more stimulating. Any of the following will add interest and credibility:
▶ Statistics
▶ Comparisons
▶ Quotations
▶ Visual aids
▶ Anecdotes/stories
▶ Examples
▶ Handouts

# ▶ Visual Aids

Visual aids support and enhance an oral presentation in the following ways:
1. They make a talk interesting and stimulating.
2. They have a strong and lasting impact.
3. They can help an audience understand the topic by:
   – illustrating with examples
   – simplifying and supporting verbal information with charts or graphs.

## Types of Visual Aid

- ▶ Models and objects
- ▶ Maps
- ▶ Diagrams
- ▶ Charts and graphs
- ▶ Drawings, paintings, sketches
- ▶ Photographs
- ▶ Posters

Fig. 7.3

## Means of Display

1. Presentation software such as Microsoft PowerPoint or Apple's Keynote are designed for presentations and are relatively easy and enjoyable to use. You will need a computer linked to a data projector and a screen. Slides that use a combination of images and a few bullet points of text will keep the audience interested. Avoid overdoing slide transition effects.
2. DVD – a relevant video clip can be used to support your speech.
3. Always prepare your equipment beforehand to make sure it is working properly.

Other visual aids:
- ▶ Whiteboard
- ▶ Blackboard
- ▶ Flipchart

These are not usually prepared beforehand, but you need to have clear handwriting or drawing skills.

- ▶ Slide projector
- ▶ Overhead projector

## Handouts

Don't make your audience read too much. They will forget about you. It is best to use handouts at the end of the presentation. They should be headed with the title of your presentation and your name.

## General Points to Remember about Visual Aids

1. Keep them simple – simple language, simple images, limit the amount of text you use – an audience doesn't like to read too much.
2. Make them big – they should be visible from the back of the room.
3. Make them relevant – use visuals only if they support and enhance the speech. Don't let them dominate.
4. They should look well – no one likes to look at unattractive or messy images.

5. Colour is more attractive than black and white.

6. For a five- to ten- minute talk, three to five visuals are sufficient.

### Effective Use of Visual Aids

1. Prepare them well in advance of the presentation.

2. Plan exactly when to use them during the talk. Don't have them all at the beginning or all at the end.

3. Practise using them.

4. Check that any equipment is working.

5. Don't block the audience's view of them.

6. When finished using them, switch them off or remove them.

7. Remember, technology can always let you down at the last moment, and you may have to speak without it.

### Font Sizes

If using written text, make sure you use appropriate-sized words. Here are some guidelines:

| Flip Charts/Blackboards/Whiteboards | |
|---|---|
| Headings | 3 inches |
| Sub-headings | 2 inches |

| | Computer Printouts | |
|---|---|---|
| | PowerPoint/Transparencies | Handouts |
| Headings | 36 point | 18 point |
| Sub-headings | 24 point | 14 point |
| Main Body of Text | 18 point | 12 point |

# ▶ Dealing with Questions

When you have finished speaking, thank the audience for listening and ask if there are any questions. Here are some hints:

▶ Listen to the question carefully.

▶ Repeat the whole question in case not everyone has heard it.

▶ When answering, address the whole audience, not just the questioner.

▶ Give answers that are complete, concise and to the point.

▶ When finished answering, ask the questioner if your reply was sufficiently clear.

▶ If you don't know the answer, don't 'wing it'. Be honest and say you'll have to look into it.

▶ Stay alert.

▶ Bring the question session to an *effective* conclusion, e.g. 'If there are no further questions . . .'

▶ Say thank you at the end.

## Finally

Preparation for an oral presentation requires sufficient practice. This means spending time rehearsing in front of a class group, at home with friends or family or on your own in front of a mirror. Without practice you will be ineffective. Each time you practise, you improve.

Practice is vital for the following reasons:

▶ To time the speech to ensure you won't go too much over or under the allotted time
▶ To get used to the layout of and the flow of words in the speech
▶ To practise using the cue cards, and filling out the keywords and phrases
▶ To get comfortable with your visual aids, if using any, and to know when to use them
▶ To improve your overall performance: voice, body language, eye contact etc.
▶ To get completely acquainted with and confident about your subject matter.

# ✳ Activity

1. Read or watch some famous speeches and observe what techniques are being used. Here are a few good examples:

   ▶ US President John F. Kennedy's inaugural speech 1961
   ▶ Martin Luther King's 'I Have a Dream' speech 1963
   ▶ President Mary Robinson's inaugural speech 1990
   ▶ President Barak Obama's inaugural speech 2009
   ▶ Neil Gaiman's commencement speech at the University of the Arts, Philadelphia 2012
   ▶ The final speech from the Charlie Chaplin film *The Great Dictator*.

2. Vocal Warm-up

It's useful to warm up your vocal cords before giving a speech. Stand comfortably straight, feet hip-width apart and imagine you are drawing the number 8 in the air with your nose for about a minute. This loosens up the neck muscles. Then 'draw' a number 8 on its side or an infinity symbol. Next, start making 'blah blah blah' sounds and really stick your tongue out as you do it. Then change that into the noise children sometimes make by flapping your tongue in and out of your mouth and loudly vocalising. Next, make a continual 'ng' sound such as at the end of the word 'sing' but using your voice to go up and down making a sound like a siren, getting higher and lower each time. Then purse your lips to make an 'ooooh' sound followed immediately by an 'eeee' sound and alternate quickly between the two really stretching your lips. Do this to the tune of 'Twinkle Twinkle Little Star'. By now your vocal cords should be warmed up nicely.

3.  Sit or stand in a circle and do a go-round, each student repeating the tongue twisters on p.45.

4.  Three-word speech
    ▶ Each student writes three words on three separate pieces of paper and puts them in a bowl/box/bucket.
    ▶ Students take turns to pick three pieces of paper and, on the spot, they must make up a story/speech that contains the three words.

# ▶ Tips for an Effective Presentation

▶ Prepare well.
▶ Keep it simple.
▶ Practise.
▶ Use good visual aids.

## Chapter Review

1.  Explain the main causes of fear of public speaking.
2.  How can we get over our fear of public speaking?
3.  What are the similarities and differences between an oral presentation and a conversation?
4.  How can you organise a speech to make it easy for an audience to understand?
5.  Why is it important to structure a speech?
6.  What are the advantages of using visual aids?
7.  Describe effective ways of opening a speech.
8.  How can you make effective use of visual aids?
9.  Explain the importance of NVC (nonverbal communication) in an oral presentation.
10. Outline how to deal with questions from the audience.

# Part 3

## Nonverbal Communication

### Some Examples

▶ Body language
▶ Facial expression
▶ Eye contact
▶ Gestures
▶ Posture

### Advantages

▶ Supports and reinforces verbal messages
▶ Adds interest
▶ Personalises messages
▶ Gives a more complete picture

### Disadvantages

▶ May be vague or ambiguous
▶ May need verbal explanation
▶ Mostly unconscious
▶ Cultural differences

# Chapter 8
## Nonverbal Communication

Nonverbal communication (NVC) means communicating without words. NVC probably accounts for over 80 per cent of what we communicate, whereas the spoken word may communicate as little as 7 per cent. A look can often reveal more accurately what we are thinking than words can. We are constantly communicating nonverbally, by the way we look, gesture, stand, sit, smile, frown, dress ourselves, wear our hair etc. This is why NVC is so important in any study of communication.

Let's look at a few general points about NVC before we examine the specific types.

1. NVC is ambiguous. There are always at least two potential meanings to any NVC, that of the sender and that of the receiver. It is not always possible to interpret the exact meaning of NVC, since it depends on both the context and the people involved. We should not attempt to attach a fixed meaning to any one form of NVC in isolation from the other verbal and nonverbal messages that may be communicated with it.

2. NVC varies from culture to culture. What might be a friendly gesture in our culture may be a serious insult in another, so be careful! The circle sign made with the thumb and forefinger means 'OK' to Irish, British, Americans and most Northern Europeans. In France it signifies 'zero' or 'worthless', in Japan, 'money', and in parts of the Mediterranean it is an obscene insult.

3. Most of our NVC is unconscious. We wave our hands about and gesticulate when talking excitedly; our face changes shape depending on our emotional state; we twitch, fidget, scratch, stretch, shift our posture hundreds of times every day without even noticing it.

4. We are much less aware of our NVC than our speech. If we become more conscious of how we communicate nonverbally, we can learn to control it and become better communicators.

5. NVC:
   - Supports speech – hand gestures reinforce, elaborate and emphasise what we say, e.g. 'I caught a fish *this* big!' 'He went *that* way'
   - Modifies speech – we can say 'Don't do that' in an angry, pleading, firm, or light-hearted way
   - Replaces speech – sign language
   - Contradicts speech – 'Yes of course I'm fine!' she snapped, avoiding his gaze, and sighing heavily.

6. First impressions count. When we walk through that door for an interview, we are immediately being judged on our appearance, how we walk, shake hands and sit down. Jobs are often disproportionately offered on this basis.

7. Actions speak louder than words. If someone says he has time to talk to you, yet continues what he is doing: gathering his books, erasing the board and checking the register, do you believe his verbal or nonverbal message? Most people, when confronted by such contradictory signs, believe the nonverbal language. Since we are more in control of our words than our body language, most of us find it easier to lie verbally than nonverbally.

8. 'Baby signing' i.e. using hand signs to support verbal communication with babies, is believed to improve communication skills, behaviour, parent–child relationships and mental development in children.

Fig. 8.1 *The Beatles*

Compare these two photographs of The Beatles, one during their heyday, and the other shortly before their split. Discuss the differences in facial expression, physical proximity and contact.

## ▶ Appearance

Fig. 8.2

Compare the appearances of the women in these two photographs. What messages might they consciously or unconsciously be communicating?

Appearance says a lot about the type of person we are. Even if we are the kind of person who dresses 'down' so as not to attract unwanted attention, we are still communicating something about ourselves. We can change how we present ourselves by making alterations to our hair, facial hair, make-up, clothes, accessories, and by using jewellery, tattoos and body piercing. By doing this we can communicate messages about our:

▶ Personality – conservative, rebellious, artistic, individual, extrovert/introvert
▶ Occupation – some jobs have specific uniforms
▶ Role – think of a few different roles you fill, e.g. at work, socialising (formal/informal, single/attached), at home, at an interview
▶ Status – in some occupations higher status is illustrated by different clothing, e.g. the army, nursing, the church, expensive designer suits etc.
▶ Nationality
▶ Gender
▶ Sexual orientation
▶ Interests and tastes
▶ Club membership

It is important to consider how we present ourselves in different situations. For example, for job interviews it is recommended that we dress formally. If we dress too formally for an occasion that is casual, we may look, and feel, out of place. Our appearance projects a certain image of ourselves, and other people will respond to that image. At work and in formal situations we tend to respond more positively to those who are well dressed, but not overdressed.

Consider the clothes you wear. Have you ever thought about the signals that you might be sending out with them? Do you wear them:

▶ For comfort/practical reasons?
▶ Because they are fashionable?
▶ To attract attention?
▶ To blend in with the crowd?
▶ To look 'cool'?
▶ To appear sexy?
▶ Because they are long lasting?
▶ To look rebellious/different?
▶ To be part of a clique?
▶ Because they have a certain logo?

What signals might the following be sending out?

▶ A male with long hair
▶ A female skinhead
▶ A male with short back and sides
▶ A Mohican haircut
▶ Dreadlocks

▶ Pierced tongue
▶ Pierced eyebrow
▶ A male with a right earring only

# ▶ Facial Expression

The face is probably the main source of nonverbal communication and the most important, authentic and direct communication takes place face-to-face. The face is the best indicator of our feelings, and it is only when we are face-to-face with someone that we really connect with him. Even though expressions like smiling and frowning are inborn, we learn how to respond facially to others through interaction with our parents, families and friends, so for example, we smile as a response to another's smile. There is a concern today that many children who don't receive enough parental interaction due to busy lifestyles, and spend much of their time using electronic games, lose out on healthy face-to-face contact. As a result they don't learn facial expression responses, and this can cause relationship problems in later life.

There are over 10,000 facial expressions caused by 44 facial muscles and two bones, the skull and the jaw. There are, however, seven primary expressions that promote a deep response in us: happiness, sadness, surprise, anger, fear, disgust and contempt.

The eyes and the mouth are the main communicators and they are the features we focus on mostly when we are looking at someone. Socrates said that the eyes are the windows of the soul and we can usually tell how someone really feels by looking at their eyes.

The mouth smiles, sneers, pouts, purses, grins, opens wide, shuts tightly etc. The ultimate facial expression, which seems to mean the same in every part of the world, is the smile. A true smile is never misunderstood and, as believed by some scientists, releases endorphins into the body that make us feel good. It also uses fewer muscles than a frown and therefore requires less energy!

Facial expression is so important that in order to avoid misunderstandings when sending emails, some of us accompany them with imitation faces.

Fig. 8.3 *The seven primary expressions*

## ✳ Activity

**Can you match the seven primary expressions of happiness, sadness, surprise, anger, fear, disgust and contempt with the pictures above?**

## ▶ Eye Contact

In western society, when we speak with someone face-to-face it is natural to look her in the eye. It is considered to show directness and integrity. Avoidance of eye contact shows lack of confidence and may indicate dishonesty. In the Czech Republic, avoiding eye contact when clinking beer glasses is interpreted as an indication that the person has something to hide and may not be trustworthy. In some Asian cultures, however, eye contact can be considered rude.

Eye contact is also a way of communicating that we are listening. It lets the speaker know we are interested. It is also used as an initial means of contact. Prior to speaking to someone we usually make eye contact with him.

Eye contact communicates:

▶ Attitudes – intense gazing into another's eyes shows trust and closeness between two people. Is there a difference between gazing and staring into another's eyes?

▶ Attraction – our pupils involuntarily dilate when we are attracted to or interested in someone or something.

▶ Personality – assertive, confident and extrovert types make more direct eye contact than those who are less confident.

▶ Emotions – avoiding or breaking eye contact can show annoyance with someone.

Fig. 8.4 Eye contact

 ## Activity

In pairs, A and B sit opposite each other and spend a minute or two on each of the following:

1. A tells B what he did at the weekend. A makes eye contact and B doesn't.

2. A tells B what he did at the weekend. B makes eye contact and A doesn't.

3. B tells A what she did at the weekend and both make constant eye contact.

4. B tells A what she did at the weekend and each behaves as normal.

Who normally makes more eye contact, the speaker or the listener?

Discuss how you felt as speaker/listener with your partner avoiding your eyes.

# ▶ Gesture

Gestures are actions we make with different parts of our body that can replace or support spoken communication. We each have hundreds of gestures that we use to communicate a vast array of messages.

## Discussion

1. What messages can we send with each of the following parts of the body?
   - ▶ Head
   - ▶ Hands
   - ▶ Arms
   - ▶ Shoulders
   - ▶ Legs

2. How do we communicate the following with gestures?
   - ▶ Hello
   - ▶ Come here
   - ▶ Go away!
   - ▶ Stop
   - ▶ Money
   - ▶ OK
   - ▶ I don't know

   - ▶ Stupid!
   - ▶ Naughty!
   - ▶ Quiet
   - ▶ Drink?
   - ▶ Well done
   - ▶ Pleased to meet you
   - ▶ Please!

There are a multitude of gestures and gesture combinations. One gesture can have many different meanings, and there are many gestures that mean the same thing. Very subtle differences between similar gestures can have widely different meanings.

## Discussion

What different meanings can the following have?
- ▶ A protruding tongue
- ▶ Hands up in the air
- ▶ The V-sign

By becoming more conscious of our gestures and by being clear in their transmission we can avoid vagueness and misunderstandings. It is useful to observe public speakers and the movements that they make when speaking. Be careful not to overdo gesturing to support speech as it may distract from what you are saying.

# Activity

It is possible to have a 'conversation' using only gestures. Try to act out the following role-play without words:

A: Hello.

B: Hello.

A: Are you alright?

B: I'm alright. And you?

A: So so.

B: What time is it?

A: I don't know.

B: Can you give me some money?

A: No.

B: Please.

A: No!

B: I'm hungry.

A: I don't have any money!

B: I'm cold.

A: Look over there!

B: What, where? I don't see anything.

A: It doesn't matter.

B: Goodbye.

A: Bye.

 # Discussion

In terms of gesture, a talk pleading for people to donate money to a cause would differ from a talk intended to incite people to revolt. What sort of gestures would you use in each case?

a      b

*Fig. 8.5 Mary Robinson and Michael D. Higgins using gestures during speeches*

# ▌ Posture

How we stand, sit, walk, lie and generally hold our body communicates a variety of messages:

1. Mood and physical state, e.g. relaxed posture = confidence
2. How we feel towards others, e.g. two people squaring up to each other aggressively stand upright, shoulders back and heads up straight
3. Status, e.g. soldiers stand to attention in front of a superior officer; in some cultures people bow before royalty; people kneel to pray
4. Situation, e.g. at an interview we sit upright showing alertness and interest.

## Activity

Match the moods with the postures below:

| Moods: | Postures: |
| --- | --- |
| Triumph/victory | Arms and legs crossed |
| Boredom | Hands held tightly in front, fidgeting |
| Interest | Hands on hips, head up and back straight |
| Nervousness/shyness | Leaning forward, head cocked |
| Confidence | Head in hands, elbows on table, shoulders slumped, body sagging |
| Defensiveness | Arms held aloft, head held high, fists clenched |

Are any of these signals ambiguous?

Fig. 8.6            a            b            c

What messages are the different individuals in these pictures sending out?

A look around a classroom often reveals a wide variety of moods, with postures ranging from interest to boredom to utter disbelief!

# ◗ Territory

Our territory is something we feel strongly about and it can make us protective and defensive. It is our space and we communicate this in a variety of ways. Animals leave their scent on trees and bushes to let other animals know who lives there, and humans mark their territory in visual ways.

There are three types of human territory: tribal, family and personal.

## Tribal Territory

Primitive tribes occupied a specific area consisting of a home base and a hunting ground around it. Members of the tribe communicated their membership by war chants, face and body paint and a unifying sense of dress. Intruders would have been identified by differences in these markers and driven away. Today, the tribe has become the nation, using nonverbal signals such as flags and national anthems to communicate its identity, and border checkpoints to show its boundary. Another example is football fans who communicate to rival fans their territory in the stadium with a display of colours, flags, scarves and chanting.

## Family Territory

The family territory is the home, with the bedroom as the core where we feel most secure. People who have been burgled and had their private possessions in their bedrooms rummaged through experience a sense of having been invaded. The house has a boundary of a wall, fence or hedge. Within the home are other markers of territory: ornaments, furniture, family photographs, pictures on the walls etc. A family often displays its territory outside the home, e.g. when at the beach, towels, rugs, bags etc. will mark the space to which the family temporarily belongs.

## Personal Territory

Each of us carries an invisible 'space bubble', our own portable piece of territory. We can see this when we get on to a bus or train. If the seats are all empty, except one, the chances are we won't sit next to the only person there. We will always sit where we give ourselves the maximum amount of space.

If someone unknown enters our bubble, we might feel threatened. If someone we know and care for keeps well outside it we might feel a sense of rejection. Our personal space bubble communicates levels of formality, friendship, intimacy and how comfortable we feel with other people. We have to know someone pretty well, or trust her, before we let her enter our space bubble. Sometimes we have no choice but to let others into our space, for example at a crowded concert or football match. In Mediterranean and North African cultures people usually like to stand closer than Northern Europeans and Americans.

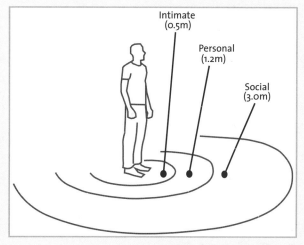

Fig. 8.7 Personal space

Sitting behind a desk is putting up a barrier, and therefore distance, between two people. It can give the impression that we are

Cyanide and Happiness © Explosm.net

Fig. 8.8 Personal space invader

unapproachable. Observe the different interview techniques of television chat show hosts. Some use desks and others don't. Which is more effective?

# Activity

List five people you feel comfortable entering your 'space bubble'.

**What do they have in common? Discuss your reasons with the class group.**

## Proximity

Proximity is how close we let someone get to us. It depends on:

1. Status – people of high status enter others' space more than vice versa, e.g. teacher and pupil, doctor and patient, Garda and criminal, officer and soldier, employer and employee.
2. Gender – women tend to be physically closer to each other than men are to other men.
3. Age – children enter each others' space more than adults enter each others' space.
4. Culture – Middle Eastern and African people tend to stand closer to one another in comparison to people from Western countries and parts of Asia.

# ▌ Orientation

This is how we position ourselves in relation to others and it communicates how we feel towards them. We sit face-to-face with someone we like or respect. Giving someone the 'cold shoulder' means we face away from her in a display of dislike or disrespect.

Two people sitting at a table can choose to orient themselves in a number of different ways:

- ▌ Side by side
- ▌ Face-to-face across the table
- ▌ At right angles to each other at one corner

What are the differences between each of these in terms of formality and intimacy? Consider, for example, which is most appropriate for a job interview. Why did King Arthur have a round table? Consider the typical classroom set-up. Are there alternative ways of arranging the seating for different types of activity?

## Discussion

If a stranger approached you and appeared to be a threat, how would you orient yourself towards him/her? If he appeared to be no threat, how would your NVC be different?

# Physical Contact

Experts say physical contact with others is good for us. It can satisfy emotional needs, increase our sense of self worth, and enhance our relationships as a means of communicating love, affection and closeness. Of course, we all experience different degrees of closeness in our different relationships. For some people it would be perfectly natural to give an affectionate hug to a friend, while to others this would be embarrassing. Touching defines relationships and communicates social status. What messages are being sent out by the people in these photographs?

Fig. 8.9 *Physical contact*    *a*                                                                              *b*

There are four types of physical contact, ranging in degree of intimacy:
1. Functional – usually done in professional situations, e.g. doctors, physiotherapists, hairdressers.
2. Ritual – the most common type of ritual touching is the greeting, e.g. handshake, embrace, nose rub, kiss on the cheek, 'high five'.
3. Playful/supportive – used to indicate encouragement, sympathy and affection, e.g. pat on the back, touching the hand or arm. This type is open to misinterpretation, especially at work. It may be viewed as patronising, as an invasion of personal space or at worst as sexual harassment.
4. Intimate – between parent and child, between lovers.

## Handshake Techniques

There are a variety of handshake techniques:
1. The firm handshake
2. The limp handshake
3. The accompanying hand on the other's elbow
4. The accompanying hand on the other's shoulder
5. The accompanying hand on the side of the other's head.

## Discussion

What does each of these handshake techniques communicate in terms of confidence, warmth and intimacy?

Physical contact varies in the following ways:

1. Status – doctors will touch patients and not vice versa (see Proximity above).
2. Gender – in Western countries, women touch each other more often than men touch each other.
3. Age – children touch each other more than older people touch each other.
4. Culture – Northern Europeans, Americans and Asians tend to touch each other less than Southern Europeans and Africans touch each other. Many Asian societies are traditionally not touch-oriented and public displays of affection are avoided.

## Discussion

You have decided to go on a world trip for one year. At the airport a number of friends and family members have come to bid you farewell. How would you say goodbye nonverbally to the following?

▶ Your mother
▶ Your father
▶ Your sister
▶ Your brother
▶ Your closest friend
▶ A colleague
▶ Your boss
▶ A casual acquaintance
▶ Your boyfriend/girlfriend

This could be done as a role-play if members of the class feel comfortable doing it.

# ▶ Paralanguage

Sometimes we communicate with the voice but not necessarily with words. There are three types of paralanguage:

1. Vocal qualities
2. Vocalisations
3. Vocal segregates

## Vocal Qualities

▶ Pitch
▶ Volume
▶ Stress/emphasis
▶ Speed
▶ Rhythm
▶ Tone
▶ Accent

These can communicate our emotional state, personality, social status, cultural background and education. We can alter the meaning of what we say by infusing it with different tones. We can convey approval or disapproval, warmth, humour, friendliness, dislike, scorn, sarcasm etc. We can sound serious or playful, firm, seductive, apologetic, angry etc.

If we are planning on working in a vocation that involves dealing with the public, it is important to be aware of how we speak. A warm, welcoming tone to our voice is preferable to sounding bored or impatient.

 **Activity**

1. How would you say 'We have a half-day tomorrow,' as a question?

2. Try to say 'That's absolutely brilliant,' first using an enthusiastic, and then a sarcastic tone.

3. Try to say, 'Shush, be quiet' first in an angry, and then in a gentle/friendly tone.

## Vocalisations

Sometimes we communicate through noises rather than through speaking. We grunt, groan, moan, shriek, weep, gulp, giggle, laugh, snigger, cry, sigh, whisper, whistle, scream, shout, yawn, sneeze, cough, belch, etc. As with other forms of NVC, noises can be ambiguous, for example, what different meanings can a sigh communicate?

# Discussion

1. What does Homer Simpson mean when he says, 'Doh!'?
2. What noises would you use to communicate the following:
   ▶ Delicious
   ▶ Disgusting
   ▶ Disapproval
   ▶ Frustration
   ▶ Boredom
   ▶ Pain
   ▶ Yes
   ▶ No
   ▶ What?
   ▶ Quiet

## Vocal Segregates

The use of pause, hesitation and fillers like, 'Em'. Many of these we use unconsciously but using pause and hesitation effectively can greatly enhance a speech.

# Activity

If it feels comfortable, pick one of the following attitudes/moods and, without telling the rest of the group, try to communicate it through a combination of posture, facial expression, eye contact, paralanguage and gesture. Have the rest of the group guess the emotion.

▶ Disappointment
▶ Fear
▶ Confusion
▶ Love
▶ Fascination
▶ Boredom
▶ Frustration

- Derision
- Victory
- Piety
- Disgust
- Shiftiness
- Disapproval
- Admiration
- Derision
- Sexiness
- Cockiness
- Astonishment

Make up others if you wish.

# Silence

In couples who are very close, silence communicates contentment as they may know each other so well they don't need to talk. On the other hand, it can mean awkwardness when two people cannot keep a conversation going. Giving someone the silent treatment is a way of slighting someone we aren't pleased with. Teachers may use it to show disapproval in a classroom, usually accompanied by a stare. In many Asian countries silence indicates politeness and contemplation.

Depending on the situation silence can mean:

- Affection
- Reverence
- Attention
- Hesitation
- Embarrassment
- Hostility
- Oppression

# The Environment

The design, shape, colour, size, temperature, lighting, smells and sounds of a place can affect how we feel and behave in a particular setting. In this way the environment communicates with us and we should be aware of how we arrange the furniture in a room for a meeting, for example. A room lit with daylight rather than artificial lighting can have a better effect on our work. A brightly lit room is easier to work in than a dark one, but dim lighting can create a romantic or relaxing mood if that is what we want.

Restaurants use environmental factors to create atmospheres that can determine how long people stay. Fast food outlets use bright lights and not very comfortable seating to prompt customers to leave soon after they've finished eating. Soft music, candles, comfortable chairs are used in more expensive restaurants. Supermarkets have spent time and money researching how light and music affects how we shop.

Feng shui (pronounced fung shway) is an ancient Chinese way of arranging furniture, objects and colours etc. so that we can feel more relaxed by a balanced energy.

## Activity

1. Look at the furniture arrangements where you are right now. Is it a comfortable, relaxed environment or not? Discuss what makes it so.

2. Survey the environmental arrangements in your college canteen. Are there any improvements you could make to improve the overall atmosphere?

# ▶ Time

How we use time communicates something about relationships, status and personality. We tend to spend more time with people we like. An employer will spend more time with an employee who is impressive than with one who is less so. People of higher status tend to keep others waiting, e.g. a doctor might keep a patient waiting, which tells us that the doctor's time is more precious than the patient's. A person who is always late may be seen as being unreliable. In western society we are more concerned with punctuality than in many other cultures.

# ▶ Music

It has been said that music can soothe the savage breast. In other words, music has the power to alter our moods. Music comes from and appeals to the emotions, with the ability to soothe, uplift, sadden, impassion or anger the listener. Listen to some different styles of music and try to identify what they are communicating in terms of mood and emotion. What do the following styles communicate to you?

▶ Rap
▶ Traditional Irish jig
▶ Psalm
▶ Punk
▶ Ambient

- Strauss waltz
- Heavy metal
- Hip-hop
- Reggae
- Bach fugue
- Techno
- Folk ballad

## Discussion

How does a live concert communicate differently from a record?

## ▶ Sounds

Bells, car horns, sirens, drum signals etc. all communicate various messages.

## ▶ Smell

Whether they come from a person or a place, smells are powerful communicators, usually either attracting or repelling. The aroma of fine food wafting from a restaurant, the scent of flowers on a May day or the odour of clothes after a night on the dance floor all provoke emotional responses and give out their own messages. Even though we have lost much of the power of our sense of smell, we still tend to cover up our own unpleasant odours with different soaps, perfumes and oils to make ourselves socially accepted, or to try and attract a partner. We might even deodorise our homes to make them more pleasant to inhabit.

## ▶ Dance

Dance is an artistic expression using many of the nonverbal techniques mentioned above such as posture and gesture, but it is also much more than that. A famous ballet like 'Swan Lake' is a powerful performance full of emotion and drama. 'Riverdance' changed traditional Irish dancing into something much more passionate than it used to be and introduced it to a worldwide audience. What does it communicate to you?

## ▶ Art

Painting, drawing and sculpture are all forms of visual art. They can communicate any number of moods, feelings and ideas, or may just be something attractive to hang on the wall.

# ▶ Other NVC Signs and Codes

Morse code, semaphore, drum signals, smoke signals, traffic lights and some road signs all use nonverbal ways of communicating messages. Computer technology uses languages that are based on numbers as opposed to words, and programs are written in a series of zeros and ones. Shorthand is a system of written symbols used to record speech quickly.

## Activities

1. Role-play the following simple situations using only NVC:

   ▶ Waiting at the bus stop in freezing weather.
   ▶ A tourist asking directions (doesn't speak the language).
   ▶ A mugging.
   ▶ Football supporters at a match in the minutes leading up to and including a goal.
   ▶ Ordering a meal in a restaurant.

2. Try to spend a break session without using words.

3. Chinese Miming:

   You may have played Chinese whispers before. This is similar. Everyone sits in a circle, and the first person sends a message by mime to the person on her left. That person passes it on to the person on his left and so on around the circle. Compare the final message to the original.

4. Four female secretaries are working at their computers. A large window is between them and the street. A man tries to pick each one up by knocking on the window to try and get them to come outside. Each secretary reacts differently.

5. Online activity:

   Watch the TED talk 'Your Body Language Shapes Who You Are' by Amy Cuddy.

## Chapter Review

1. Give a brief explanation of: eye contact; face-to-face communication and facial expression; gestures; territory; paralanguage.
2. Explain the significance of NVC with regard to cultural differences.
3. Describe ways in which NVC can be ambiguous.
4. Make a list of the NVC types you are now more aware of and consider how you might consciously use them in future.

# Chapter 9
## Visual Communication

> ### In This Chapter
>
> - The Image
> - Visual Language
> - Visual Interpretation
> - Visual Production
> - Posters and Flyers
> - Data Representation

## Examples

- Pictures
- Photographs
- Drawings
- Paintings
- Posters
- Diagrams
- Charts
- Maps
- Flags

## Advantages

- Reinforces spoken word
- Interesting
- Attractive
- Can simplify written and spoken word
- Has impact
- Easy to remember
- Crosses language barriers

## Disadvantages

- Can be vague
- Open to misunderstanding
- May need written/spoken support
- May be time-consuming to produce
- May be expensive

# ▶ The Image

Verbal communication uses words to send messages; visual communication uses images. While it is not known exactly how the earliest humans communicated, it is certain that they did paint pictures on the walls of caves. We are not sure what kind of language our early ancestors used, but for thousands of years the spoken word has been the main means of communication for humans. In the Middle Ages, especially after the invention of the printing press, the written word became more important as a source of information. With the emergence of photography, cinema, television, video and the internet the image has almost overtaken the written word as a means of communication.

Today we are constantly being bombarded by visual messages in advertising, magazines, on television, film, video, the internet and with social media and smartphone applications. We are also exchanging more images than ever before on social media sites and with smartphones.

Images can be used in numerous ways to communicate effectively in order to:

▶ Educate
▶ Advertise
▶ Inform
▶ Aid meaning
▶ Express ideas
▶ Persuade
▶ Entertain

## Activity

Write down one or two examples of each of the above and discuss as a group.

We can often read and understand a visual message more quickly than a written one. An image is easier to remember than words and can cross language barriers. It may also have much more immediate and emotional impact. The image is a very powerful means of communication.

*Fig. 9.1*

This photograph of the Earth rising above the surface of the moon was taken by astronaut William Anders during the 1968 Apollo 8 mission to the moon. It was the first time Earth had been photographed from deep space and this image is said to have inspired the environmental movement.

## ❝ Discussion

There is an old saying that 'a picture is worth a thousand words'. What does this mean? Could we ever say that a word is worth a thousand pictures? ❞

Images are not necessarily superior to words but they are equally important. The most successful communication is when there is a combination of words and pictures. Some images on their own can be ambiguous and even meaningless. This is why captions are used to explain photographs in newspapers and magazines, and why slogans accompany pictures used in advertisements. In this way, words *anchor* the meaning of the image. Words and images complement each other and should be carefully chosen. Look at a cover of *Phoenix* or *Private Eye* magazine to see how humour is created out of inserting slightly inappropriate, but often hilarious, speech bubbles into photographs of celebrities and politicians.

## The Camera Lies

These photos of a model show how the camera can cover up the truth of the subject in a photograph. The image on the far right has been altered using image-enhancing software to make the model appear more 'beautiful'.

Fig. 9.2

Visual communication also has the power to manipulate, especially in the modern media. Photography, film, television, video and the internet, as communication media, are deliberately manipulated to produce a specific effect on the viewer. It may be to persuade him to buy a product, to make him laugh or cry, to seduce him into wanting to watch another episode or just wonder at the beauty of the image. It used to be said that the camera never lies, but it does, very effectively.

One major disadvantage of visual communication is that images cannot give detailed descriptions, which words can. Nor can they easily express abstract ideas like hope, fate or knowledge, or complex feelings like resentment or rejection. It is easier to visualise words that refer to concrete objects, such as *dog*, *ball* and *hat*.

# ▶ Visual Language

Verbal language has rules of grammar and punctuation in order to give it meaning. We don't usually consider visual language to have such rules but we can look at some of the basic elements of visual communication. These are:

- ▶ Colour/light
- ▶ Form/shape
- ▶ Size
- ▶ Texture
- ▶ Depth

- Perspective
- Boundaries
- Position
- Movement/direction

## Colour

Colour is essentially a combination of different shades of light and dark and it can communicate a variety of meanings. Light and darkness can affect our moods, lightness being linked with daytime, spring and summer, positive feelings of hope, celebration and joy. Darkness we associate with night-time, winter and negative feelings of fear, despair and depression. Not everyone will have the same feelings, of course. Some people love dark colours and wear them all the time. They can look smart and sophisticated. How we view colour is highly subjective.

## Discussion

1. In the film *Reservoir Dogs* the chief characters were named after colours, Mr White, Mr Black etc. The two unpopular colours were Mr Pink and Mr Brown. Why did no one want to be called by these names? Why was there competition for the name Mr Black?
2. What words, feelings and ideas do you associate with these colours?
   - Red
   - Orange
   - Yellow
   - Green
   - Blue
   - White

When using colour in a visual message we must remember that it can affect the emotions of a viewer more than other attributes. If used well it can draw attention to certain aspects of an image. If poorly used it can damage the overall effect.

## Size

In image production, size counts. We tend to notice large images more easily than smaller ones. When designing an image we need to consider its size in relation to the page on which it will appear.

## Texture

Texture refers to the feel or appearance of a surface, or of an image. Look at the table or desk nearest to you. Is its surface rough or smooth, is its colour plain or dappled?

## Depth

We perceive the world as having three dimensions. In other words, we can see the actual volume of objects which shows that they have weight and mass. A square, a circle and a triangle each has two dimensions, but a cube, a sphere and a pyramid each has three.

## Perspective

Perspective gives the impression of distance in a picture. A picture of a railway track disappearing into the distance shows perspective by the way the lines get closer together as they 'get further away'.

## Boundaries

The boundary of an image is the edge or frame that contains it. Borderlines or designs can enhance a poster but they can also distract from the main image if they are too prominent.

## Position

The positioning of an image in relation to the boundary is quite important. The most obvious thing is to place an image in the centre. When taking photographs of people, we often 'cut off' their feet or the tops of their heads by mistake. Filling the frame of a photograph means not having the object too far away or chopped in two. Do we want just someone's face, or their entire body in the picture?

## Movement/direction

Getting a viewer to perceive movement in a still image needs 'visual vibration'. The use of wavy lines is applied to cartoons to show a character moving or shaking, and high-contrast straight or wavy lines can create the illusion of something moving in a particular direction.

*Fig. 9.3 Movement*

# ▶ Visual Interpretation

As with all forms of communication, an image can have more than one specified meaning. The meaning is determined by a combination of the sender, receiver and the context. A national flag is literally a symbol of the country it represents. It can also fill one person with patriotic pride, but to another, it could represent an offence or a threat. A Union Jack in the Falls Road, a predominantly Republican/Catholic street in Belfast, will have a completely different meaning to one hanging in the Shankill Road, a largely Loyalist/Protestant area. As well as the literal meaning, there is an implied meaning, or connotation.

 **Activity**

What is the connotation of the photograph below?

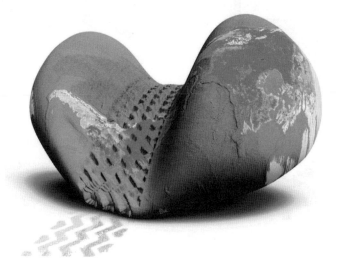

*Fig. 9.4 What was that bump?*

## Symbols

A symbol is a particular kind of image or sign that represents something. Initially the meaning is not always clear: it has to be learned. Then it becomes easily recognisable.

What do the following symbols represent?

Fig. 9.5

## Logos

Logos are symbols used by companies and organisations to promote easy recognition and are a key part of branding and brand recognition. They may be purely graphic (i.e. use a symbol only) or may combine the organisation's name in a particular style of text, such as a trademark.

Can you recognise these logos? Which ones are the most effective? Why? What other logos can you think of which work well to promote particular brands?

a  b  c

d  e

Fig. 9.6

# ▶ Visual Production

More and more we find we need to create visual messages or images for college assignments, presentations at work, to promote a business, product or an event, or for social media sites where we can share our colourful lives with family and friends.

# ▶ Posters and Flyers

Posters and flyers can be created using readily available computer software. A poster must be large, preferably A3 size, and should have enough impact to compete with other posters in, say, a shop window or community notice board. Use appropriate colours, fonts and eye-catching imagery to create the best possible visual message.

## Font Selection

Look at the following list of film titles. Is there anything strange about them? We have seen the titles written before but the way they are written seems to be at odds with the themes of the films. *Frankenstein* is a horror film, yet the font used is humorous and playful. The connotations of the film are monsters, mad scientists, middle Europe in the eighteenth century and the font does not suit these connotations. Make a similar analysis of the other titles, their connotations and the fonts used.

# Frankenstein

# The Wizard of Oz

# SHAKESPEARE IN LOVE

# Pulp Fiction

Fig. 9.7

If you are using text to accompany an image, choose a font that is appropriate for the message.

# ▶ Data Representation

Charts, graphs and diagrams are very useful for showing statistics in a simple and interesting way. They can give written assignments, projects and oral presentations a bit of added impact and interest, condensing and clarifying certain types of information. A computer makes them fairly easy to produce with a range of styles and colours and even three-dimensional effects.

*Line graphs* are useful for showing trends that rise and fall.

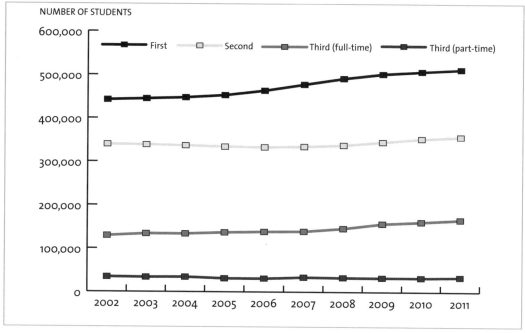

Fig. 9.8 Line graph                                    *Source: Department of Education and Skills*

*Bar charts* are effective for illustrating differences in quantity. They can be horizontal or vertical.

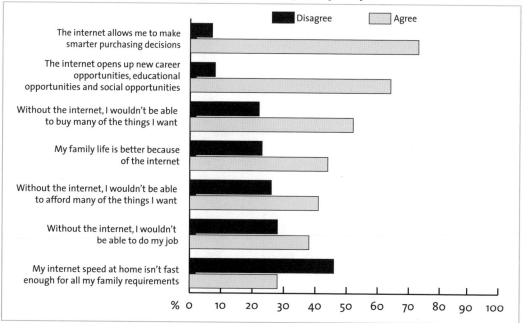

Fig. 9.9 Bar chart

**Note:** *Histograms* are similar to bar charts, except the columns represent the frequency of occurrence (how often something occurs) and have no spaces between them.

*Pie charts* can be used to display percentages of a whole.

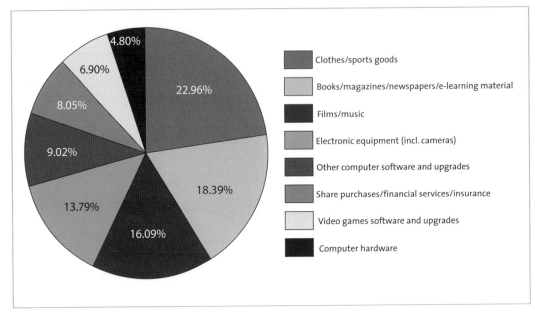

Fig. 9.10 Pie chart

*Pictograms*, as the name suggests, consist of a picture or series of pictures that can add a touch of humour, although they are not as precise as other charts.

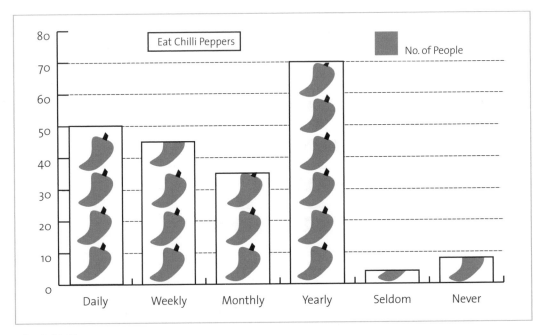

Fig. 9.11 Pictogram

The following methods of data representation are not strictly visual, but they do help simplify information:

*Organisation charts* are used to show the structure of authority in an organisation.

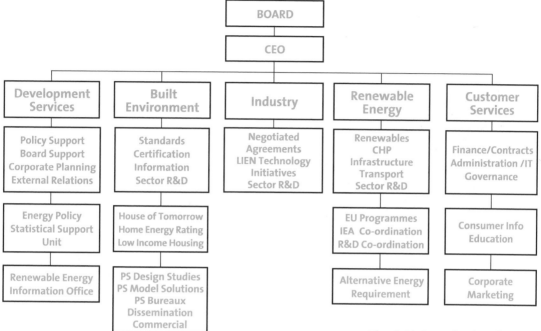

Fig. 9.12 Organisation chart

*Flow charts* show how an activity is to be carried out in a series of logical stages.

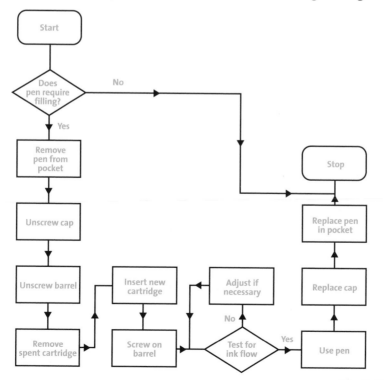

Fig. 9.13 Flow chart

*Tables* can be used to compare and contrast data in a clear and simple way.

| TOP TEN COUNTRIES WITH THE HIGHEST POPULATION | | | |
|---|---|---|---|
| # Country | 2009 Population | 2000 Population | Pop. Increase 2000–2009 |
| 1 China | 1,338,612,968 | 1,268,853,362 | 69,759,606 |
| 2 India | 1,156,897,766 | 1,004,124,224 | 152,773,542 |
| 3 United States | 307,212,123 | 282,338,631 | 24,873,492 |
| 4 Indonesia | 240,271,522 | 213,829,469 | 26,442,053 |
| 5 Brazil | 190,010,647 | 176,319,621 | 13,691,026 |
| 6 Pakistan | 174,578,558 | 146,404,914 | 28,173,644 |
| 7 Bangladesh | 156,050,883 | 130,406,594 | 25,644,289 |
| 8 Nigeria | 149,229,090 | 123,178,818 | 26,050,272 |
| 9 Russia | 140,041,247 | 146,709,971 | (6,668,724) |
| 10 Japan | 127,078,679 | 126,729,223 | 349,456 |
| TOP TEN countries | 3,988,712,105 | 3,618,894,827 | 369,817,278 |
| Source: Miniwatts Marketing Group | | | |

*Fig. 9.14 Table*

**Points to Remember**
1. Always title charts
2. Keep them simple and clear
3. Don't clutter them with too much information
4. Colour looks better than black and white
5. Keep text to a minimum and make it legible
6. Fill up as much of the page as possible.

## Diagrams

A diagram is essentially a drawing or sketch of an object showing its various parts. It would obviously be preferable to see a diagram of the inner workings of a camera than have someone try to explain them to us!

## Maps

To show locations, transport networks, or any geographical features, maps are ideal.

# Activities

1. Produce a poster and/or flyer for one of the following:

   ▶ A concert
   ▶ A newly opened leisure centre/restaurant/shop/business
   ▶ A college social
   ▶ A sporting event
   ▶ A fashion show
   ▶ A circus
   ▶ A charity/fundraising event
   ▶ An international day against racism
   ▶ An international day of AIDS awareness.

   Think of other occasions, perhaps related to your own vocational studies.

2. Produce a card for one of the following occasions:

   ▶ Birthday
   ▶ Christmas
   ▶ Passing exams
   ▶ Wedding anniversary
   ▶ Condolence
   ▶ St Patrick's Day
   ▶ St Valentine's Day
   ▶ Easter
   ▶ Newborn baby
   ▶ Mother's Day
   ▶ Father's Day

 # Further Activities

1. Page 138 shows the image on a plaque attached to the Pioneer spacecraft with a message from humankind to whoever finds it on its journey through space. What does it communicate? Do you think it is effective? If you had to convey an image of humankind to extraterrestrials, what would you draw?

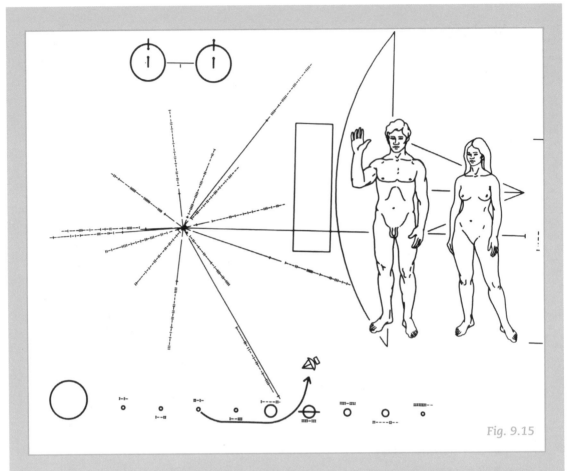

Fig. 9.15

2. The US Department of Energy wants to design a sign that will warn people of its nuclear waste dump in Nevada. The waste will remain dangerous for 10,000 years, so the sign must last for that long and keep its meaning for whoever inhabits that part of the world at that time. Consider that about 10,000 years ago humans were evolving from hunter gatherers to farmers. We don't know what language they will speak 10,000 years from now. Maybe Earth will be dominated by things other than humans. How would you design a 'Keep Out' sign for the future? What kind of message would you use?

## ▶ Chapter Review

1. What advantages does visual communication have over verbal communication?
2. Why is it important to learn about visual communication?

# Part 4

## Reading and Writing

### Some Examples

- Letters
- Memos
- Reports
- Assignments
- Notices
- Agendas
- Reviews
- Notes
- Postcards
- Poetry
- Stories

### Advantages

- Provides a written record
- Can be used as evidence/contract
- Can be re-read, copied, stored/filed
- Time to conceive message carefully
- Can relay complex detailed ideas
- Provides analysis, evaluation, summary
- Can confirm, interpret, clarify spoken and visual messages

### Disadvantages

- Takes time
- More formal and impersonal than spoken
- Harder to convey tone, emotion
- No instant feedback
- Once sent, difficult to change
- Slow exchange of views/opinions

# Chapter 10
## Reading Skills

# ▶ Purpose of Reading

## Discussion

Make a list of the things you've read in the past twenty-four hours. Discuss with the class group.

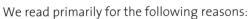

We read primarily for the following reasons:

1. Information
2. Entertainment/leisure
3. Personal contact
4. Education.

Another very sound reason for reading is that it improves our command of the language we speak by increasing our vocabulary and this in turn helps improve our communication skills. Reading helps us to expand our range of words so that we can express ourselves more eloquently.

Our reading will improve with practice and our communication skills will improve by reading. Although it is tempting to take the easy way out and read what is unchallenging, we won't improve unless we read material that introduces us to new words and new ways of expression. Reading regularly and widely is the main thing. Don't always read the same type of material. If you've been used to magazines, try a newspaper. If you read novels, try a work of non-fiction. If non-fiction is your thing, try a comic for a change.

It is also useful to have a good dictionary at hand to look up new words.

Fig. 10.1

## Reading Self-check

How well do you read? We all read at varying speeds and levels of concentration and efficiency. Here are some of the most common problems that people have with reading:

1. Reading all kinds of text at the same speed.
2. Slow reading.
3. Re-reading words or passages.
4. Inability to find the main idea in a passage.
5. Losing concentration while reading.
6. Pronouncing or mouthing words while reading them.
7. Study-reading intensely for a long period of time without taking a break.

If you do any or all of the above you have developed some bad habits over the years, but by and large they are problems that can be overcome with a little effort. In the following few pages we will look at some of the ways in which our reading can be improved.

## Different Texts, Different Speeds

If you think about what you've read in the past 24 hours you will notice the sheer variety of texts. We don't use the same method of reading for all of them. For example, when looking at a bus timetable we don't read every single word on the page. We scan it for the particular item relevant to us. We would use a different method for reading a novel. With a novel we would read every word but not as intensely as if we were studying a book for an exam.

# ▶ Types of Reading

There are four types of reading:

1. Scanning
2. Skimming
3. Normal reading
4. Close reading.

## Scanning

This is very fast reading to find specific information that is only relevant to our needs. We scan timetables, dictionaries, small ads, notice boards and telephone directories for specific words or names. We scan newspapers for articles that interest us and web pages on the internet for relevant pieces of information or for links to other pages. Scanning is useful for finding information as part of a research project.

# Activity

You've decided you want to learn how to swim so you get a brochure from the local pool. Scan the timetable of the various sessions to find a suitable time for a lesson. Your working hours are 9.00 am to 5.00 pm Monday to Saturday with Wednesdays free, and you work until 8.30 pm on Tuesdays.

|       | Monday | Tuesday | Wednesday | Thursday | Friday | Saturday | Sunday |
|-------|--------|---------|-----------|----------|--------|----------|--------|
| 7.30  | Early Swim | Early Swim | Early Swim | Early Swim | Early Swim | Closed | Closed |
| 9.00  | Open Swim | Open Swim | Adults | Open Swim | Adults | Closed | Closed |
| 10.00 |  |  | Adult Lesson | Child Lesson | Child Lesson | Family | Closed |
| 11.00 | Open Swim | Club | Club | Open Swim | Club | Child Lesson | Family |
| 12.00 |  |  |  |  |  | Child Lesson | Family |
| 13.00 | Lunch Swim | Lunch Swim | Lunch Swim | Lunch Swim | Lunch Swim | Adults | Family |
| 14.00 |  |  |  |  |  | Open Swim | Open Swim |
| 15.00 | Child Lesson |  |  |  |  | Open Swim | Open Swim |
| 16.00 | Open Swim | Family | Child Lesson | Child Lesson |  | Open Swim | Open Swim |
| 17.00 | Open Swim | Lane Swim | Open Swim | Lane Swim | Open Swim | Open Swim | Open Swim |
| 18.00 | Family | Open Swim | Family | Open Swim | Family | Closed | Closed |
| 19.00 | Club | Club | Child Lesson | Club | Club |  |  |
| 20.00 | Adult Lesson | Adult Lesson | Club | Open Swim | Open Swim |  |  |
| 21.00 | Adults | Adults | Club | Adults | Adults |  |  |

How did you scan the timetable? Did you do it methodically starting from Monday at 7.30 am and carefully work your way down each day? Or did you scan it haphazardly looking all over the place with no apparent system? Having a methodical system can sometimes help us find information more quickly.

Fig. 10.2

## Skimming

When we skim-read a passage we swiftly glance across the surface to get an overview of what it is about. Passages may be skipped because they are irrelevant. We skim advertisements, newspaper articles and brochures. For study or research purposes a skim-read lets us know if the material is relevant to our needs, and if it is, we can then go back and read it in detail. Topic sentences are often placed either at the beginning or at the end of paragraphs. When skimming we can focus on these to get the gist of the text. It is good to skim-read any piece of writing before reading it fully. Then when we go to read it at a normal pace we will absorb the information more easily.

### Signposts

In most textbooks and some news articles, headings, subheadings and headlines indicate what is to follow in the main body of the text, acting as signposts. Words and phrases that are underlined, in **bold**, in *italics*, numbered, lettered or in bullet points are often signposts and make it easy to skim-read.

## Normal Reading

This is reading at moderate speed, for example: novels, letters, newspaper articles and magazines. A lack of speed is considered to be a major reading problem. It is often found that with increased speed comes better understanding. The average person reads at about 240 words per minute with a comprehension rate of about 60 per cent. This means that most of us do not remember 40 per cent of what we read. Most of us could do with improvement in both our speed and comprehension. If you are curious about your reading speed, there is a free test at this website:

▶ http://www.readingsoft.com

When we read, our eyes do not move smoothly across the page from left to right, because every now and then they stop very briefly to take in a word or a phrase. These stops are called *fixations* and normally last from one quarter to one and a half seconds. The number of words we focus on during each fixation is referred to as the *recognition span*. Fast readers can read vertically down a page, fixating on each line just once and taking in its whole meaning. These people have a large recognition span. So, obviously, the greater the recognition span, the fewer fixations we need and the faster we will read. Slower readers make more fixations because they have a smaller recognition span. Unfortunately, meaning in sentences does not come in single words but in chunks of words, phrases and sentences. When we try to take in meaning one word at a time, by the time we reach the end of a sentence we have forgotten what was at the beginning. Because the human brain can function much faster than this, we are leaving time for our mind to drift off and think about something else. So we lose concentration and start to daydream.

## Activity

Read the following passage slowly, one word at a time, covering up each word in front of the one you are reading:

*In...spite...of...what...you...might...think...reading...can...be...improved...by... fixating...on...groups...of...words...rather...than...on...single...words...because... single...words...don't...mean...much...on...their...own.*

As you will have noticed, this very slow way of reading makes it more difficult to understand the sentence quickly. We don't find any meaning at all in the first few words and things only start to make sense once we reach the word 'improved'. A more efficient reader will read the sentence in clusters of meaning like this:

In spite of what you might think...reading can be improved...by fixating on groups of words...rather than on single words...because single words don't mean much on their own.

We need to push ourselves to practise reducing our fixation time, and at the same time try to expand our recognition span. This should increase our speed, our comprehension and also help reduce concentration loss.

### Re-reading
Re-reading words or phrases in a passage naturally decreases our reading efficiency. To reduce this habit we can use a pointer when reading. This might seem a little childish,

but it helps our eyes move more smoothly across the page. Alternately, we can cover up the lines already read with a sheet of paper, card or another book, and even push it down a little faster than we think we can go. This means we will concentrate better on what we are reading the first time and it helps us break the habit.

These techniques should be practised regularly for our reading efficiency to improve.

## Close Reading

This is reading which is slow and intensive because the text is demanding and needs to be properly understood. We might close-read poetry, class notes, textbooks, instructions for operating equipment or for examinations, leases, contracts and other detailed documents so that we understand them fully.

It is not a good idea to read long, difficult passages for more than about forty minutes at a time. After this time we tend to lose our ability to concentrate, and a short break of five to ten minutes is usually sufficient to refresh ourselves.

### Tips for Close Reading

1. Have a pen, paper and dictionary handy.
2. Start with a skim-read of the entire passage. If it's a book, look at the title, contents, introduction, conclusion, heading and subheadings. Scan the index for specific subjects.
3. Read the passage *actively*. This means asking yourself questions such as:
   (a) Why is it written this way?
   (b) What does the writer mean by this?
   (c) Do I agree with this?
   (d) Do I find this information new, interesting, boring?
   (e) What are the main points?
   (f) Does this make sense?
   (g) Is the information correct?
   (h) Is the language formal/informal, objective/subjective, emotive/factual/opinionated?
4. Note information that you already know.
5. Note information that you find particularly interesting, relevant, irrelevant, or even ridiculous.
6. Write down, highlight or underline difficult words or passages.
7. Look up any unfamiliar words.
8. When you've read the passage, try to recall it in your mind. What are the main points of the passage? Write down what you can remember in your own words.
9. Finally go over the passage again in case you've missed any important points.

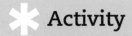 ## Activity

Read the following article, using all four methods of reading. Scan it first for words you don't understand and underline them. Look them up in a dictionary or consult your tutor. Skim the article to get the gist of what it's about. Read it normally to get the details and finally close read it.

## SOCIAL MEDIA AND INTERPERSONAL COMMUNICATION

Glance around a restaurant and you'll be hard-pressed to find people who don't have their heads down using their cell phones to text, Tweet, or update their Facebook statuses—all while sharing a meal with others at their table.

Social media's effect on our ability to interact and communicate is visible throughout all areas of society, so what does this mean for interpersonal communication? According to Paul Booth, PhD, an assistant professor of media and cinema studies in the College of Communication at DePaul University in Chicago, social media certainly affects how we engage with one another across all venues and ages. 'There has been a shift in the way we communicate; rather than face-to-face interaction, we're tending to prefer mediated communication,' he says. 'We'd rather e-mail than meet; we'd rather text than talk on the phone.'

According to Booth, studies have shown that people actually are becoming more social and more interactive with others, but the style of that communication has changed so that we're not meeting face-to-face as often as we used to.

That said, our interactions on social media tend to be weak ties—that is, we don't feel as personally connected to the people at the other end of our communication as we do when we're face-to-face. 'So while we're communicating more, we may not necessarily be building relationships as strongly,' Booth says.

Three key issues are surfacing regarding the role social media now plays in people's communication styles, Booth notes. First, when we communicate through social media, we tend to trust the people on the other end of the communication, so our messages tend to be more open. Second, our social connections are not strengthened as much through social media as they are face-to-face, so we don't tend to deepen our relationships—they tend to exist in the status quo. Last, we tend to follow and interact with people who agree with our points of view, so we aren't getting the same diversity of viewpoints as we've gotten in the past.

'Certainly, with every new communication technology comes changes in the style and type of interpersonal communication,' Booth says. 'Obviously the bigger the influence of the technology, the more changes we see in communication styles.'

*Far-Reaching Effects*

Nicholas David Bowman, PhD, an assistant professor of communication studies in the Eberly College of Arts and Sciences at West Virginia University, says actions that trigger a bad online relationship likely are the same ones that trigger a bad relationship in real life—only the modality has changed. 'For example, cyberbullying has largely the same antecedents and behavioral, emotional, and affective consequences as does [noncyber] bullying,' Bowman says. 'Yet the difference is the "more"—that is, social media allows for more contact, more communication, and in a more public manner.'

In a bullying event, often the person being bullied can remove himself or herself from the environment, at least temporarily. For example, a child being bullied at school can escape the playground when he or she goes home each night. 'However, cyberbullying is marked by its persistence,' Bowman says. 'The bullying messages don't stay in a particular space, such as a playground, but can follow the child home. If we consider that bullying's effects on an individual can build over time, then there is a real concern that increasing contact between bullies and their targets in persistent and digital interactions might exacerbate the problem.'

## Information Overload

One big concern surrounding social media's impact is communication overload – learning how to handle and make sense of this 'more' information we now have.

As Bowman explains, we're getting more information about more people than ever before, and we feel a need to process and perhaps even respond to it all. 'In fact, there has been some very early recent data suggesting that teens are perhaps pulling away from Facebook because it's just too much for them to handle,' he says.

Another concern lies in technology addiction, when individuals spend more time with their smartphone than interacting with the people around them, to the detriment of those face-

to-face relationships. 'It may be the parent checking his or her e-mail during a family dinner or the young college student updating Twitter while on a first date,' Bowman says. 'For these people, they likely feel such a strong sense of identity online that they have some difficulty separating their virtual actions from their actual ones.'

With the release of the fifth edition of the DSM, internet addiction now will be listed as a mental illness marked by emotional shutdown, lack of concentration, and withdrawal symptoms, so we may be closer to diagnosing and understanding socially detrimental human–technology relationships.

'However, many of us caution that internet addiction might be an inaccurate portrayal,' Bowman says. 'After all, if social media is designed to connect people with people, then is it really a human–technology relationship or is it a human–human relationship mediated by technology?'

## Protecting Privacy

One potentially negative consequence of social media is a lack of privacy. 'Because interpersonal communication is changing, we're finding ourselves more apt to share on social media the sort of information we might have previously shared privately face-to-face,' Booth says. 'We always have to keep in mind that our social networks are searchable – even when privacy settings are set extremely high, it's always possible to find out personal information.'

Of course, the negativity surrounding social media is countered by positive influences, including the ability to communicate with more people across greater distances and with increased speed. 'Your message can be shared and spread farther and faster than at any other time in human history,' Booth says. 'We can do a lot of good by spreading positive messages in this way.'

*Future of Social Media*

Experts agree that clinicians must be aware that people are changing the way they communicate. 'We may rely on the weak connections we're making on social media more than on the strong connections we might have when we're meeting face-to-face,' Booth says.

What does the future hold for social media and its potential continuous effect on interpersonal communication within society? Bowman believes social media likely will continue to become increasingly integrated into the normal human experience like most of the communication technologies that preceded it.

'They will continue to increase the volume of the human communication process, and we will continue to learn how to use them for good and for bad,' he says.

'We must remember that social media is really only a decade old. That's very young in the history of communication technology,' Booth adds. 'It's been influential, but it hasn't really settled into a routine yet. As social media becomes more normalized, we'll stop seeing it as changing things and start seeing it as the way things are. As a society we'll be OK – we've always adjusted to new technology. So whether it's wearable communication media, such as Google glasses, or more cloud computing, we'll change and adapt.'

Maura Keller, *Social Work Today*, May/June 2013 (vol. 13, no. 3, p. 10)

# ▶ Writing a Summary

To summarise a message means to condense it down to its main points. Writing a summary shows that you have understood a text and that you can communicate its overall meaning to others. It is a useful skill in that it helps to identify the essential meaning of a piece of writing while leaving out the unnecessary points.

# ▶ Guide to Writing a Summary

Here are some guidelines to help you write summaries.

1. Skim-read the text to get the overall gist. Focus on any headings, subheadings, words or phrases in bold and 'topic sentences', which are usually the first or last sentence in a paragraph and encapsulate the subject matter of the paragraph.
2. Do a normal read of the text.
3. Close-read the text and underline topic sentences.
4. Write one sentence that explains the overall theme. This is sometimes called a 'theme sentence'.

5.    Write down the main idea of each section.
6.    Omit specific details such as examples, dates, statistics etc.
7.    Write a draft of your summary, using the key points you identified, keeping to the same order of information as the original and adding words and phrases to link them together, e.g. *then, however, despite this* or *because of this.*
8.    Re-read your summary to make sure you've included all the important elements.
9.    Rewrite if necessary.
10.   Proofread for spelling, grammar and punctuation.

# ▶ Tips for an Effective Summary

- ▶ Stick to the same tense as in the original.
- ▶ Include the author's name and title.
- ▶ If there is no title, create your own from your theme sentence.
- ▶ Be concise: your summary should be shorter than the original.
- ▶ Don't add your own opinions.

# ▶ Critical Evaluation

An ability to analyse and critically evaluate information, be it in written, spoken or visual communication, is a useful life skill that can improve our interpreting and problem-solving skills. The analytical process involves a methodical examination of something, looking closely at its different parts to see how each contributes to the whole, in order to evaluate and understand it better. Then we are in position to make a more informed opinion about its value or worth.

In a piece of writing we need to examine the following:

## Structure

- ▶ How well is it put together?
- ▶ Does it have a good beginning, middle and end?
- ▶ Is there a logical sequence of paragraphs and subjects?
- ▶ Does it argue a case and if so how well is the argument structured?
- ▶ Does the author have an agenda, i.e. might he/she be putting forward one particular point of view or are both sides of an argument presented?
- ▶ Do you agree or disagree with the author?

## Language

- ▶ Is it well written?
- ▶ Is the language clear or is it vague or ambiguous?
- ▶ Is it subjective (personal) or objective (impartial)?

▶ Consider the style: is it fluent, easy to read, or does it contain unnecessarily difficult language?

▶ Consider the tone: is it serious, humorous, factual, creative, formal, informal etc?

### Information

▶ Is the information accurate?

▶ How do you know?

▶ Distinguish between information that is relevant and information that is not.

### Strengths and Weaknesses

▶ What are the strengths and weaknesses of the piece?

## Informed Opinion or Personal Opinion

Informed opinion is always based on facts and when you have done the analysis, you are in a better position to give a more informed opinion rather than just a personal opinion having read it through without any analysis.

## Activity

1. Write a summary of the article on pp.146–8 using the process described.
2. Write a short critique of the same article.
3. Select a variety of pieces of writing such as newspaper/magazine articles, academic articles, blogs, professional documents, essays etc. and distribute amongst the class. Singly or in pairs, summarise one article and relay the information to the rest of the class group. Give a critical evaluation of each piece.
4. Read and write a summary of a professional document based on your own vocational area.

## Chapter Review

1. Give four good reasons for reading.
2. List five bad reading habits.
3. Explain the four types of reading.
4. What does active reading mean?
5. Why is summary writing useful?
6. List five components of critical evaluation.

# Chapter 11
## Writing Skills

### In This Chapter

▶ Types of Writing
▶ Punctuation
▶ Confusing words
▶ Grammar Basics
▶ Answers to Selected Activities

'Writing is perhaps the greatest of human inventions, binding together people who never knew each other, citizens of distant epochs.'

*Carl Sagan*

Writing as a form of communication probably evolved in ancient cultures as a way of exchanging information, keeping financial accounts and recording historical events.

## Activity

Make a list of the things you have written in the past 48 hours.

## ▶ Types of Writing

Different types of writing require different approaches and styles. Some are formal and some informal. Some use descriptive and some use plain language. The following is a list of examples.

**Instructive writing** such as a recipe, instruction manual or list of directions, uses clear and simple language, short sentences and avoids any unnecessary words.

## Activity

1. Write out your favourite recipe.
2. Write instructions for using a mobile phone.
3. Imagine an English-speaking alien has landed in your classroom. Write precise, detailed and clear directions for him on how to get from the classroom to your home.

**Descriptive writing** uses words that appeal to the senses to create an image in the reader's mind. There is usually a lot of detail. For example, a travel journal might describe the sights, sounds, smells, tastes and other sensations experienced by the traveller to give the reader a vivid impression of the holiday location. The writer's feelings may also be included and figures of speech such as similes and metaphors also add to the description. Precise language, especially adjectives, should also be included.

## Activity

Describe a day or an event during your last holiday. Use as much detail as possible to create a picture in the reader's mind.

**Narrative writing** tells a story, true or fictional, using a series of connected events. See Short Story section on p.175.

## Activity

Write a short story beginning with this phrase: 'I woke up this morning...'

**Persuasive writing** presents a particular viewpoint and tries to convince the reader that the writer's opinion is correct. It may try to convince the reader to do something such as take action or it might consist of an argument for or against a particular issue. Advertisements persuade people to buy certain products.

Key elements in persuasive writing include:

▶ Repetition of certain words or phrases
▶ Facts that supports the viewpoint
▶ An appeal to the reader's emotions
▶ A clear writing style to eliminate any contradictions in the argument
▶ Rhetorical questions (questions that make the reader think but don't need an answer), e.g. 'Who would want to live in that place?', 'How can we stand by and let this happen?'

The main goal of persuasive writing is to win over the reader in some way.

## Activity

1. Write a short persuasive piece on one of the following statements.
   ▶ 'The use of college computers for social networking should be banned.'
   ▶ 'We must stop using fossil fuels if we are to prevent runaway climate change.'
2. Write some keywords you would use in an advertisement for a new chocolate bar.

**Creative writing** includes stories, poems, novels as well as non-fiction and the purpose is for the writer to use her imagination and to express her thoughts, feelings and emotions.

## ✳ Activity

1. Choose an ordinary household object and pretend it can perceive the world as humans do. Write its thoughts.
2. Think of someone you love and write a poem describing their attributes, good and bad, using similes ('Her eyes shone like stars') and metaphors ('Her eyes were stars').
3. 7×7×7×7
   Grab the seventh book from your bookshelf, open it on the seventh page, choose the seventh sentence, begin a poem/piece of writing with that sentence and write the rest of the piece using only seven lines/sentences.
4. Write about each member of your family but limit the number of words about each to the age of that person, e.g. seventeen sentences about your 17-year-old brother.
5. Make two columns on a sheet of paper. In one column make a list of ten nouns and in the other a list of ten verbs. Put them into random pairs and write a sentence for each pair. Create a story using all ten sentences.

**Academic writing** is usually serious, factually based, objective and aimed at the critical and well-informed reader. Though it is primarily aimed at academics such as professors, teachers and students, it may also be of interest to the general reader. Some academic books that become bestsellers are often called 'popular' or 'pop', e.g. popular science and popular psychology.

**Business writing** can vary in style from conversational to very formal, though it is advisable in the first contact to be formal. Information must be presented clearly and concisely to avoid misunderstandings and wasting time, and ultimately to make a good impression on a potential client, employer or business partner. Use simple English and see Formal/Business Letters on p.196 and Business/Formal Email on p.268.

# ▶ Punctuation

Punctuate the following sentence:

> ▶ Woman without her man is nothing

There are two possible solutions:

> ▶ Woman: without her, man is nothing.
> ▶ Woman, without her man, is nothing.

*"PUT SIMPLY, J.B., WE CAN SAVE €1,000 PER ANNUM ON TIME AND TONER IF WE ELIMINATE ALL FULL STOPS, SEMI-COLONS AND OTHER FORMS OF PUNCTUATION."*

Fig. 11.1

Two sentences with the same words and two very different meanings. This is why we punctuate written communication, so that the reader understands clearly and without ambiguity the meaning of the written word. Writing cannot convey meaning as speaking does – with tone of voice, volume, speed etc. – so punctuation is our best way of doing this. Computer technology can help with automatic checks and predictive writing, but these tools can cause our writing skills to become rusty if we become too dependent upon them. So we still need to know the basics in order to produce good, meaningful pieces of writing.

## Capital Letters

The capital letter is used:
- To begin all sentences including direct speech: **H**e said, '**H**ello.'
- For proper nouns, i.e. names of people, countries, organisations, buildings, geographical features, historical events and festivals: **J**im, **E**stonia, **G**reenpeace, the **T**aj **M**ahal, the **A**mazon, the **T**reaty of **V**ersailles, the **E**dinburgh **F**estival.
- For proper adjectives, i.e. derived from proper nouns: **S**panish, **T**arantinoesque
- For the personal pronoun '**I**'
- For acronyms: **NAMA, UNESCO**
- For well-known geographical regions, e.g. the **N**orth
- For titles of books, newspapers, magazines, television and radio programmes, plays, songs, poems, films, people (conjunctions – and, but, because etc. – prepositions – of, in, by, beside, for, from etc. – and 'a' in the middle of a title are not capitalised) '**T**he **W**izard of **O**z', '**R**omeo and **J**uliet'.
- For days of the week and for months, not for seasons of the year: It was a fine **M**onday in **M**arch. At last, spring had arrived.

 ## Activity

Rewrite the following, putting in capital letters where necessary.

1. paula, robert and i are studying a course at drumlinn college of further education.

2. it's a vec-run college, i'm doing a fetac course and I have temporary accommodation in a b&b.

3. the college isn't far from ballylinane and the m25.

4. next summer we are going on a sponsored hike in the french alps to raise money for concern.

5. i do work experience at setanta designs every tuesday, just behind the customs house.

6. they dyed the liffey green on st patrick's day.

7. the students aren't all irish. one comes from nigeria and another is lithuanian.

8. last wednesday we went to see the curious case of benjamin button, starring brad pitt.

9. she said, 'why don't you come in?'

10. last year I went to the electric picnic and the festival of the fires.

11. we had our debs in the royal hotel and the dj was rubbish.

12. there's a module in customer service, but we don't have to do german any more.

13. i want to become a physiotherapist with manchester united when i'm finished.

## The Apostrophe (')

The apostrophe is used in the following ways.

### It indicates possession in nouns:

Fred's cat.

The Chief Inspector's slightly shabby raincoat.

So we add an apostrophe and an 's'. The same applies for possessors that don't have an 's' in the plural:

The children's toys.

The women's scarves.

However, when the possessor is a plural *with* an 's' the apostrophe goes after the 's':

The students' assignments.

The ladies' handbags.

For possessors that end in an 's' in the singular, we add an apostrophe and an 's' if it doesn't sound too silly:

> The boss's office.
>
> Mr Burns's nose.
>
> Bridget Jones's Diary.

But if we want to talk about the feet of Moses, we say:

> Moses' feet.

Adding another 's' to Moses sounds silly.

 # Activity

Change the following phrases and add apostrophes where required:

e.g. 'The cage of the hamster' becomes 'The hamster's cage'.

1. The goggles of the swimmers

2. The plays of Shakespeare

3. The tomb of Rameses

4. The toys of the children

5. The bones of the dog

6. The Green of St Stephen

7.. The wool of the lambs

8. The Square of St Thomas

Note the Expressions:
- A fortnight's holiday
- Two weeks' holiday
- One week's time
- One euro's worth
- Five euros' worth
- For God's sake
- For goodness' sake

Also:

▶ She went to the dentist's.

▶ We are off to the butcher's.

In each case a word has been left out – surgery and shop.

### Omission of letters

The apostrophe is used to indicate that a letter has been left out, e.g. He doesn't know wha' he's talkin' about (He does not know what he is talking about).

Who'd 'a' thought you'd be head o' the company (Who would have thought you would be head of the company)?

A word like 'doesn't' is known as a contraction because it has been contracted, i.e. shortened, from 'does not'.

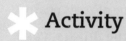

# Activity

Rewrite the following, contracting and inserting apostrophes where necessary:

1. I could not eat another thing.

2. They are all we have got.

3. Do you not have your umbrella with you?

4. Who will sit in the back with Sarah?

5. She is the best hope there is to win.

6. It has been raining.

7. Who would have thought you had it in you?

### The Apostrophe is Not Used

▶ For plurals: The band played all their hits. (Not hit's)

▶ Do we have to do Communications? (Not Communication's)

▶ Verbs: She saves her money each week. (Not save's)

▶ Possessive pronouns: hers, its, ours, yours, theirs

▶ Plurals of numbers/years: the 1960s

▶ Plurals of abbreviations: PCs, B&Bs, DVDs.

'DVD's' and '1960's' are frequently used today, but these usages are incorrect.

Confusables

▶ Its = belonging to it

The government did its best to curb inflation.

▶ It's = it is/it has

It's only rock 'n' roll but I like it.

▶ Whose

The man whose wife sang at the opera was wearing green trousers.

▶ Who's = who is/who has

Who's been eating my porridge?

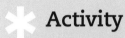 ## Activity

Insert apostrophes (and an 's' if necessary) into the following:

1. Were tired of reading Shakespeares plays. Cant we read some of Yeats poetry?

2. The buses didnt stop at St Stephens Green because the drivers wage increase wasnt enough.

3. Were goin to Donegal for a fortnights holiday.

4. Ill get an hours work done if Peter doesnt disturb me.

5. Theres nothin but rocks on Mars surface.

6. If Goldilocks hunger hadnt got the better of her, shed have passed by the bears house and none of this wouldve happened.

7. Ive got to go to the doctors cause my tonsils swellings got worse.

8. Heres Dereks jacket. Its covered in dogs hairs.

9. The pubs windows look great but its doors colours dont.

10. For heavens sake, if its such a big deal well all go to Helens.

11. The medias got to curtail its habits of prying into peoples lives.

## Hyphen (-)

The hyphen is used in many compound words, i.e. words formed by joining two or more other words to create a new meaning, e.g. well-being, merry-go-round.

Compound adjectives are hyphenated when they come before the noun but not after, e.g.

▶ We played a well-known song for the encore.

▶ The song was well known by the audience.

Phrasal verbs are not hyphenated, e.g.

▶ You need to build up your strength.

But when used as a noun they are hyphenated, e.g.

▶ We enjoyed the build-up to the game.

A hyphen is also used to divide a word that won't fit at the end of a line, e.g. dis-
connected. When word-processing this is unnecessary as the words are automatically
fitted into the page.

## Dash ( – )

The dash separates:

1. Words and phrases in the middle of a sentence, e.g.
   ▶ The band – the best in the country – has just embarked on a world tour.
   ▶ Two young men – both beginners – joined the course yesterday.
2. Words or phrases added on to the end of sentences, e.g.
   ▶ The street has a lively atmosphere – just what we were looking for.
   ▶ We drove down the coastline – one of the most beautiful I'd ever seen.

The dash is often regarded as slightly informal. When word-processing, use the same key for
a dash as for a hyphen, but put a space either side for a dash.

## Activity

The following passage needs six hyphens and seven dashes:

> My sister in law came to stay for the weekend she didn't even ring to warn
> us! Her husband my brother Harry is a long legged evil looking man he even
> scares the dog. We watched the semi final on television and then were
> about to have a big feed of pasta my favourite when we noticed the sell by
> date on the packet two weeks old!

## Colon (:)

The colon:

1. Indicates that something is following on from the previous phrase or sentence, e.g.
   You know what will happen if you miss the deadline: you'll fail the assignment.
2. Introduces a series or list:
   Here's what I'm having: soup, lasagne, a side salad, ice cream and coffee.
3. Introduces a quotation:
   As Bob Dylan said: 'Keep a good head and always carry a light bulb.'

## Semi-colon (;)

The semi-colon:

1. Is used to separate two parts of a sentence which are too closely connected to be separated by a full stop, e.g.

    ▶ I love apples; Granny Smiths are my favourite.
    ▶ I remember him when he couldn't put two notes together; now he's top of the charts.
    ▶ She was delighted; I was delirious.

    These could be written as separate sentences.

2. Can sometimes be replaced with a conjunction such as 'but' or 'and'.

3. Can also be used for a list in which the items are lengthy:

John's travels took him far and wide: a week by the sea on a beautiful Greek island; a month exploring the rugged Turkish coastline; three weeks travelling south through the scorched landscape of the Middle East; and finally a month in Egypt exploring the ancient archaeological wonders.

 **Activity**

Put a colon or semi-colon into the following sentences:

1. Out came the sun off came the shirts.

2. We'll need the following a hammer, nails, wood and paint.

3. To err is human to forgive divine.

4. Here's the suspect's description 6'2" brown hair, brown eyes and a moustache.

5. The speaker began 'Good evening, Ladies and Gentlemen.'

6. Luxembourg is a small country France is a large one.

## Full Stop (.), Question Mark (?), Exclamation Mark (!)

The full stop is used:

1. At the end of sentences, normally followed by a capital letter to begin the next sentence

2. After initials: W.B. Yeats

3. After abbreviations: 25 Dec.

There is no full stop in a sequence of capitals – USA, UN, etc.

A sequence of three full stops, called an *ellipsis*, means an omission of a section of text:

Everyone . . . seems to have used the internet these days.

A *question mark* is used after questions instead of a full stop and is followed by a capital letter. It is not used after indirect questions.

An *exclamation mark* is used instead of a full stop after exclamations, which usually express some strong feeling, emphasis or humour.

 ## Activity

Put a full stop, question mark or exclamation mark after each of the following sentences:

1. I don't know whether she's in or not

2. Do we know if there is alien life in the universe

3. Help

4. I wonder if I could borrow your hammer

5. He told me why he was late

6. Don't you dare

7. How far do we have to travel

8. What a great idea

## The Comma (,)

The following sentences can be very confusing without commas:

1. The discussion over the game continued.
2. The student thought the teacher was going to do very well.
3. The tiger having eaten the children walked on.
4. Granny has eaten Brian.

Where would you put them?

### Separating Mark

The comma is a *separating mark*. It separates:

1. Two clauses that could be two complete sentences and are joined by conjunctions such as 'and', 'but', 'or', 'yet' and 'while':
   ◗ We wanted to go to the beach, but it had started to rain.
   ◗ They booked into a nice hotel, while we had to camp in the field.
2. Descriptive phrases in the middle of a sentence, which are not essential to the meaning of the sentence:
   ◗ The novel, a murder mystery, will probably become a bestseller.
   ◗ Mrs Malone, who was wearing a bright pink frock, poured the tea.
   BUT
   ◗ The woman who was wearing a bright pink frock poured the tea.
   (This is essential to the overall meaning.)
3. Items in a list of three or more items, but not before 'and':
   ◗ We bought tea, milk, sugar and bread.
   ◗ She climbed to the top of the wall, took out her binoculars, scanned the horizon and prepared for the worst.

## Words that Introduce Direct Speech

◗ He said, 'You know, that's the worst sentence I've ever read.'
◗ 'You know,' he said, 'that's the worst sentence I've ever read.'
◗ 'You know, that's the worst sentence I've ever read,' he said.

## Non-essential Additions to Sentences (including interjections like 'aha', 'oops', 'er', 'um' etc.)

◗ Aha, there you are!
◗ Janey Mac, would you look at the state of him?
◗ It's a really brilliant film, like, you know what I mean?

## Question Tags (also non-essential additions)

◗ It's cold today, isn't it?
◗ You saw it, didn't you?

## Vocatives (addressing a person or thing) and Salutations

◗ Mr President, I'd like to congratulate you.
◗ It's nice to see you again, Helen.
◗ Dear Sandra,

## Sentence Adverbs (like 'however', 'nevertheless', 'meanwhile', 'finally', 'at last')

◗ There is, however, a good reason for studying this.
◗ Yes, I'd like that.

No, I disagree.

Of course, she'll never make the grade.

### Participial (-ing) Phrases

Feeling energetic, he went for a run.

The class having finished, the students left the room.

### Parts of a Sentence to Avoid Confusion

The discussion over, the game continued.

The student, thought the teacher, was going to do very well.

The tiger having eaten, the children walked on.

Granny has eaten, Brian.

### Incorrect Uses of the Comma

I walked to the window, it was still open.

At the end of the game, the players, were exhausted.

Addresses: 12, Stephen Street.

People, who live in glass houses, shouldn't throw stones.

# Activity

Insert commas into the following sentences:

1. So Joe do you think we have a chance of winning?

2. The doctor a large friendly man prescribed some pills.

3. Singing at the top of his voice Steve prepared a splendid dinner.

4. Josephine meanwhile was reading the paper.

5. 'Don't you think' she enquired 'we should call the vet?'

6. The Delaneys live in number 46 and their dog chases cars up and down the road.

7. The train travelling at 120 mph had fourteen carriages.

8. The concert having finished they took the last bus home.

9. I put on my coat picked up my things bade farewell and left the building.

10. It was like the worst book I've ever read.

11. I told you yesterday we had to submit the assignment.

12. You're finished now aren't you?

## Inverted Commas/Quotation Marks (' ') ("")

Use either single ' ' or double " ". If using a quotation within a quotation use single for the first and double for the second:

>   She said, 'In the words of Roosevelt, "The only thing we have to fear is fear itself," and I must say I have to agree.'

### Direct Speech

'You know,' she said, 'maybe we'll meet up again sometime.'

>   Punctuation marks that belong to the quote remain within the quotation marks. In a written passage a new speaker is indicated by a new paragraph.

### Quotations

Quotations are used for what someone else said or wrote: As Descartes said, 'I think, therefore I am.'

### Titles

Quotation marks indicate titles of poems, songs, articles in newspapers or magazines and short stories: 'The Lake Isle of Innisfree' is a favourite poem in Ireland.

### Jargon/Slang

Jargon, slang or words that have new or strange meanings can be indicated by the use of quotation marks:

- I'm not going to that town again, it's full of 'gombeens'.
- The team tried out their new 'shock and awe' tactics during the match.

Quotation marks can be used around a word or phrase to imply doubt about its meaning or to question its validity:

- In today's technological world, devices can 'talk' to each other. (In other words they don't really talk to each other.)

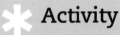

## Activity

Insert quotation marks, if necessary, into the following sentences:

1. It's all right she said everything will be better in the morning.
2. What kind of a word is bodacious anyway he enquired.
3. What do you mean I'm a babe she asked.
4. Give us your rendition of As Time Goes By.
5. Teachers to Strike yelled the headline across the front page.
6. In the words of Samuel Beckett: We are all born mad. Some remain so.

## Brackets/Parentheses ( )

These are used to enclose explanations, translations, definitions and added information to the text:

His philosophy was always *carpe diem* (seize the day).

(If an entire sentence is enclosed in brackets, the full stop must come within the final bracket.)

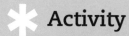

## Activity

Put brackets into the following sentences:

1. The ship if you could call it that will sail at 10.30 pm.

2. We sat in the shade it was too hot to do anything else drinking ice-cold water.

3. The people who are really stressed these days not counting nurses are senior management.

4. The books both thrillers lay on his desk gathering dust.

5. She shouted after him, 'Ich liebe dich I love you,' but it was too late. He was gone.

6. This steady increase in temperature known as global warming is set to get worse over the coming century.

## ❯ Confusing Words

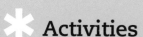

## Activities

Delete whichever words are incorrect from each of the following sentences:

1. There/their/they're is a group of men outside and there/their/they're carrying umbrellas under there/their/they're arms.

2. I've been/being at this bus stop for 45 minutes and I'm sick of been/being kept waiting.

3. Where/were/we're all going to Donegal, which is where/were/we're we where/were/we're last year for our holidays.

4. There are two/too/to gunslingers coming two/too/to this town. That is two/too/to two/too/to many.

5. It's/its been a long time since the union got it's/its way.

**Two words or one?**

1. Is there a post office near by/nearby?
2. Communications is easy, whereas/where as Maths is hard.
3. She fell in to/into his arms with a heavy sigh.
4. On the count of three, altogether/all together now.
5. When he found it in the river, the brief case was still intact/in tact.
6. He slammed his fist on the table, there by/thereby breaking his wrist.
7. We have to do a practical as well/aswell as a theoretical exam.
8. Who knows what's instore/in store for us?
9. Don't you get a lot/alot of ice with your drink?
10. In fact/infact Ireland need three points to qualify.
11. Bring an umbrella incase/in case it rains.
12. That holiday has left me deeply in debt/indebt.
13. It will be all right/alright on the night.

## Numbers

Newspapers and other publications often pick a style of numbering. For example, when writing numbers from one to nine use words, and from 10 upwards use numbers.

## Frequently Used Latin Abbreviations

- i.e. – id est (that is)
- e.g. – exempli gratia (for example)
- etc. – et cetera (and the rest)
- et al. – et alibi (and elsewhere), et alii/alia (and other people/things)

Beware of the following confusing phrases:
I could have been a contender. √
I could of been a contender. X
She should have stayed. √
She should of stayed. X
It would not have been possible. √
It would not of been possible. X

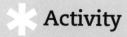 **Activity**

In each of the following sentences, select the correct word, decide what the other word means and put it into another sentence (it may have more than one meaning):

1. We dropped into the off-licence/license to get some beer for the party.
2. Is this a licensed/licenced premises?
3. She decided to brake/break off/of their relationship.
4. I have an awful pain in my back. I hope I don't have a slipped disc/disk.
5. We saw a fantastic programme/program on television last night.
6. After all the Christmas eating and drinking, he was scared to way/weigh himself.
7. He called to say he'd be late due to a bored/board meeting.
8. Police are investigating an incidence/incident in a city centre shopping mall.

# ▶ Grammar Basics

It would be impractical to cover the grammar of the English language in its entirety in this book, but a few basic points are worth making here.

## Sentence

A sentence is often described as a set of words that has a complete meaning. It starts with a capital letter and ends with a full stop, question mark or exclamation mark. For a sentence to have complete meaning, it almost always has to have two things:

1. Subject: who or what does the action, or about whom or what something is stated.
2. Predicate: refers to what the subject is or does.

Example:

The student submitted the assignment.

This is a complete sentence, 'student' being the *subject*, and 'submitted' being the *predicate*; 'assignment' is what is called the *object*. 'Student' is also a *noun* (the name of a person, place or thing) and 'submitted' is a *verb*, which describes an action or state of the noun.

To make this sentence more interesting we can add:

1. An adjective:

   The **brilliant** student submitted the assignment.
2. An adverb:

   The brilliant student **hastily** submitted the assignment.
3. A preposition (and indirect object):

   The brilliant student hastily submitted the assignment **to** the tutor.
4. A pronoun:

   The brilliant student hastily submitted the assignment to **her** tutor.

## Phrase

A phrase is a set of words that doesn't always have a complete meaning. For example:
 'to her tutor' is a phrase that doesn't mean anything on its own.
 'The brilliant student' is a phrase that could mean something if for example it was a response to a question such as, 'Who submitted the assignment?'

## Subject/Verb Agreement

The subject in a sentence must 'agree' with its verb. We cannot say 'The student submit the assignment' because the subject and verb do not agree. So both subject and verb should be either singular or plural, not a mixture.

### Singular/Collective

These words take the singular: each, every, either, neither, any.
With collective nouns the singular and plural are both acceptable these days:
▶ The Government has/have raised taxes again.
▶ The audience was/were thrilled with the performance.

## ✳ Activity

Correct the following sentences so that there is agreement between subject(s) and verb:

1. There is 450 students in the college.

2. Hector, together with his sister, Hattie, walk to school every day.

3. The wages they pay is very low.

4. The driver and passenger is happy.

5. That herd of cattle have BSE.

6. Which one of you two are the manager?

7. All four of them has a PhD.

8. Each of them were studying for years.

9. 'The Simpsons' are my favourite TV programme.

## Paragraph

A paragraph is a section of writing that usually deals with one specific topic. The writer states the topic in either the first or last sentence. In a handwritten piece the first sentence is indented. When word-processing, paragraphs are normally separated from each other by a line space. Paragraphs give a piece of writing a tidy, ordered appearance and can make it easy for the reader to read.

# ▶ Answers to Selected Activities

## Capital Letters

1. Paula, Robert and I are studying a course at Drumlinn College of Further Education.
2. It's a VEC-run college, the course is a FETAC course and I have temporary accommodation in a B&B.
3. The college isn't far from Ballylinane and the M25.
4. Next summer we are going on a sponsored hike in the French Alps to raise money for Concern.
5. I do work experience at Setanta Designs every Tuesday, just behind the Customs House.
6. They dyed the Liffey green on St Patrick's Day.
7. The students aren't all Irish. One comes from Nigeria and another is Lithuanian.
8. Last Wednesday we went to see *The Curious Case of Benjamin Button*, starring Brad Pitt.
9. She said, 'Why don't you come in?'
10. Last year I went to the Electric Picnic and the Festival of the Fires.
11. We had our debs in the Royal Hotel and the DJ was rubbish.
12. There's a module in Customer Service, but we don't have to do German anymore.
13. I want to become a physiotherapist with Manchester United when I'm finished.

## Apostrophes

1. The swimmers' goggles
2. Shakespeare's plays
3. Rameses' tomb
4. The children's toys
5. The dog's bones
6. St Stephen's Green
7. The lambs' wool
8. St Thomas's Square

1.  I couldn't eat another thing.
2.  They're all we've got.
3.  Don't you have your umbrella with you?
4.  Who'll sit in the back with Sarah?
5.  She's the best hope there is to win.
6.  It's been raining.
7.  Who'd have thought you had it in you?

1.  We're tired of reading Shakespeare's plays. Can't we read some of Yeats's poetry?
2.  The buses didn't stop at St Stephen's Green because the drivers' wage increase wasn't enough.
3.  We're goin' to Donegal for a fortnight's holiday.
4.  I'll get an hour's work done if Peter doesn't disturb me.
5.  There's nothin' but rocks on Mars' surface.
6.  If Goldilocks' hunger hadn't got the better of her, she'd have passed by the bears' house and none of this would've happened.
7.  I've got to go to the doctor's 'cause my tonsils' swelling's got worse.
8.  Here's Derek's jacket. It's covered in dogs' hairs.
9.  The pub's windows look great but its doors' colours don't.
10. For heaven's sake, if it's such a big deal we'll all go to Helen's.
11. The media's got to curtail its habits of prying into people's lives.

## Six Hyphens and Seven Dashes

My sister-in-law came to stay for the weekend – she didn't even ring to warn us! Her husband – my brother Harry – is a long-legged evil-looking man – he even scares the dog. We watched the semi-final on television and then were about to have a big feed of pasta – my favourite – when we noticed the sell-by date on the packet – two weeks old!

## Colon/Semi-Colon

1.  Out came the sun; off came the shirts.
2.  We'll need the following: a hammer, nails, wood and paint.
3.  To err is human; to forgive divine.
4.  Here's the suspect's description: 6'2", brown hair, brown eyes and a moustache.
5.  The speaker began: 'Good evening, Ladies and Gentlemen.'
6.  Luxembourg is a small country; France is a large one.

## Full Stop/Question Mark/Exclamation Mark

1.  I don't know whether she's in or not.
2.  Do we know if there is alien life in the universe?

3. Help!
4. I wonder if I could borrow your hammer.
5. He told me why he was late.
6. Don't you dare!
7. How far do we have to travel?
8. What a great idea!

## Commas

1. So Joe, do you think we have a chance of winning?
2. The doctor, a large friendly man, prescribed some pills.
3. Singing at the top of his voice, Steve prepared a splendid dinner.
4. Josephine, meanwhile, was reading the paper.
5. 'Don't you think,' she enquired, 'we should call the vet?'
6. The Delaneys live in number 46, and their dog chases cars up and down the road.
7. The train, travelling at 120 mph, had fourteen carriages.
8. The concert having finished, they took the last bus home.
9. I put on my coat, picked up my things, bade farewell and left the building.
10. It was, like, the worst book I've ever read.
11. I told you yesterday, we had to submit the assignment. (Or: I told you, yesterday we had to submit the assignment.)
12. You're finished now, aren't you?

## Quotation Marks

1. 'It's all right,' she said, 'everything will be better in the morning.'
2. 'What kind of a word is "bodacious" anyway?' he enquired.
3. 'What do you mean I'm a "babe"?' she asked.
4. Give us your rendition of 'As Time Goes By'.
5. 'Teachers to Strike' yelled the headline across the front page.
6. In the words of Samuel Beckett: 'We are all born mad. Some remain so.'

## Brackets

1. The ship (if you could call it that) will sail at 10.30 pm.
2. We sat in the shade (it was too hot to do anything else) drinking ice-cold water.
3. The people who are really stressed these days (not counting nurses) are senior management.
4. The books (both thrillers) lay on his desk gathering dust.
5. She shouted after him, 'Ich liebe dich (I love you),' but it was too late. He was gone.
6. This steady increase in temperature (known as global warming) is set to get worse over the coming century.

## Confusing Words

1. There is a group of men outside and they're carrying umbrellas under their arms.
2. I've been at this bus stop for 45 minutes and I'm sick of being kept waiting.
3. We're all going to Donegal, which is where we were last year for our holidays.
4. There are two gunslingers coming to this town. That is two too many.
5. It's been a long time since the union got its way.

## Two words or one?

1. Is there a post office nearby?
2. Communications is easy, whereas Maths is hard.
3. She fell into his arms with a heavy sigh.
4. On the count of three, all together now.
5. When he found it in the river, the brief case was still intact.
6. He slammed his fist on the table, thereby breaking his wrist.
7. We have to do a practical as well as a theoretical exam.
8. Who knows what's in store for us?
9. Don't you get a lot of ice with your drink?
10. In fact Ireland need three points to qualify.
11. Bring an umbrella in case it rains.
12. That holiday has left me deeply in debt.
13. It will be all right on the night.

## Subject/Verb Agreement

1. There are 450 students in the college.
2. Hector, together with his sister, Hattie, walks to school every day.
3. The wages they pay are very low.
4. The driver and passenger are happy.
5. That herd of cattle has BSE.
6. Which one of you two is the manager?
7. All four of them have a PhD.
8. Each of them was studying for years.
9. 'The Simpsons' is my favourite TV programme.

## Tip

Always proofread your writing before sending a message or submitting an assignment. Check for punctuation, spelling and grammar.

# Chapter 12
## Personal Writing

## ▶ Writing as a Response

Writing is often done in response to something. Personal writing can be a response to something we've experienced or felt. We might be responding to our own emotions, thoughts or experiences and we express them in poetry, a story, diary etc. Or we could be responding to events in society that prompt us to write a letter to a newspaper. A letter of thanks is a response to a favour done or gift received; a review is our response to a film, book, play etc. Functional writing could be in response to a brief we might have been given by an employer or a college tutor.

### Personal Writing

Personal writing is about expressing our own personal experiences, thoughts and feelings. In effect we are communicating our personalities, which should come across in a piece of writing whether it be a letter, poem, story, review etc. It may also stem from simply reflecting on our lives, the lives of others or the world at large and expressing these reflections in writing.

Some people keep journals or diaries in which they regularly express their innermost thoughts and desires. This type of writing can be therapeutic and liberating, helping to unload psychological burdens that we may be carrying. Since we are doing it purely for ourselves it doesn't matter if its grammar or punctuation is weak.

# ▶ Preparation

No matter what type of personal writing we are faced with, we all begin with the dreaded blank page and a head bereft of fresh ideas. How do we start? First of all we need to be clear *what* we are writing:

1. *Purpose/intention* – What do we want to achieve; what effect do we want to have on the reader?
2. *Topic* – What is it going to be about?
3. *Form* – What way is it going to be written – a poem, prose, story or dialogue? This will be strongly influenced by our purpose.
4. *Language* – The kinds of words we use will create the style, e.g. language using imagery and metaphor suits poetry but not a letter of application.
5. *Personal style* – Certain words or expressions that we commonly use and even the kind of sentence structure we usually employ (long/short etc.) denote our own particular style.
6. *Punctuation and grammar* – Obviously these need to be correct. (See Chapter 11.)

There are several stages we need to go through to put together a piece of writing:

### Plan/Rough Notes

We cannot hope to write a piece from scratch and submit it as it is. There will always be mistakes and room for improvement. A brainstorming session to get all our ideas on the topic down onto a page is useful. We can then link them together by subtopic.

### Draft

We then try to organise these notes to give them some kind of shape. We work out how to order each idea, how to begin and end the written piece and how we structure the main points in between.

### Redraft/Edit

We might find some words we don't like. We might change them, make additions, omissions, polish, refine etc.

### Proofread

It is wise to get someone else to proofread our work, as he will see the mistakes that we don't notice.

## Where Do We Get Our Ideas?

*Memory* – is one source of ideas. Experts often say, 'Write what you know.' If we can tap into our memory for experiences, events etc. we will be truly communicating our own personality.

*Imagination* – we can imagine scenarios, characters, situations and build a story around them.

*Observation* – look around you and write about what you see: people, nature, objects, events etc.

## ✳ Activity

1. To get over 'writer's block' try the following:
   Handwrite three pages about whatever comes into your head without stopping or worrying about spelling, grammar or punctuation. This can free up your inner creative juices and free you from your inner censor ('I'm no good at writing'). It can also provide you with some good ideas for a story or a poem.

2. Sit somewhere quietly and simply record in writing everything you see, hear, smell, touch and taste. These ideas can then be developed into a poem or part of a story.

3. Create two characters by giving them names, physical descriptions, jobs, hobbies, habits, likes, dislikes, activities, ways of talking and walking. Put them in a setting. What happens next? Now you have the start of a story.

## ▶ Short Story

A good story needs to hold the reader's attention and make her want to read on to find out what happens at the end. The beginning and the end should be strong, the former to hook the reader and the latter to leave them feeling satisfied. Sometimes the best stories are the ones we have experienced ourselves. We can always adapt them to make them more exciting and dramatic.

A short story usually has five key elements:

### 1. Characters
Create few characters or just one. Make them come alive by giving them descriptions and making them say and do things.

### 2. Setting
Start by giving the story a time and a place. This can help create a mood e.g. 'A dark and stormy night in the woods' is very different from 'A sunny afternoon by the sea'. You can also give social setting, i.e. what kind of life do the characters lead? Are they wealthy, poor, dull, adventurous, young, old etc?

### 3. Theme
This is the main idea of the story or an underlying message.

### 4. Conflict
All great stories from Shakespeare's plays to modern soap operas would be very dull without people arguing or involved in some kind of struggle. Introduce conflict early on.

### 5. Plot
This is what happens to the character(s). It should contain these key elements:

- Introduction – setting the scene and introducing the character(s).
- Problem or conflict – the character(s) has to deal with this by taking some action. This is sometimes called the rising action.
- Climax – the high point of the action, involving some element of danger or the main challenge the character(s) must face. It is a turning point in the story or a change to the main character(s). This should occur near the end.
- Resolution – the conclusion to the story with an outcome that shows what has happened to the character(s) as a result the climax. Here the conflict is resolved.

A short story should focus on one event in a person's life. Every sentence should either develop the character(s) or move the plot forward. Use a variety of writing forms to make it interesting: dialogue, description and action. Decide on the type of narration you will use. First person narration, in which the narrator is part of the story, can make it sound more personal and believable. Third person narration gives it a more objective, detached feel. Write about what you already know and keep it simple.

Here is a short story written for Twitter in under 140 characters.

Nothing happened. Then it did. Adventures ensued. Helpers, adversaries came. He lost everything. Then, redemption. He was changed – forever.

Tim Lott, *Short Story Tweet*, The Guardian, *Saturday 26 January 2013.*

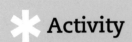 **Activity**

Write a short story in under 140 characters.

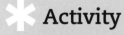 **Activity**

Read this short story and discuss the setting, characters, structure, plot, narration, language etc. It illustrates how short and simple an effective story can be. What is your opinion of it?

### ANGEL

Sitting on the drippy, cold steps of Penn Station, sharing a smoke with a boyfriend. This Saturday night is scattered with drunks, and for once, we are not the drunkest; we do not smell the worst. Late-night, paranoid tourists don't even stare – a few ask for directions. We are spreading our wet, waiting bodies all over that stone, watching stumbling silhouettes wrestle with the escalator. She shuffles up the steps with the last of her strength. Her pink sweatpants are tinged with brown, and her feet are buried in city-stained bunny slippers. Her eyes look like they've seen so much sadness they're forever doomed to apathy. They are eyes dazed with the work it takes to stay warm, and weary of the excess of privileged people. I'm looking at those glass eyes and thinking that she reeks of survival; that I'm too cold to move, and all I'm doing is waiting for the first train home. Out comes her wrinkled, begging hand. We turn out our pockets and find nothing. The mouth of the station swallows her descending, dejected frame. Light another smoke. We are pushing reluctant time forward as it digs its heels in at the dusty smells and sounds of old stories, at the sucking of smoke, at our involuntary shivers. She's back again. The wrinkled hand, heavy with pleading, is now answering. She drops four warm quarters into my palm and says, 'Get yourselves a cup of coffee. Merry Christmas.' The station gulps her up again before we can say thank you.

**Maria Raha**
1999 from *www.storybytes.com*

## ▶ Poetry

Some people think poetry is about the lives led by the poets who write the stuff, but in fact poetry can be about anything and can be written in a variety of styles including dialogue and free verse (no formal structure).

If you haven't written poetry before, it's probably not a good idea to submit your first attempt for a communications assignment. A poem should have something special that will inspire the reader. This could include any or all of the following:

1. Language that is clever, beautiful, rhythmic, humorous or that uses sounds to good effect. Some techniques used for creating effective sounds:

▶ Assonance – words sharing similar vowel sounds, e.g. 'The fire smouldered in the cold but the old man couldn't scold her.'

▶ Alliteration – words that share the same initial letter or sound, e.g. 'The rich may rule the world but the rebels rightly riot.'

▶ Onomatopoeia – words that sound like their meaning, e.g. 'splash'.

▶ Rhyme.

2. Imagery that the reader can 'see'. Imagery can be created by:

▶ Metaphor – an imaginative description comparing something to an object or action that is not literally applicable, e.g. 'the whispering breeze'.

▶ Simile – a comparison using the words 'like' or 'as', e.g. 'she sang like an angel'.

3. Emotions that will inspire, move or entertain the reader.

4. Ideas that will provoke thought.

As with all personal writing, you should tap into your own memories and experiences for subject matter.

## Activity

Read this poem by Seamus Heaney and consider the use of memory, observation and the senses as writing aids. Look also at his use of imagery, sounds and language. What does the poet say about poetry?

**Digging**

Between my finger and my thumb
The squat pen rests, snug as a gun.

Under my window, a clean rasping sound
When the spade sinks into gravelly ground:
My father, digging. I look down

Till his straining rump among the flowerbeds
Bends low, comes up twenty years away
Stooping in rhythm through potato drills
Where he was digging.

The coarse boot nestled on the lug, the shaft
Against the inside knee was levered firmly.
He rooted out tall tops, buried the bright edge deep
To scatter new potatoes that we picked
Loving their cool hardness in our hands.

By God, the old man could handle a spade.
Just like his old man.

My grandfather cut more turf in a day
Than any other man on Toner's bog.
Once I carried him milk in a bottle
Corked sloppily with paper. He straightened up
To drink it, then fell to right away.
Nicking and slicing neatly, heaving sods
Over his shoulder, going down and down
For the good turf. Digging.

The cold smell of potato mould, the squelch and slap
Of soggy peat, the curt cuts of an edge
Through living roots awaken in my head.
But I've no spade to follow men like them.

Between my finger and my thumb
The squat pen rests.
I'll dig with it.

**Seamus Heaney**
1966 from *Death of a Naturalist*.

## Poetry online

▸ Seamus Heaney, 'Digging': http://www.youtube.com/watch?v=dIzJgbNANzk
▸ Allen Ginsberg, 'Howl': http://www.youtube.com/watch?v=IM9BMVFpk8o
▸ Benjamin Zephania, 'Faceless': http://www.youtube.com/watch?v=l9IzHm9GCzk
▸ Dylan Thomas, 'Do Not Go Gentle into that Good Night': http://www.youtube.com/watch?v=1mRec3VbH3w

# ▸ Review

The purpose of a review is to give an *informed* opinion and criticism of a book, play, film, album or concert. There should be sufficient detail to let the audience decide whether or not they want to go and see/buy it.

A film review, for example, should contain information about the following:

▸ *Director* – has he/she created a good film? How? Compare it to other films he/she has made.
▸ *Actors* – have they played their parts well?

▶ *Characters* – are they believable and well developed? What kind of characters are they? Heroic, funny, sad, evil etc?
▶ *Plot* – is it exciting, suspenseful, realistic, full of holes, complicated? The ending should not be revealed.
▶ *Setting* – where and when does it take place?
▶ *Genre* – what type of film is it (comedy, drama, science fiction, thriller etc.)? Is it a successful example of its genre?
▶ *Script* – is it well written? Perhaps you could give a good quote or two from the film.

Sometimes a film review might include further information about the budget, soundtrack, lighting, cinematography, special effects etc.

A book review should contain information about:
▶ *Author* – compare the book to other works by the same author.
▶ *Language* – is it simple/complicated, easy/hard to read, well written/poorly written/ beautifully written?
▶ *Style* – is it snappy, slow, fast-paced, a page-turner, gripping, 'unputdownable', dull, exciting etc?
▶ *Characters* – see film review (above).
▶ *Setting* – see film review (above).
▶ *Plot* – see film review (above).
▶ *Genre* – see film review (above).

A CD review should contain information about:
▶ *Recording artist/band/singer*
▶ *Genre* – folk, rap, rock, pop, hip-hop, classical etc. Is it a successful example of its genre?
▶ *Different songs/pieces of music* – are they moving, exciting, sad etc?
▶ *Lyrical content* – are the words any good?
▶ *Sound quality/production* – is it raw, polished, clean, dirty etc?
▶ How it *compares* to other albums by the same artist or of the same genre.

A concert/gig review should contain information about:
▶ *Artist/band/singer/musicians* – did they play, sing, dance well?
▶ *Performance* – was it entertaining, funny, moving, beautiful etc?
▶ Whether the performer(s) *related* to the audience?
▶ *Special effects* – lighting, explosions etc.
▶ *Sound quality* – e.g. could you hear the lyrics/various instruments?
▶ *Audience reaction* – were they happy, pleased, ecstatic, miserable etc?

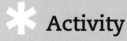 Activity

Read the following review of *Donnie Darko* and discuss the reviewer's references to the director, actors, characters, plot, genre etc.

**Donnie Darko**

It is early October 1988, and the US presidential election is on. Donnie Darko (Jake Gyllenhaal) is a likeable, sleepwalking, troubled teenager who might be schizophrenic. He lives with his family in leafy suburban Middlesex, Virginia and goes to the local high school. One night a six-foot evil-looking rabbit called Frank leads him out of the house on a sleepwalk and tells him the world will end in 28 days, 6 hours and 42 minutes. He arrives home the next morning to find a jet engine has crashed into his bedroom. Miraculously, none of his family is hurt, and had he been in bed he surely would have been killed. But strangely no aeroplane with a missing engine is found. As he tries to work out what all this means, Frank continues to haunt him and instructs him to commit various acts of destruction. At the same time he has to deal with the assorted characters in his life. His parents (Mary McDonnell and Holmes Osborne) are naïve but compassionate and tolerate his insulting behaviour because they know he is ill. His sister, played by real-life sister, Maggie Gyllenhaal, is as sweet and sarcastic as you'd expect. His science teacher has to stop a conversation he has with Donnie about time travel because it is veering into religious territory. Donnie soon starts going out with Gretchen, the new girl in class played by Jena Malone, and an awkward romance starts.

Gretchen: 'You're weird.'

Donnie: 'Sorry.'

Gretchen: 'No, that was a compliment.'

Directed by first-timer Richard Kelly, this has become something of a cult favourite since its release in 2001. Its success partially lies in the fact that it doesn't fit neatly into any one specific genre but manages to dip into high school drama, black comedy, supernatural sci-fi, romance, psychological thriller and because of this it remains free from clichés and utterly unique.

   Jake Gyllenhaal is superb as the central character, giving a subtle yet emotionally powerful performance as a highly intelligent but disaffected teenager searching for answers and questioning authority. The film is also peppered with some wonderful minor characters and subplots to keep the interest up. Drew Barrymore plays the liberal English teacher who gets fired for teaching literature that is considered to be offensive; Patrick Swayze is a smug motivational guru who has a nasty skeleton in the closet; Katherine Ross is Donnie's psychiatrist who prescribes him drugs and, in one of the film's funniest scenes, hypnotises him and foolishly asks him what he thinks about at school. One character, the isolated Grandma Death, might just have the answers to Donnie's probing questions. The performances are all impeccable, played with conviction and doing justice to the fabulously witty script.

As the film counts down the 28 days, after which we expect some kind of apocalypse (coinciding with Halloween), the tension builds and Donnie's questions about fate, chaos and time travel force us to ask, is he really living in some parallel time sequence or is he delusional and hallucinating? At one point he asks Frank, 'Why are you wearing that stupid bunny suit?' to which Frank replies, 'Why are you wearing that stupid man suit?'

The film's ending, with Tears for Fears' 'Mad World' playing over various characters chewing over their actions or overcome with emotion, is incredibly moving, leaving the viewer with many questions on many levels yet strangely satisfied. Hilarious, heartbreaking, surreal, profound and thought-provoking, this is as much a treat for those with enquiring minds as it is for the hopelessly romantic. Some people will find it a little too strange and puzzling, but for those who want something beyond the ordinary this is just the ticket.

*Martin Scott 2005*

# ▶ Personal Letters

With the communications revolution in full swing and new technologies appearing all the time, letter writing would appear to be a dying art. Today it seems much more efficient to send an email, text message or to telephone. Yet there is something special about receiving a personal letter from someone. Somebody has taken the time and effort to put pen to paper, to compose words with more thought than goes into a text message or email, to buy a stamp and to post the letter in a letterbox. An email can be deleted at the touch of a button, whereas a letter can be read and re-read and may be stored away to be discovered years later. How many text messages or emails will be found and savoured in years to come?

A personal letter, be it a letter of thanks, condolence or congratulations, should be handwritten. Its purpose is to express personal thoughts, and if it is typed it becomes less personal, and the less personal, the less its effect. The receiver of a handwritten letter will note and appreciate personal touches.

The informal nature of personal letters means that the rules are not as strict as for formal letters. Nevertheless a basic layout is required.

## Layout of a Personal Letter

49 Bridge Street,
Bray,
Co Wicklow

23.9.14

Dear Philip,

It was great to see you and Erica in Boston over the summer holidays. Thanks for putting us up in your house for the week. We really had a brilliant time. Next year you can come and stay with us and I'll show you some Irish hospitality.

I've just started a course at a college of further education so I'm really busy studying hard and making lots of new friends. I'm working part-time in a local café at the weekends, but I make sure I have time for socialising too.

I bought myself a new bike last week with some of the money I saved from working in the States. It's great for getting to college every day and for keeping fit, though the traffic can be pretty dangerous at times. Mum keeps telling me to get a helmet!

Give my love to Erica, Ted and Sue.

All the best,

Martin

The sender's address should go at the top right-hand side of the page. The date goes below this. The salutation begins below the date but on the left-hand side. Indent the first and all subsequent paragraphs. There are a variety of ways to close a personal letter depending on how well we know the recipient. 'Yours sincerely' may be too formal for some people. 'Yours affectionately' for close relations or friends, or simply 'Yours' for a close friend. For people we know well, familiar endings such as 'Love', 'All the best' or 'Best wishes' are also typical.

## Thanks

A letter of thanks is not only showing appreciation for a favour or a gift, but also acts as acknowledgement of receipt. It does not have to be very long, but should be sincere and contain a personal touch. It may be used as a reply to invitations, on receipt of gifts/presents, after weddings, parties and visits or in response to help given or acknowledgement of expressions of condolences. Two short paragraphs are sufficient.

### Paragraph 1

Suggestions:

▶ 'Many thanks for the book you sent me. It was very kind of you. I haven't been able to put it down since . . .'

▶ 'Thank you very much for the wedding present you gave us. It is proving to be very useful.'

### Paragraph 2

Could contain some simple news about yourself or about the receiver:

▶ 'It was good to see you . . .'

▶ 'I have been really busy lately, studying hard at college . . .'

## Condolences

A letter of condolence can be a difficult and sensitive piece of writing. It is important to find the right amount of sincerity, without going over the top and sounding false. It should contain words of sympathy:

▶ 'I was sorry to hear about the death of . . .'

▶ 'We were so shocked to hear the sad news about . . .'

### Words of Comfort

▶ 'She was a wonderful person, kind and generous . . .'

▶ 'We are thinking of you at this sad and difficult time.'

▶ 'He was a great friend and will be greatly missed.'

If practical, some offer of assistance:

▶ 'If there is anything I can do . . .'

To personalise a letter of condolence, we can include a personal memory we ourselves had of the deceased or an anecdote about a time spent in his company: 'I remember the time when . . .'

## Congratulations

Offering congratulations is a simple matter and may be used for the following occasions: passing exams, engagement, wedding, promotion, birth of a child, a new home.

Some useful phrases:

- ▶ 'We wish you every success in your new position'
- ▶ 'I am delighted to hear the good news'
- ▶ 'We were overjoyed to hear the news about the birth of your son'
- ▶ 'You should be proud of such a fine achievement'
- ▶ 'Well done'
- ▶ 'Congratulations'.

There is even scope here for humour such as:

'I never thought you had it in you' (not for the birth of a child!).

## Tip

Some people are naturally more imaginative than others and have no problem finding inspiration to write a story or a poem. If you feel you aren't that creative, writing a book or a film review might be easier – or maybe a personal letter. Remember that a teacher will have to read many pieces of personal writing, so you should try to make your writing as original as possible.

## Confusing Words

In each of the following sentences, select the correct word, decide what the other word means and put it into another sentence (it may have more than one meaning):

1. There is ample/amble opportunity to get to know each other.
2. Tourists can wonder/wander through the beautiful gardens at leisure.
3. She didn't except/accept my apology.
4. The film had a powerful effect/affect on me.
5. There was a full compliment/complement of members at the meeting.
6. There was a continuous/continual flow of water from the tap.
7. Don't loose/lose your keys.

## Lost in Translation

The following are signs that have been poorly translated into English. Work out what is wrong with them, what each is trying to communicate, then rewrite them to make their meaning clear.

**Swiss restaurant menu:**
Our wines leave you with nothing to hope for.

**Rhodes tailor:**
Order your summers suit. Because is big rush, we will execute customers in strict rotation.

**Bucharest hotel lobby:**
The lift is being fixed for the next day. During that time we regret that you will be unbearable.

**Athens hotel:**
Visitors are expected to complain at the office between the hours of 9 and 11 am daily.

# Chapter 13
## Workplace Documents

During your career you are bound to come across various types of documents that relate to the workplace, such as letters, memos and invoices. You may be required to produce such documents. Therefore, it is important to know how to prepare and write them. Most workplace documents follow certain formats and use language that is clear and concise. This chapter will look at how to create these.

## ▶ Application Form

Filling in a job application form sounds simple enough but many opportunities are lost due to carelessness. Here are a few tips:

1. Make a photocopy of the original and fill it in first. If you make mistakes you have a chance to correct them.
2. Skim-read the whole form before completing it.
3. Keep handwriting as neat and clear as possible.
4. If it can be word-processed, it will look more professional than if it is handwritten.
5. Check all instructions, e.g. using block capitals, ink colour etc.
6. Don't rush it.
7. Double check all information you give 'for accuracy'.

8.  Include information that is accurate – you might have to explain it in an interview.
9.  Get permission from referees before you use their names.
10. Get someone to proofread it when finished.
11. Make a photocopy of the completed form for your own use, e.g. to prepare for the interview.
12. Take the same care when addressing the envelope.

## Sample Job Application Form

Job Title: _____

Surname: _____

First Name(s): _____

                                        Title: _____

Address: _____

_____

_____

Telephone Number: _____

Mobile: _____

Email: _____

Date of Birth: _____

**EDUCATION**

List in reverse chronological order.

| Schools/Colleges | Dates | Subjects/Courses | Results/Grades |
|---|---|---|---|
| | | | |
| | | | |
| | | | |
| | | | |
| | | | |
| | | | |
| | | | |

**EMPLOYMENT**

**Current/most recent position**

Dates

From: _____  To: _____

Salary: _____

Name and address of employer: _____

_____

Job title: _____

Main duties and responsibilities: _____

_____

_____

_____

Period of notice required: _____

**Previous employment**

List in reverse chronological order.

| Name and address of previous employer(s) | Dates | Position held | Reason for leaving |
|---|---|---|---|
| _____ | _____ | _____ | _____ |
| _____ | _____ | _____ | _____ |
| _____ | _____ | _____ | _____ |
| _____ | _____ | _____ | _____ |
| _____ | _____ | _____ | _____ |
| _____ | _____ | _____ | _____ |
| _____ | _____ | _____ | _____ |

Have you ever suffered from any serious illnesses? _____

If so, give details: _____

_____

Do you have a full current driving licence? _____

Have you ever been charged for a driving offence or been involved in a serious accident? _____

If so, give details: _____

_____

Have you ever been convicted of a criminal offence? _____

If so, give details: _____

_____

Language proficiency: _____

Computer proficiency: _____

How did you learn about this vacancy? _____

Have you worked for this company before? _____

If so, when? _____

**INTERESTS**

Give details of any interests, pastimes and achievements:

_____
_____
_____
_____
_____
_____
_____

Outline your reasons for wanting this position:

_____
_____
_____
_____
_____

Additional information that you think might be relevant:

_____
_____
_____
_____
_____

Please give names and addresses of two referees:

Name: _____

Address: _____

_____

Telephone Number:_____

Name: _____

Address: _____

_____

Telephone Number: _____

Signature: _____

Date: _____

# ▶ Curriculum Vitae

Latin for 'course of life', a CV is a document giving a brief account of your life to date. It should be word-processed, neatly presented, well laid out, putting the most important information first, and all of it should be relevant. There are various ways of presenting a CV, but it should be no longer than two A4 pages. It will contain the following information:

### Personal Details
Name, address, phone number and email. You do not need to include your date of birth, marital status or nationality.

### Personal Profile
This is a brief summary of your unique selling points, skills and qualities that should encourage the reader to read further. Try to tailor it to the job for which you are applying.

### Education
List in reverse chronological order i.e. the most recent first. Include names and addresses of schools and colleges, dates, course/award titles, subjects/modules and final third level dissertation/thesis if relevant. Leave out primary school.

### Employment History
List in reverse chronological order, list dates, names and addresses of employers, job titles or description/responsibilities. Keep job descriptions concise.

### Further Training
Add any other courses you have done outside of mainstream education such as first aid, ECDL. Include dates, name and address of the place you completed the training.

### Hobbies and Interests
Include pastimes, membership of clubs, societies, community groups and voluntary work.

### Achievements
This section could include any medals, awards or prizes won, e.g. for sport, debating or other competitions.

### Additional Information
Here you can include other skills and abilities that might be useful such as computer or language proficiency or full clean driving licence.

### Referees
Use one academic and one non-academic, such as a previous employer. Ask for permission to use their name on your CV.

# CURRICULUM VITAE

Stephen Loughran

Riverside House, Bridge Street, Bandon, Co. Cork.

086 0000000

sloughran@internetmail.com

## PERSONAL PROFILE

Highly skilled horticulturalist with excellent attention to detail, motivated and flexible with a desire to experiment with new crop varieties. A good team player, able to work on own initiative, striving for high standards and efficiency.

## EDUCATION

| | |
|---|---|
| 2013–2014 | Drumlinn College of Further Education, Drumlinn, Co. Monaghan. |
| | FETAC Level 6 in Organic Horticulture |
| | Grade: Distinction. |
| 2011–2013 | Drumlinn College of Further Education, Drumlinn, Co. Monaghan. |
| | FETAC Level 5 in Organic Horticulture |
| | Grade: Distinction. |
| 2005–2010 | Kinsale Community School, Kinsale, Co. Cork. |
| 2010 | Leaving Certificate |

## EMPLOYMENT HISTORY

| | | |
|---|---|---|
| 2011–2012 | Ballywhelan Organic Farm, Dunderrow, Kinsale, Co. Cork. | |
| | Responsibilities | Sowing seeds |
| | | Crop maintenance |
| | | Harvesting crops for market |
| | | Selling produce at weekly market |
| 2010–2011 | Coughlan's Bar, Bridge Street, Bandon, Co. Cork. | |
| | Position | Barman |
| | Responsibilities | Serving customers |
| | | Cash and card handling |
| | | Ordering stock |
| | | Opening and closing premises |
| | | Cleaning premises |

2008–2010    Supervalu, Riverview Shopping Centre, Bandon, Co. Cork.

Position           Storehouse assistant

Responsibilities    Stacking shelves

Stock-taking

Ordering stock

Taking deliveries

## INTERESTS

* Swimming, music, reading
* Member of Sandycove Swimming Club, Kinsale
* Volunteered for Kinsale Arts Festival 2011

## ACHIEVEMENTS

* Took part in 1 mile swim to raise money for Cork Simon Community
* Photography – winner West Cork People under 18 Photo of the Year Award 2010
* Chess – School Chess Champion 2008

## ADDITIONAL INFORMATION

* Excellent command of French
* Full clean driving licence

## REFEREES

Colin Whelan

Ballywhelan Organic Farm

Dunderrow

Kinsale

Co. Cork

087 0000000


Paul Flynn

Organic Horticulture Course Co-ordinator

Drumlinn College of Further Education

Drumlinn

Co. Monaghan

086 0000000

# ◗ Letter of Application

Many applications are now made online via email but often employers still require a letter, sometimes called a cover letter, to accompany your CV. It will be the first impression you make on an employer so it should be well written and presented. Its purpose it to encourage the employer to read your CV and to be impressed enough to invite you for an interview. Here are a few guidelines:

1. Find out the name of the person to whom you should apply and address the letter to that person.
2. Find out the details of the job, e.g. title and specifications.
3. Use language that is formal, positive, enthusiastic and confident.
4. Use short and simple sentences.
5. Send copies of references or certificates and keep the originals.
6. Keep copies of all letters you send.

## Breakdown of a Letter of Application

### Paragraph 1
◗ Say that you would like to apply for the job.
◗ Say where you found out about it.

### Paragraphs 2 and 3
◗ Say why you would like the job.
◗ Say why you are qualified for the job and refer to any specific details on your CV.
◗ Say what skills and qualities you can bring to the job.

### Paragraph 4
◗ Say you can supply more information if required.
◗ Say when you are available for an interview.
◗ Say you look forward to their reply.

Sample Letter of Application

Riverview
Bridge Street
Bandon
Co. Cork
Tel: 086 0000000

20 May 2013

Shane Cochrane

Manager

Coolmain Outdoor Education Centre

Kilbrittain

Co. Cork

**Re: Assistant Instructor Position**

Dear Mr Cochrane,

I would like to apply for the job advertised in *The Examiner* on Friday 14 May.

As you can see from my CV I have just completed a FETAC Level 5 Outdoor Instructor Award, during which I greatly improved my skills in kayaking and rock-climbing as well as developing group facilitation and instruction abilities.

I am highly motivated and outgoing and have always been interested in the outdoors. I believe this job would give me the opportunity to further develop my skills and to share my enthusiasm with your clients.

If you require any further information, please do not hesitate to contact me. I am available for an interview at any time and look forward to your reply.

Yours sincerely,

_____

Ronan O'Neill

# ▶ Formal/Business Letters

All formal and business letters should be typed/word-processed. When typing a letter it is practical to use the fully blocked style. This means everything, address, date, salutation etc. starts from the left-hand margin and is frequently used with open punctuation, in other words, only the body of the letter contains commas, full stops etc. The style for business letters today is short and to the point. Software that provides templates for formal letters is readily available on most computers.

## Sample Business Letter

E-Zee
Internet Services and Web Design
31 Main Street
Kilkenny
Co. Kilkenny
Email: ezee@ireland.com
Tel: 056 2144781
Fax: 056 2144795

**①**

Ref BO/RD

**②**

13 March 2010

**③**

Ms Tanya Fitzpatrick
Principal
Drumlinn College of Further Education
Drumlinn
Co. Monaghan

**④**

Re: Quotation for design of website

**⑤**

Dear Ms Fitzpatrick

**⑥**

Thank you for your enquiry of 4 March concerning our web design services which were recently advertised in *The Irish Times*.

Although we are a relatively new company, we already have a reputation for a fast, efficient service, state-of-the-art technology and a design team, which has many years' experience.

I have consulted with my chief designer and am pleased to submit a quotation for the requirements you outlined in your letter. I hope this meets with your approval.

Please do not hesitate to contact me if you require any further information.

**⑦**

Yours sincerely

**⑧**

*Brian O'Neill*

**⑨**

Brian O'Neill

**⑩**

Manager
Enc

**⑪**

## Layout

The layout of a business letter is as follows:

1. The sender's address, unless the paper has a company letterhead, which will include the address, phone number, fax and email address.
2. A reference which is used for filing purposes and is usually the sender's and typist's initials (optional).
3. The date like this: 13 March 2010. The 'th' after numbers is usually omitted these days and avoid abbreviations such as: 13/3/10.
4. The recipient's name, title and address.
5. The heading if required: 'Re: Quotation for design of website'.
6. The salutation:
   ▶ 'Dear Sir/Madam' (if the recipient is unknown)
   ▶ 'Dear Sir' (if recipient is known to be male)
   ▶ 'Dear Madam' (if recipient is known to be female)
   ▶ 'Dear Mr/Mrs/Ms/Miss Fitzpatrick'
   ▶ 'A Chara'.
7. The body of the letter. A simple rule is: keep it clear, concise and courteous. If it can be written in three paragraphs, that is enough, with one main idea per paragraph. The breakdown of the body of the letter should be as follows:
   ▶ Paragraph 1: State the background or context of the letter, e.g.
     – 'Thank you for your letter of 13 July last in which you stated . . .'
     – 'I would like an estimate for . . .'
   ▶ Paragraph 2: The reason for writing, the 'main thrust' of the message.
   ▶ Paragraph 3: Round off with an indication of an expected outcome, or further communication.
     – 'I look forward to hearing from you at your earliest convenience'
     – 'Please do not hesitate to contact me, should you require any additional information'.
8. Complimentary closure:
   ▶ 'Yours faithfully' if begun with 'Dear Sir'/'Dear Madam'
   ▶ 'Yours sincerely' (sometimes shortened to 'Sincerely') if begun with 'Dear Mr'/'Ms' etc.
9. Signature (handwritten).
10. Name and title of signatory (typed/word-processed).
11. Enc for an enclosed document or Encs for more than one.

## General Guidelines

1. Always make notes or do at least one rough draft before you start to write your letter.
2. Use an appropriate tone.
3. Proofread.
4. Spelling, grammar and punctuation should be accurate.
5. Use good-quality paper and matching envelopes if possible.
6. Write on one side of the page only.
7. Keep copies of all letters you send.

# ▶ Other Formal Letters

## Letter of Enquiry

1. Make sure you give complete and precise details about the information you require.
2. Ask someone to proofread your letter as if he is the recipient.

## Reply to an Enquiry

1. Begin with a reference to the enquiry.
2. Information can be presented clearly by using numbered or bulleted headings.
3. As above, ask someone to proofread.

## Letter of Complaint

1. Reasons for sending:
   - ▶ On receipt of shoddy goods
   - ▶ On receipt of poor service
   - ▶ Environmental nuisance/disturbance
   - ▶ To record your annoyance
   - ▶ To seek an end to a situation
   - ▶ To seek redress for damage/inconvenience caused.
2. Always write a letter of complaint as soon as possible after the situation or event.
3. Start with a statement of regret.
4. When complaining use a tone that is polite but firm.
5. Explain the inconvenience caused to you and the dissatisfaction you felt, using I-statements, not you-statements, e.g. 'I was very distressed . . . ', not 'You caused me great distress . . . '
6. Avoid being offensive, rude or overly dramatic.
7. Supply details to support complaint – dates, times, numbers, documents etc.
8. Offer a suggestion of how the matter might be rectified – by compensation, replacement etc.

## Letter of Adjustment (Reply to a Complaint)

1. Whether a complaint is justified or not, be tactful.
2. If it is justified accept responsibility, offer an expression of regret, an explanation, an apology and an intention to rectify the matter by compensation etc.
3. If it is not justified (and be quite certain that it isn't), politely make this clear.
4. If a complaint is mishandled, it could result in loss of business, loss of goodwill or adverse publicity.

# ▶ Memorandum

A memorandum (memo for short) is a brief message used internally in organisations to convey or request information, to confirm spoken communication or to give instructions. The word comes from the Latin for 'something to be remembered'. It can often be quite informal in style, depending on the organisation. Since a memo is such a short document, A5 paper is normally used, although A4 is also acceptable. As in business letters, a reference number/initial can be used, Cc indicates copies sent to other parties and Enc means there is an accompanying note or document. A memo may be typed or handwritten, and deals with just one item of business.

Many companies have their own standardised memo forms. There are a variety of items that may be included on a memo but generally the following are the most important: the sender, the recipient, the date and the subject matter. Open punctuation and fully blocked style is usual today.

## Sample Memo

**MEMORANDUM**

TO              All Staff

FROM            P. Jacob

DATE            10 August 2010

SUBJECT         New Computer Software

The new computer software has just been installed. As most staff members will be unfamiliar with its operation, I would suggest a demonstration for an hour on Thursday 15th at 10.30 a.m. in the main office. Des Griffin has kindly volunteered to show us how to use it.

# ▶ Invoice

An invoice is a document given to a customer or client, which serves as a record of goods or services provided to them. The vendor needs to keep a copy as a sales record and the customer should retain a copy as a purchase record.

An invoice should include the following:

▶ The word 'Invoice', often in capitals or bold
▶ Company name, letterhead/logo, address, phone number, email and website if available
▶ Company number
▶ VAT registration number if VAT-registered
▶ Invoice number – each invoice should have a unique number
▶ Date
▶ Date payment is due, usually 30 days after invoice date
▶ Customer/client name
▶ Description of goods/services including quantities, units of measure, etc., with cost per item
▶ Subtotal
▶ VAT
▶ Total amount due.

Sample Invoice

## INVOICE

St Brogan's Community Farm
St Brogan's Hill
Bandon
Co. Cork
Tel: 023 0000000
Fax: 023 0000000

Tax Reg No: 1284950T

23 October 2014

**To:**
Treacy's Garden Centre
Cork Road
Kinsale
Co. Cork
Tel: 021 0000000

Invoice No. TG002
Payment due: 23 November 2014

| Quantity | Description | Unit Price | Total |
|----------|-------------|------------|-------|
| 5 | Bags Radar over-wintering onion sets | 8.00 | 40.00 |
| 7 | Bags Record seed potatoes | 12.45 | 87.15 |
| 2 | Empire apple trees | 14.80 | 29.60 |
| | | Subtotal | €156.75 |
| | | VAT 21.5% | €33.70 |
| | | Total | €190.45 |

# ▶ Press Release

A press release is a written message for the media to announce a news item, an event such as a concert or festival, awards, new products or services or the opening of a new business. It is a useful promotional document and, if done well, it increases the likelihood of your news story being published in a media outlet such as a newspaper.

A press release should contain:
- ▶ Headline
- ▶ Main body.

### Headline

Create an eye-catching headline that will make the reader interested and want to read further. It should be clear and to the point. Use a bold or upper case font to highlight it. A subhead can go underneath in italics, giving a little more information.

### Main Body

Write the press release as you would like it to appear in the publication. Save the newspaper editors and reporters time by giving them all the important details in the first paragraph using around 25 words and answering the questions: who, what, why, when, where and how. Any additional content should elaborate on it. Start with the date, venue and town. Use as much factual information as possible and write in clear, short sentences and simple language. Include a quote from a reliable source and add a single line about the organisation and contact information at the end. A link to a website is useful.

IMMEDIATE RELEASE

Kinsale College of Further Education presents:

# Love's Labour's Lost

Written by William Shakespeare and Directed by Belinda Wild.

– a comic celebration of young love and its pitfalls –

The King of Navarre and his friends vow to study in seclusion for three years and deny themselves food, sleep and women! When the desirable Princess of France and her feisty female companions arrive at the gates, the young men's resolve is severely tested, with hilarious results.

As the men struggle and the women delight in outwitting them, they are aided and abetted by an eccentric cast of characters featuring a flamboyant Spanish knight, a pedantic schoolmistress, an unctuous parson and a vengeful clown. Full of clever verbal tricks and comic invention, Shakespeare's exuberant comedy proves that the course of true love never does run smoothly.

Belinda Wild has extensive experience of directing accessible, dynamic and imaginative versions of Shakespeare's plays and *Love's Labour's Lost* follows the riotous success of previous Shakespearean productions from Kinsale College including, *A Midsummer Night's Dream* and *The Merry Wives of Windsor*.

'The audience laughed with uncontrollable abandon…wonderful team spirit.'
Wrap up warm and bring a friend to enjoy a theatrical treat in Kinsale College's unique outdoor venue.

Performances on May 6, 7, 8, 12, 13, 14, 15 at 8pm
School matinee: May 11 at 12 noon.
Advance Bookings: 086 0000000 or in person at Kinsale Bookshop

Venue: Kinsale College Amphitheatre, Bandon Road, Kinsale

(Supplied by Belinda Wild, Kinsale College of Further Education)

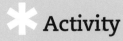 **Activity**

1. Fill in the application form on p.188 as if you were applying for a job in your own vocational area.

2. Create/update your own CV using the guidelines and sample in this chapter.

3. You are working in a department store. Write a memo to your colleagues informing them about your Christmas party. Include details about the date, time, venue and cost.

4. Write a memo to your classmates informing them that there is a student council meeting next week. Include the date, time and room.

5. You are the manager of a company/organisation (select appropriate vocational area). Write a memo to your staff informing them of some new equipment that has been installed, with instructions for use/suggestion for a demonstration at a particular time and place.

6. You are the manager of a company/organisation (select appropriate vocational area). Write a memo to your staff informing them about the importance of punctuality in the workplace, as some members have been arriving late in the mornings and leaving early in the evenings.

7. Find an advertisement for a job related to your area of study and write a letter of application for it.

8. Write a letter applying for work experience.

9. Write a letter of complaint to a travel company about a disastrous holiday they sold you.

10. Write a letter of complaint to a company/organisation about poor service/shoddy goods you received from them.

11. Create an invoice for a service or goods supplied by you/your company (select appropriate vocational area).

12. Write a press release for the launch of a new service/product by you/your company (select appropriate vocational area).

## Confusing Words

In each of the following sentences, select the correct word, decide what the other word means and put it into another sentence (it may have more than one meaning):

1. Write to the personal/personnel manager.
2. Who is the principle/principal of this college?
3. The forest was very quiet/quite at night time.
4. No dogs are aloud/allowed.
5. The awards ceremony will precede/proceed the speeches.
6. You can hire/higher a car at the airport.
7. It looked like a scene/seen out of a disaster movie.
8. The couple decided to steel/steal away in the dead of night.

## Lost in Translation

The following are signs poorly translated into English. Work out what is wrong with them, what each is trying to communicate, then rewrite them to make their meaning clear.

**Leipzig elevator:**
Do not enter the lift backwards, and only when lit up.

**Yugoslav hotel:**
The flattening of underwear with pleasure is the job of the chambermaid.

**Moscow hotel, next to cemetery:**
You are welcome to visit the cemetery where famous Russian and Soviet composers, artists, and writers are buried daily except Thursday.

**Austrian skiing hotel:**
Not to perambulate the corridors in the hours of repose in the boots of ascension.

**Hong Kong dress shop:**
Ladies have fits upstairs.

## Tips

1. The following websites are useful for information on CVs and job applications:
   - www.cvireland.ie
   - www.monster.ie
   - www.jobs.ie
   - www.irishjobs.ie
   - www.recruitireland.com
   - www.bestjobs.ie

2. More Tips
   - Check you have the correct document layout.
   - Keep information clear and concise.
   - Always proofread for punctuation, spelling and grammar.

# Chapter 14
## The Report

Like other forms of written communication, reports vary in length, content, format and style depending on the purpose for which they are intended. Essentially a report is a presentation of facts following an investigation or examination. For example the manager of a company may ask for a report on the company's sales figures for the past year. A fire officer might be asked to carry out a report into the adequacy of the fire safety procedures in an organisation. Large corporations and state bodies often commission lengthy reports that take many months to prepare and are the size of a book.

# Types of Report

### Routine Reports

These are submitted regularly, are brief and often written on specially provided forms, for example a doctor's report on a patient or a teacher's report on a student.

### Special Reports

Special reports are normally carried out and written for a specific purpose. For example, a fire officer may be called in to a firm to investigate the necessary improvements needed so that a building meets the requirements of the fire department. These reports are usually short and may be approximately 500–1000 words in length. Some reports may be so brief that they take the form of a memo.

## Long Reports

As the name suggests, these are lengthy documents, often taking the form of a book. Large corporations and State bodies will commission long reports and they may take many months to prepare, for example the Report of the Special Group on Public Service Numbers and Expenditure Programmes, published in 2009, was commissioned by the Department of Finance.

Reports may also be categorised as *formal* or *informal*.

# ▶ The Short Report

This section looks at the short structured report, as it is the kind we are most likely to come across in our working lives and it is an assessment requirement for FETAC Level 5.

The short structured report consists of the following components:

- ▶ Title
- ▶ Terms of Reference
- ▶ Methodology
- ▶ Findings
- ▶ Conclusions
- ▶ Recommendations.

## Title

Use a separate cover page and a short title stating precisely what the report is about, e.g. 'Report on Fire Safety at Dun Laoghaire Music Centre'.

## Terms of Reference

This states the purpose of the report or why it was carried out. If the report is simply to provide information it will go something like this: 'As requested by the management, to provide information on the adequacy of fire safety procedures at Dun Laoghaire Music Centre.'

If the report is required to make recommendations then the wording would be as follows: 'As requested by the management, to provide information on the adequacy of fire safety procedures at Dun Laoghaire Music Centre and to make any necessary recommendations.'

## Methodology

This is how the report was carried out and should state what kind of research was done (see p.214 for Research methods). The methodology section can range in length from one sentence to a few short paragraphs.

## Findings

This is the main body of the report and shows the results of the research or investigation. The information here must be factual and presented in a clear, objective and impersonal style. Avoid using the first or second person pronouns 'I', 'me, 'my', 'you' and 'your'. This keeps the language impersonal and helps avoid biased statements. For example, write 'this report' instead of 'my report' and 'in conclusion' instead of 'I can conclude that'.

Factual statements must be supported by evidence of research. See References on p.212.

Divide the findings into logically sequenced sections, using subheadings for subsections and bullets and/or numbers for lists.

Use visual supports such as charts, diagrams, photographs or drawings to help present the findings and enhance the overall presentation of the report, but only use them if they are relevant.

## Conclusions

These must be based on the findings and summarised into three or more main points. They should be unbiased, supported by the facts presented in the findings and should answer the questions in the terms of reference. They should be written in descending order of importance.

Never introduce new information in the conclusion.

## Recommendations

Not all reports need to make recommendations, so include them only if they are relevant or part of the terms of reference. They should be positive suggestions for future implementation that could improve a situation or an organisation. List them in descending order of importance. See p.224 for an example of how a finding must progress logically to a conclusion and from there to a recommendation.

## Appendix/Appendices

This contains any additional information such as results of a survey or questionnaire, questions asked in an interview or notes taken during an observation.

## Bibliography

A bibliography is a list of all the secondary research sources you have used for your report and should go at the end of the report. Its purpose is twofold:

1. To show that you have done some research
2. To acknowledge the creators of the work you have used.

Different source types require different entries. Here is the layout using the Harvard Style of bibliography.

### Books

- Author (surname, initials),
- Year of publication,
- *Title of book* (italics or underlined),
- Edition (if applicable),
- Place of publication (city, country if necessary).

Example:
Harvey, N., 2014, *Effective Communication*, 4th edition, Gill & Macmillan, Dublin.

### Newspaper article online

- Author (surname, initials),
- Year of publication,
- 'Title of article' (single quotation marks),
- *Newspaper name* (italics),
- Date,
- Page number(s) (if applicable).

Example
Freeman, H., 2013, 'How to use the internet without being a loser', *The Guardian*, 30 July 2013.

### Websites

- Author/editor (if identified) (surname, initials),
- Last update (if identified),
- *Title of article* (italics or underlined),
- Date accessed,
- <URL> (full website address).

Example:
Riebeek, H., 2010, *Global Warming*, accessed 31 July 2013, http://earthobservatory.nasa.gov/Features/GlobalWarming/

### Encyclopaedias

▶ *Title* (italics or underlined),
▶ Year of publication,
▶ Publisher,
▶ Place of publication,
▶ Volume number,
▶ Page number(s).

Example: *Philip's Concise Encyclopaedia*, 1997, George Philip Ltd, London, p.132.

### Pamphlets, Brochures, Leaflets

▶ *Title* (italics or underlined),
▶ Year of publication,
▶ Publisher,
▶ Place of publication.

Example: *Ireland's Environment, Take Action Now!*, 2000, Environmental Protection Agency, Wexford.

### Edited Works (books with a selection of essays by different authors)

▶ Author(s),
▶ Year of publication,
▶ 'Title of essay/chapter' (single quotation marks),
▶ in name of editor(s), (Ed.)/(Eds)
▶ *Title* (italics or underlined),
▶ Publisher,
▶ Place of publication.

Example: Fiske, J., 1991, 'Postmodernism and Television', in Curran, J. and Gurevitch, M. (Eds) *Mass Media and Society*, Edward Arnold, London.

### Video

▶ *Title* (italics or underlined) [Video],
▶ Year of publication,
▶ Publisher,
▶ Place of publication.

Example: *Body Language* [Video], 2001, Simply Communication, Galway.

### Email

▶ Author(s),
▶ Year of publication,
▶ *Title/subject* (italics or underlined) [Personal email],
▶ Date of access.

Example: Brophy, J., 2001, *Punctuation* [Personal email], 14 April.

### Interviews

▶ Name of interviewee,
▶ Year of interview,
▶ Position of interviewee [Interview],
▶ Date of interview.

Example: McLelland, S., 2002, Manager of Leitrim Tourist Office [Interview], 14 November.

**You can now create bibliographies easily using software such as EndNote.**

# ▶ References

A report should be written in your own words. Under no circumstances should passages of text be copied, word for word, from other sources, and passed off as your own work. You need to show evidence of the research carried out and this is done by including references to other works and written material. Any information taken from a secondary research source should be referenced. You do not need to reference information that is common knowledge. Here are the main types of referencing:

## Quotations

Quotations must be taken from the original text word for word. Short quotations should be placed within quotation marks and be followed with the author's surname, year of publication and page number.
Example:

'A report must be written in your own words.' (Harvey, 2014, p.212)

This means the quotation is taken from a book by someone by the name of Harvey, published in the year 2014, and is taken from p.212. The reader can then refer to the bibliography and check the details of the book.

*Long quotations* (three lines or more) are separated from the rest of the text and indented.

Example:

> A report must be written in your own words. Under no circumstances should passages of text be copied, word for word, and passed off as your own work. (Harvey, 2014, p.212)

Words omitted from a quoted piece are indicated by an *ellipsis* ( . . . ). This is useful if a passage contains words in the middle that are irrelevant, and you want to leave them out.

Quotations from an interview should be presented the same way, but followed in brackets by the name of the interviewee and the word 'interview' and if possible the date the interview took place.

A *citation* is a reference to another author's work, which must include the year of publication.

Example:

> Harvey (2014) states that a report should be written in your own words.

Again, the reader can then check in the bibliography for books by Harvey.

# ▶ Language and Format

The language of a report should be formal, objective (unbiased) and impersonal. To avoid personal language you can use the passive voice, e.g. 'A survey was conducted' instead of 'I conducted a survey.'

Consider the reader and use language and terminology that he will understand. If you use any technical terms add a glossary at the back to explain them.

Use a standard formal font to make your report easy to read. Use 10pt or 12pt font for main text, and 14pt or 16pt for main headings. Be consistent throughout the report: don't use a variety of fonts.

# ▶ Choosing a Topic

If you have the option of choosing a topic, then choose something that interests you and that is easy to research. Begin by brainstorming the topic and writing down everything you already know about it. Follow this by working out what information is missing. This will be the start of your research.

# ▶ Research

You cannot write an assignment based purely on what you already know, or from class notes and handouts. You have to go and do some thorough research yourself. The strength or weakness of an assignment often rests upon how much research has been done, how it has been carried out and how it is presented. Extensive and relevant research will yield a good result.

There are two types of research:

1. Primary Research – Information that is gathered first hand by means of surveys, interviews, questionnaires, observation, experiments and testing.
2. Secondary Research – Information that is gathered from material that has already been produced by someone else, e.g. books, brochures, leaflets, magazines, newspapers, the internet, reports and other research papers.

## Primary Research

There are two types of primary research:

1. **Quantitative research** refers to quantities, for example, data that can be measured and turned into statistics. Surveys and questionnaires are typical forms of quantitative research and often require large numbers of participants. This type of research answers the questions *who, what* and *where*. The results can be displayed in charts or graphs.

2. **Qualitative research** is about how good or useful something is and is often based upon people's opinions and behaviour. For example, you might conduct an interview or set up a focus group to find out people's attitude to something. Fewer numbers of participants are needed. Since the results are not measureable, they are presented in written form. This type of research answers the questions *why* and *how*. Observation is another example of qualitative research.

A combination of both types of research can be very useful to get a complete picture. For example, market research might be done on how many people bought a certain product (quantitative) and then some of these people might be interviewed to find out why they bought it (qualitative).

## Types of Quantitative Research

### Survey

A survey is a way of collecting information, usually by means of a questionnaire, from a sample of the population. A sample here means a selection, such as a group of people being asked how they might vote prior to an election. Surveys can be carried out by post, telephone or email. They can also be carried out using free online software such as SurveyMonkey (*www.surveymonkey.com*). Before carrying out a survey, consider the pros and cons of each method of survey, e.g. a postal survey will take time; telephone surveys might prompt interviewees to hang up; and email surveys can be efficient but sometimes respondents can be slow to reply.

## Questionnaire

A questionnaire is a method of collecting data using a series of questions and should be designed so that it is as concise and user-friendly as possible. If possible, do a test-run on classmates or friends and make any necessary adjustments before undertaking the real survey. You should aim for twenty or thirty respondents for a short structured report. When designing a questionnaire consider the following:

1. Exactly what information is required?
2. Who will supply the information?
3. Will the respondents understand the questions and be able to answer them?
4. Are the questions clear and unambiguous?
5. In what sequence should the questions be arranged?
6. Is the layout clear?
7. How will the results be formulated, i.e. in tables, charts, graphs etc.?

When distributing questionnaires, try and get them filled out and returned by respondents immediately rather than leaving them in locations where they may go missing or simply be ignored.

### Layout of the Questionnaire
1. Title of survey
2. Some factual questions
3. More complicated, multiple-choice questions
4. Open-ended questions
5. Identification questions (age, gender, nationality etc.).

### Types of Question
*Closed-ended questions* require an answer of either yes or no. Boxes may be used for the respondent to tick. Tick boxes like these are very user-friendly, as respondents don't have to spend too much time thinking or writing.
Example:
Do you drive a car?  Yes ❑  No ❑

*Multiple-choice questions* supply a number of possible answers from which the respondent can choose. Leave a space for 'other' in case there is an option you haven't considered.

Example:

Do you travel to work:

by bus     ❏

by car      ❏

by train    ❏

by bike     ❏

on foot     ❏

other (please specify) _____

*Open-ended questions* give the respondent the option of giving a more lengthy and detailed reply, so remember to leave a few lines before the next question. Use a limited amount of these questions as they can be time-consuming for the respondent and are also difficult to quantify unless some answers are the same, in which case they can be converted into statistics.

Example:

What improvements would you like to see? _____

_____

_____

*Scaling questions* ask the respondent to rate something. There are three types of scale:

1.  The *Likert Scale* asks the respondent to agree or disagree with something.
    Example:
    The internet is a useful means of research.

| Strongly agree | Agree | Neither agree nor disagree | Disagree | Strongly disagree |
|---|---|---|---|---|
| | | | | |

2.  The *Semantic-differential* presents the respondent with a scale of two opposing adjectives, and he indicates with a mark on that scale his attitude toward a specific issue or product.
    Example:
    Monkstown Leisure Centre is:
    Well maintained _____ Poorly maintained
    A mark on the very left means he thinks it is very well maintained and a mark on the very right means he thinks it is poorly maintained. A mark in the middle indicates average.

3. The *Staple Scale* consists of one adjective in the middle of a numbered scale.

   Example:

   Do you think the staff in the centre are:

   | -5 | -4 | -3 | -2 | -1 | friendly | +1 | +2 | +3 | +4 | +5 |
   |----|----|----|----|----|----------|----|----|----|----|----|
   | -5 | -4 | -3 | -2 | -1 | helpful | +1 | +2 | +3 | +4 | +5 |
   | -5 | -4 | -3 | -2 | -1 | efficient | +1 | +2 | +3 | +4 | +5 |

   ## Sample Questionnaire

   Questionnaire on Social Networking Use

   Which of the following social networking websites do you use?

   Facebook ❏

   Google+ ❏

   Twitter ❏

   Pinterest ❏

   LinkedIn ❏

   Ask.fm ❏

   Other (please specify) _____

   How often do you check your social networking site(s)?

   Several times a day ❏

   Once a day ❏

   Three to four times a week ❏

   Once a week ❏

   Once a month ❏

   How much time do you spend on social networking sites during each visit?

   Less than 30 minutes ❏

   30 minutes to one hour ❏

   More than one hour ❏

   How many 'friends' do you currently have?

   _____

   How many of your friends have you met in person?

   _____

What do you mainly use social networking sites for?

Keeping in touch with friends      ❑

Keeping in touch with family      ❑

Meeting new friends      ❑

Sharing photos      ❑

Sharing information      ❑

Other (please specify) _____

Are you concerned with privacy issues around social networking?

Yes ❑         No ❑

Are you concerned with security issues around social networking?

Yes ❑         No ❑

Have you ever experienced bullying while on a social networking site?

Yes ❑         No ❑

Have you modified your settings to make them as safe as possible?

Yes ❑         No ❑

What improvements would you like to see in your social networking experience?

_____

_____

_____

_____

Social networking is a fun way of keeping in touch with people but it is also a huge time-waster.

Strongly agree     ❑         Agree         ❑

Disagree       ❑         Strongly disagree   ❑

To which age group do you belong?

❑ Under 18

❑ 18–24

❑ 25–34

❑ 35–50

❑ Over 50

## Analysis of the Results

When the questionnaires have been completed and collected, they need to be analysed and the results presented. Some results, for example responses to closed-ended questions, can be simply converted into charts.

Supposing there were twenty respondents to the questionnaire and the results for Question 2 were as follows:

How often do you check your social networking site(s)?
▶ Several times a day                         5
▶ Once a day                                      10
▶ Three to four times a week              3
▶ Once a week                                     2
▶ Once a month                                   0

Now you have a frequency table showing how respondents replied to Question 2 and the results can be converted into percentages as follows:

▶ Several times a day                      25%
▶ Once a day                                     50%
▶ Three to four times a week           15%
▶ Once a week                                   10%
▶ Once a month                                  0%

## Charts

The results shown in the frequency table can be presented in charts.

A **bar chart** works well for this type of question, since the data is displayed quite clearly.

*Fig. 14.1 How often do you use social networking sites?*

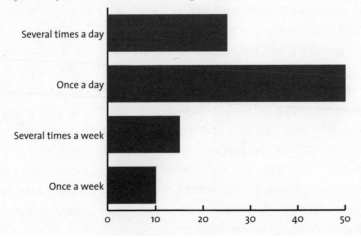

A **pie chart** is also effective for this question because the information is clear and can be read and understood quite quickly.

Fig. 14.2 How often do you use social networking sites?

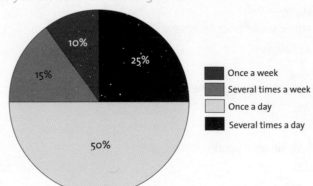

For more on charts and graphs, see Chapter 9, Visual Communication.

## Types of Qualitative Research

### Focus Group

A focus group is where you bring a group of people together to discuss and determine their attitudes, opinions and beliefs on a certain topic. It is often used for market research to determine how popular or effective a new product or service will be.

### Interview

If you decide to interview someone, consider how you will conduct the interview. If you are going to meet the person face-to-face you should contact her by email, letter or telephone to request and set up a meeting. It is useful to follow up an email or letter with a phone call. It is also possible to conduct an interview over the telephone. Whichever way you decide to proceed, you need to be prepared. The seven questions at the start of the questionnaire section will apply here also. It is important to know exactly what information you are looking for.

Always prepare a list of questions before the interview. If you arrive ill-prepared you will appear unprofessional and the interview will take longer. Some people might get annoyed if you are unprepared, as they will feel their time is being wasted. If well prepared, you can tell an interviewee how long the interview might take. It is worth considering that they may find the work you are doing useful and therefore a professional approach on your part will increase their co-operation.

Decide how you will include the information from your interview in the main body of your assignment. You might quote the interviewee in relevant sections (see section on Quotations, p.212) or refer to points made by her (see section on References, p.212). Avoid simply reproducing the interview at the end.

### Observation

This means observing people, activities, organisations, events, and patterns of behaviour, objects etc. and making careful notes on your observations.

For example, in childcare observation, a detailed factual account is written about what the child says and does and how the child behaves, plays and interacts with other children. There are descriptions of tone of voice, facial expressions and body language used.

An observation could be made of a particular bus route, such as what times and how many people get on and off at a particular bus stop during the day.

### Experiments

An experiment is a test carried out in a controlled procedure to determine the truth or otherwise of a hypothesis. Experiments can vary from an informal test to see what is the most regularly visited social network site by students in a particular college, to a rigorous scientific test using measuring equipment in a laboratory.

## Secondary Research Sources

If you are researching an organisation, your first source of secondary research will be from within the organisation itself in the form of company reports, policies, statements, website, press releases databases etc. Of course, not all of these may be made public but there is no harm in asking.

### IPA Yearbook

The Institute of Public Administration Yearbook contains an extensive database of Irish companies, state bodies, public and private organisations both national and international as well as a detailed calendar of events and a wealth of useful statistical information (www.ipa.ie).

### Central Statistics Office

The Central Statistics Office (CSO) is a government agency that provides statistics on all social and economic trends in Ireland. Its website (www.cso.ie) has a handy 'Student's Corner' with quick links to a range of topics.

Other sources:

▶ World wide web
▶ Newspapers and journals
▶ Books
▶ Government departments
▶ State agencies
▶ Reports
▶ Brochures and leaflets.

When starting your secondary research, all four types of reading will come into play (see Chapter 10). To recap: skim to get an overview, scan to locate specific facts and details, read at normal pace for general understanding and close read for more difficult material.

When you find material that you think is useful, skim-read the following in particular:
▶ Title
▶ Table of Contents
▶ Introduction
▶ Conclusion.

These will give you a broad overview of what the material is about. Scan the table of contents, index or the bibliography for more details.

As soon as you start to use published material for research it is crucial to record the following:
▶ Title
▶ Author(s)
▶ Date of publication
▶ Publisher
▶ Place of publication.

For information retrieved from the internet, record the title of the page or article, author if there is one, the URL or address and the date you accessed the website. This information will be included in your bibliography.

## Sample of a Short Structured Report

---

### REPORT ON FIRE SAFETY AT DÚN LAOGHAIRE MUSIC CENTRE

*Terms of Reference*
As requested by the management, to investigate the adequacy of the fire safety procedures and facilities at the Centre and to make any necessary recommendations.

*Method of Procedure*
The local fire officer was contacted and requested to make a visit to the Centre for a consultation with the Centre's Health and Safety Officer.

He made a thorough inspection of the building to check fire-fighting equipment, alarm system, fire exits, notices and procedures for fire drills and emergency evacuation, and reported to the Health and Safety Officer.

Members of staff were asked if they knew how to operate the different types of fire extinguisher, how to recognise them and if they were well acquainted with the evacuation procedures already in place.

### Findings

Present position

- There are five fire exits in the Centre. Each room in the Centre is within walking distance of a fire exit.

- The alarm system is functioning properly.

- Fire notices in rooms are old and worn, and difficult to read clearly.

- No fire drill has taken place in the past two years.

- There are three fire hoses and seven fire extinguishers in the building: three water, two dry chemical and two carbon dioxide ($CO_2$) extinguishers. None had been tested in the past four years. One of the water and one of the dry chemical extinguishers were faulty and one of the $CO_2$ extinguishers was almost empty. The rest of the extinguishers were in order.

- Staff members do not know the difference in appearance between the three types of fire extinguisher in the Centre, nor their uses for different classes of fire.

### Conclusions

- No one is up to date with the emergency evacuation procedures. Staff are not sure which exits correspond to the different rooms.

- It is not known if all the fire-fighting equipment is in full working order.

- Members of staff do not know how to use the various types of fire-fighting equipment.

### Recommendations

- Devise new procedures for fire prevention and emergency evacuation.

- Design new fire notices for each room indicating which exit is to be used for each room.

- Invite the local fire officer to the Centre to:

— Talk to all staff about the various uses of each type of fire extinguisher, and to give a demonstration of each

— Advise on the upgrading and purchasing of new fire-fighting equipment

— Purchase new fire-fighting equipment

— Appoint a member of staff to be Fire Officer, in charge of fire prevention and safety and to maintain equipment and notices.

Thomas O'Sullivan

Date: 20 February 2014

Note how there is a logical progression from Findings to Conclusions to Recommendations:

▶ Findings       Staff members do not know the difference in appearance between the three types of fire extinguisher in the Centre, nor their uses for different classes of fire.

▶ Conclusion       Members of staff do not know how to use the various types of fire-fighting equipment.

▶ Recommendation       Invite the local fire officer to the Centre to: Talk to all staff about the various uses of each type of fire extinguisher, and to give a demonstration of each.

This sample shows a very short structured report giving a simple basic layout. The report required for the FETAC Level 5 Communications module needs to be a good deal longer and more detailed with evidence of research.

 **Activity**

Write a report on your place of work experience. Here are some suggested guidelines for topics:

1. The history and background of the organisation/company/business

2. The ownership and management

3. Identification of the key personnel, their duties and responsibilities

4.  A full description of the organisation/company/business, its buildings, facilities, resources, access, security, maintenance, daily routine, e.g opening and closing times

5.  The impact of the organisation/company/business on the local community, economy, culture, environment etc.

6.  A survey of the clients and customers, their use of the facilities and how they rate them etc.

7.  A SWOT analysis, i.e. a list of strengths, weaknesses, opportunities and threats

8.  Conclusions and recommendations as to any improvements that would enhance the organisation/company/business.

## Chapter Review

1. What is the purpose of a report?
2. Briefly explain the meaning of:
    (a) Terms of reference
    (b) Methodology
    (c) Findings
    (d) Conclusion
    (e) Recommendations.
3. Give a brief explanation of primary and secondary research.
4. What is the purpose of a bibliography?
5. List the ways in which the findings of a survey can be presented.

## Tips

▶ Start your report good and early. It's better to spend a little time on it each week than a lot of time on it during the final week.
▶ Give yourself plenty of time at the end for putting together the table of contents and bibliography, and for proofreading.
▶ Keep a record of your secondary research as you do it, e.g. websites, authors and titles.
▶ Keep the language clear and concise.
▶ Always draft, redraft, edit and proofread.
▶ Keep your writing accurate and factual.

## Confusing Words

In each of the following sentences, select the correct word, decide what the other word means and put it into another sentence (it may have more than one meaning):

1. I'm going to give him a peace/piece of my mind.
2. The king's rain/rein/reign lasted for only two years.
3. The speeding juggernaut collided with a stationary/stationery car at the side of the road.
4. I wonder weather/whether the weather/whether will get any better.
5. We did an in debt/in depth study of the situation and then wrote a report.
6. I think I've past/passed all my exams.
7. I'm off to the club to practise/practice my moves.
8. My car is bigger then/than your car.
9. She thought/taught English as a foreign language in Spain for a year.

## Lost in Translation

The following are signs poorly translated into English. Work out what is wrong with them, what each is trying to communicate, then rewrite them to make their meaning clear.

### Swedish furrier shop:

Fur coast made for ladies from their own skin.

### Tokyo car rental brochure:

When passenger of foot heave in sight, tootle the horn. Trumpet him melodiously at first, but if he still obstacles your passage tootle him with vigour.

### Acapulco hotel:

The manager has personally passed all the water served here.

### Sign in Germany's Black Forest:

It is strictly forbidden on our black forest camping site that people of different sex, for instance, men and women, live together unless they are married with each other for this purpose.

### Norwegian cocktail bar:

Ladies are requested not to have children in the bar.

# Part 5

## Communications Technology

### Some Examples

- Computers
- Internet
- Email
- Mobile telephones

### Advantages

- Speed over distance
- Cheap to use
- Convenient (once set up)
- Good sources of information
- Can store information easily
- Global access
- Mobility

### Disadvantages

- Expensive to buy/set up
- Open to abuse
- Impersonal
- Open to misunderstanding
- Lead to decline in face-to-face communication and social skills
- Dependent on power/technology/coverage
- Privacy and security issues

# Chapter 15
## Introduction to Communications Technology

> **In This Chapter**
>
> ▶ Communications Technology Timeline
> ▶ Convergence
> ▶ Appropriateness

'Technology has democratised self-expression.'

*Patti Smith*

## ▶ Communications Technology Timeline

1831   Louis Daguerre developed first form of photography
1844   Telegraph invented by Samuel Morse
1876   Telephone invented by Alexander Graham Bell – first message: 'Watson, come here: I want you'
1879   Light bulb invented by Thomas Edison
1883   George Eastman produced the first camera film roll, paving the way for amateur photographers
1894   First radio message sent by Guglielmo Marconi
1901   First transatlantic radio transmission
1926   Television invented by John Logie Baird
1943   First working computers built
1946   ENIAC (Electronic Numerical Integrator and Computer), the first general purpose computer, invented
1957   ARPA (Advanced Research Projects Agency) set up by US State Department in response to Soviet launch of Sputnik satellite

1959  Silicon chip developed

1962  First Telstar satellite broadcast

1971  Fifteen computers connected by ARPAnet

1972  First email sent

1973  First handheld mobile phone

1978  First successful personal computer

1982  Birth of the internet

1989  World Wide Web developed by Tim Berners-Lee

1993  Internet accessible from private homes

1995  Telecommunications digitalised – sound, images and data travel the world at high speed

1996  Dramatic increase in mobile phone use

2002  New Year's Eve – eight million text messages sent in Ireland

2004  Almost half of all Irish adults use the internet and 96 per cent of children aged between ten and fourteen own a mobile phone

2004  Facebook founded by Mark Zuckerberg

2005  YouTube launched

2006  Twitter created

2009  One billion internet users worldwide; social networking sites overtake email in popularity

2012  One billion Facebook users worldwide

2013  500 million photos uploaded daily. Over 100 hours of video per minute uploaded to YouTube

2014  Google Glass launched

# ▶ Convergence

There are so many communication tools available these days that it is impossible to include them all in one section of a communications book, and the rate at which new devices and applications are being created means that some of this information will be dated after a couple of years.

We are still in the midst of a communications technology revolution involving three technologies: the telephone, the television and the computer. The history and development of CT is one of ever-increasing speed and efficiency of communications over ever-greater distances at ever-decreasing costs, and some of the world's biggest companies are at the forefront, e.g. Google, Microsoft, Yahoo and Apple.

The communications revolution has been about technologies coming together to form new, faster, cheaper and more powerful means of exchanging information. The technologies associated with the telephone, television and computer have converged to bring us the internet. Mobile phones and television both use computer technology to speed up their basic functions. The borders between telecommunications, the internet and mass media are disappearing. Unified messaging is a means of accessing all of our messages and information using one device such as a mobile phone, computer or TV set.

All these technologies have transformed and continue to transform our lives. Education, business, work, health, travel, shopping, entertainment, culture and socialising are all utterly different from what they were twenty years ago.

According to the International Telecommunications Union (ITU), in 2013, 96 per cent of the global population had a mobile phone subscription and 38 per cent use the internet. A 2012 survey by the global independent market research company Ipsos reported that 85 per cent of internet users go online for email, 62 per cent use the internet for social networking and 14 per cent use it for VoIP or online telephone calls.

The next few chapters look at some of the key components and issues that relate to communications technology.

# ▌ Appropriateness

## Activity

### Technology Appropriateness

With so many technologies available today, it is important to choose the right tool for the right job. Do you phone, text, Skype, email, use social media or instant messaging? Some technologies are more appropriate for formal and work situations and others are better for personal and leisure. Which technology (if any) would you choose for the following situations and why?

1. Your employer needs three quotations for a new printer.
2. You want to let your colleagues know about the annual Christmas party.
3. You are booking a holiday.
4. You need to call an urgent meeting at work tomorrow morning.
5. You want to ask someone out on a date.
6. You need to check your bank account details.
7. You are running late by 30 minutes for dinner with your friends. How do you let them know?
8. You are giving a talk at your old school about the course you are now studying.

9. You need to let your employer know that you are sick and cannot come to work.

10. You want to find out what your partner is wearing to the Halloween party.

11. You need to inform class representatives of the next Student Council meeting.

12. Your employer wants suggestions from staff for improved staff facilities at work.

13. You are due to meet a client for a business lunch, but she doesn't know where the restaurant is. You need to give her directions.

14. You want to invite your friends to your birthday party.

15. You have done the new staff rota, but need to run it by your colleagues to make sure it's ok. Many of your colleagues are away on holiday.

16. You want to publicise your new business venture.

17. You are planning a conference in Berlin with a group of volunteers from five different EU countries.

18. You want to share news of your engagement with your friends.

19. You are discussing plans with family members, who live in different parts of the country, to go to your cousin's wedding in Edinburgh.

20. Your sister, who lives in Australia, has just had a baby. You want to hear her news. Your parents also want to hear her news and they have just got a home computer and the internet.

21. You want to get your CV checked before sending it for a job application. There is no one nearby who can do it for you, but friends living a few miles away might be able to help.

## Discussion

Mobile phones interrupt conversations and meetings. The average web user spends less than 60 seconds on each website before quickly flitting to the next one. With the increasing use of CT are we shortening our attention span? Are we becoming too used to being interrupted and distracted and losing our ability to focus and concentrate for more than a few minutes at a time?

# Chapter 16
## The Telephone

## Discussion

What are the differences between talking to someone on the telephone and talking to them face-to-face?

Since the 1950s there have been several failed attempts to introduce the videophone into the mainstream market, with the belief that everyone would want one. What are the advantages and disadvantages of being able to see (or be seen by) the person at the other end of the line?

## ▶ Telephone Technique

It is important to be able to use the telephone effectively, especially in the workplace. A lot of time and money can be wasted when a telephone call is badly made, and often business can be lost due to poor telephone technique. Customers must be impressed, and a telephone call may be their first impression of an organisation/company. Improving our telephone skills and telephone manner is simple and can help us avoid being misunderstood or losing business.

A number of simple rules apply:

1. Speak clearly – phone line quality can vary greatly due to the different types of phone in use today. Many people, unconsciously or not, adopt a 'telephone voice', speaking more slowly, politely and neutralising their accent in order to be clear.
2. When making a call, be clear about what you want to say and how you want to say it.
3. Have a pen and paper handy.
4. Make notes of the information you need to give and receive.
5. Keep records of calls – in case you make two calls to the same person by mistake.
6. Pave the way for further contact – there may be new and unexpected developments, or simply more business to be done.
7. Be patient.
8. Use good manners at all times.
9. Use an appropriate tone of voice.
10. Try to be as efficient as possible, avoiding delays.
11. Apologise for any delays.
12. Empathise with the caller.

## Discussion

### Answering Calls

1. In some countries, people answer the phone by just stating their name. Is this a good idea?
2. What are the pros and cons of each of the following ways of answering the phone? Discuss the suitability of each one in social and vocational contexts.
   ▶ 'Hello.' (This can range in tone from friendly to abrupt)
   ▶ 'Hello, Drumlinn College of Further Education, Orla speaking.'
   ▶ 'Drumlinn College of Further Education, Orla speaking, how can I help you?'
   ▶ 'Drumlinn College of Further Education, good morning.'
   ▶ '631907.'

### Placing Calls

What are the pros and cons of each of the following statements in placing calls? Discuss their suitability in social and vocational contexts.
▶ 'Hello, may I speak to Mr O'Reilly please?'
▶ 'Is Karen there?'
▶ 'Hello, my name is Joe Dunne, is Alan there please?'
▶ 'I was wondering if I could speak to Simon.'
▶ 'Hi, I was looking for Sharon Wallace.'

Remember that when using the telephone, the person at the other end cannot see our non-verbal signals, so we should remember to be aware of the tone and pitch of our voice. Try to sound friendly and interested.

## Leaving/Taking Messages

If the person we want to speak with is unavailable, it is appropriate to ask to speak to someone else who may be able to help, or we may be asked to leave a message. Usually we will be asked for our name and number and we will be contacted later on. However, messages can go astray or be taken down incorrectly. It is advisable to find out who is taking the message. Exchanging names establishes rapport between two people and also acts as a kind of guarantee that it will be passed on. Depending on the type of call, it may be more courteous to call again, especially if we require the information or are selling something. In this case we can find out when the person will be available for us to call again.

When taking a call, if the person asked for is unavailable we should find out if anyone else can help. If not, the following information should be taken down:

1. Who the message is for
2. Caller's name and company/organisation
3. Caller's number
4. Date and time of the call
5. Reason for the call, i.e. the message
6. Your name.

It is important to *repeat this information* back to the caller. It only takes a minute and is worth it to prevent mistakes. Sometimes there are phone message slips, which are simple to fill out. A caller should never be left on hold for too long without frequent voice contact, or she may wonder if she has been cut off, or forgotten about. If she has been waiting for a few minutes, we can give her the option of whether she wants to continue to hold or leave a message.

**Sample Phone Message Slip**

Message for _____

Telephone Message _____

_____

_____

Caller _____

Of _____

Number _____

Time received _____

Date _____

Message taken by _____

# ▶ Voice Mail

Many of us are still terrified of leaving voice messages and yet they are a regular part of daily communication. One reason we find them so disconcerting is that there is no feedback, and it feels like we are speaking into a vacuum. The best thing to do is leave a simple message with our name, number and just a few details.

Fig. 16.1

# ▶ Mobile Phones

It has been said that the mobile telephone is the most successful new communication medium ever seen. Since its invention in 1973, it has evolved into a device that is far more than a tool for making phone calls. By the 1990s it had reached widespread mainstream use and by 2009 mobile phone use in Ireland was at 119 per cent. By 2012 over 50 per cent of Irish mobile phone users had smart phones.

## ▶ Smart Phones

Although most mobile phones have a range of features above the normal calling and texting capability, smart phones have functions that allow more advanced computing and connecting. One distinguishing feature is the use of apps (mobile software applications), which enable a huge range of information and connection services such as email, social networking, news, travel, gaming, GPS and banking. In 2010 'app' was declared Word of the Year by the American Dialect Society, and in 2012 in the US the use of apps grew by 35 per cent and web browsing fell.

Fig. 16.2

The increased use of smart phones with numerous functions, internet access and a range of apps at our fingertips raises many questions and concerns about the impact of smart phones on our lives. Are we spending too much time on our devices and not enough actually connecting with others face-to-face?

Fig. 16.3

Two image-sharing apps, Instagram and Snapchat, became technology phenomena in 2013. Instagram, which reached 150 million users in just two years, provides a filter to enhance photos that can be shared on social networking sites such as Facebook (which owns Instagram). With Snapchat, the image is deleted up to ten seconds after it is viewed. In 2013 150 million snaps were being shared daily. This illustrates the growing popularity of image-sharing software.

Is the growing popularity of image-sharing (e.g. Snapchat, Instagram) an indication of the need for face-to-face communication?

Some people prefer to have mobile phones just for calls and texts, as opposed to smart phones. What are the advantages and disadvantages of smart phones over simpler mobile devices?

# ◗ Mobile Etiquette

Knowing how to use mobiles effectively and with respect for other people is as important as knowing how to get the most from the technology. Are you a mobile phony, or a mobile savvy? For example, should we interrupt a face-to-face conversation to take a call? It has been said that by doing so, we are telling the person we are with that we have more important things to do. Frequent interruptions caused by mobile phone use may also damage our ability to focus for any length of time.

Here are some common-sense tips:
- ◗ Avoid loud private conversations in public places
- ◗ Obey 'No Mobile' signs
- ◗ Consider how irritating your novelty ring tone may be to others – use a simple ring tone
- ◗ Switch to the vibrate setting when in public places
- ◗ Avoid accidental dialling
- ◗ Keep texts brief – the receiver might have to pay to read them
- ◗ Respect others by not answering the phone when in an important conversation or a meeting.

# ◗ Text Messaging

Text messaging – has become the unexpected success story of mobile telephony. It is the most immediate, direct and personal form of electronic communication and as such is still relatively new and constantly evolving. It is an interesting combination of the chattiness of the spoken word with the physical display of writing. Its immediacy is one of its greatest appeals and yet this speed is what sometimes causes messages to be poorly conceived by the sender and misunderstood by the receiver. Emoticons (see Chapter 19 Email) sometimes help, but cannot replace the support of tone of voice or facial expression. With this in mind it is good advice never to text when under the influence of alcohol or when angry.

With texting, the normal rules of spelling and punctuation tend to be dropped and a whole new form of writing has developed. Here are some examples:

Anyone – ne1
Are you ok – ruok
At – @
Before – b4
Can – cn
Excellent – xlnt
For, four, fore – 4
Forward – fwd
Great – gr8

One, won – 1
See you later – cul8r
Someone – sum1
Thanks – thnx
Today – 2day
Tomorrow – 2moro
Tonight – 2nite
Want to – wan2
cool – c%l

Fig. 16.4

Such linguistic creativity can be fun and useful for quick informal exchanges but may occasionally be slipped by mistake into more formal contexts such as letters, reports and college assignments.

Another concern is that predictive texting might be eroding literacy skills as users become more dependent on this facility than thinking for themselves about grammar, spelling and punctuation.

Text messaging apps such as iMessage, Facebook Messanger, WhatsApp and Viber are becoming more popular than SMS (Short Message Service) because they are cheaper, since they use the internet as opposed to a phone network.

# ❯ Health Risks

There has been much debate regarding the potential health threat, due to radiation, from mobile phones. The manufacturers usually say that their research shows no correlation between mobile phone use and damage to human health. However, hundreds of independent studies show a possible link between mobile use and cancer, anxiety, increased blood pressure, sleep loss and heating of the brain. The debate is still ongoing, but expert advice is to err on the side of caution. Here are some tips for the safe use of mobiles:

1. Keep calls short – no longer than 15 to 20 minutes at a time.
2. Young people should use them only for essential purposes.
3. Employers who require employees to use mobiles should make them aware of the risks.
4. Consider the SAR (Specific Absorption Rate – amount of radiation the body is exposed to during mobile use) when buying a new mobile.
5. Avoid texting while driving or crossing the street.

## ✳ Activity

Make a list of the advantages and disadvantages of mobiles and smart phones under the following headings:

❯ Work
❯ Leisure
❯ Family/home life
❯ Health
❯ Security

❯ Socialising
❯ Relationships
❯ Language/communication
❯ Education
❯ Discuss with the rest of the class group.

# ▶ Fax

A fax machine is really a long-distance photocopier that can send copies of documents electronically via the telephone line to another machine anywhere in the world. It is gradually being replaced by email (see Chapter 19), but for the moment it is still in use. Dial the receiver's fax number, insert the document and it feeds through, sending a copy to the receiver for the price of a phone call. Sometimes a cover sheet is sent with the message. It usually includes details such as the sender's name, receiver's name, date, subject heading and whether it is a routine or an urgent message.

## Further Activities

If the facilities are available, make some real phone calls. Here are some suggestions:

1. Make an enquiry (e.g. travel times and costs)

2. Make an appointment (dentist, doctor)

3. Make a reservation or cancellation

4. Make a complaint or apology

5. Make a date

6. Offer congratulations or sympathy

7. Enquire about a service (plumbing, window-cleaning).

## Chapter Review

1. List five rules for effective telephone technique.
2. What is a suitable way of answering the telephone in a vocational (formal) situation?
3. What information needs to be recorded when taking a phone message?
4. What are the advantages and disadvantages of text messaging?
5. What precautions should we take to avoid health risks associated with mobile phones?
6. Explain the differences between a simple mobile phone and a smart phone.

# Chapter 17
## Computers

'Computers are incredibly fast, accurate and stupid. Human beings are incredibly slow, inaccurate and brilliant. Together they are powerful beyond imagination.'

Albert Einstein

A computer is an electronic machine that performs tasks such as storing, processing and exchanging information according to a set of instructions called a program.

## ▶ Computer Types and Uses

The number of computers and computer related devices available to us today is staggering when you consider that the founder of IBM, Thomas Watson, said in 1943 that there was a world market for about 5 computers.

From the supercomputers that forecast the weather or carry out simulated nuclear testing to the tiny microprocessor chips found in many household electric appliances, computers are used in ways we may not even realise. Most offices and many homes now have a desktop computer for word-processing documents, making calculations, storing and organising files and data, surfing the internet and sending emails. More portable devices such as laptops, notebooks and tablets are becoming increasingly popular and are enabling users to do most of the above while on the move. A phablet is a cross between a smart phone and a tablet, combining the larger screen of a tablet and the functionality of a phone. It also has a stylus/pen for writing on the screen.

*Fig. 17.1 Tablet*

The next phase in portable technology will be wearable. Smart watches are being developed by most technology companies and Google Glass is a hands-free, voice-operated computer that has similar functions to a smart phone and is worn on the face like a pair of spectacles. A similar device, Telepathy One, consists of a headset with ear pieces, an eye piece and a camera and connect to the wearer's mobile phone using Bluetooth.

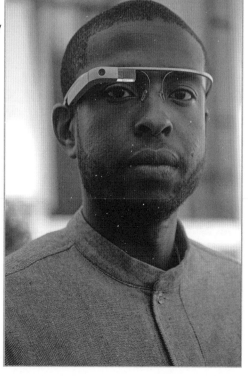

*Fig. 17.2 Google Glass*

# ▶ Computer Components

Computers essentially consist of:

*Hardware* – the physical components such as casing/body, screen, keyboard, wires, electronic circuitry, disks, chips etc.
*Software* – the instructions given to computers to enable them to perform tasks, often using programming languages.

# ▶ Computers in Education

Education is being transformed by constantly evolving computer technology making it more interesting and entertaining. Interactive whiteboards (IWB) are touchscreen displays connected to a computer and a projector that enable teachers and students to use software such as Word, Excel and PowerPoint, play games, store information and connect to the internet.

Fig. 17.3

Microsoft PowerPoint is a program for presenting information in a slideshow on a computer and projected onto a screen. The slides can contain text, images, sound and movies. The entrance and exit of each of these can be controlled using the Animations tool. If used well, PowerPoint can greatly enhance an otherwise ordinary oral presentation into something more stimulating, colourful and professional looking.

# ▶ E-Books

In 1949, a Spanish teacher, Angela Ruiz Robles, created a device to reduce the number of books her pupils had to carry to school. It consisted of a spool containing text and graphics and was named the Mechanical Encyclopaedia. This was one of the first examples of an e-reader or e-book. Nowadays e-books are widely available and can potentially store thousands of publications in one handy tablet-shaped device. They have a range of features including readability in low light, font enlargement and search tools for words and other information. They offer financial savings, since electronic texts can be cheaper than printed books. They are environmentally friendly, since they are produced by using less water and raw materials than it takes to produce a printed book.

# ▶ Portable Media Players

These devices can usually download, store and play digital music, video files and display images. Many smart phones are also media players and some also have recording capabilities. An MP3 player, named after the format for storing digital sound files (MPEGs), is mainly used for playing music but can also be used for audiobooks and podcasts.

# ▶ Video Game Consoles

It is estimated that video game consoles use 25 per cent of global computer power. A video game console is an interactive computer that can be used with a television set or computer monitor to play video games. Games can be bought in DVD format or downloaded from the internet.

# ▶ Cloud Computing

Sometimes abbreviated to 'the cloud', this process refers to computer services provided over a shared network such as the internet. Instead of storing files or applications on your own computer, you can store it in the cloud, saving on space, time, cost and power. Google Docs, for example, allows users to create, edit and store documents online in collaboration with others. Dropbox enables users to share files, often too large to exchange via email, using a folder on their computer that is synchronised with other users that are sharing the files.

Despite its obvious convenience, there are security and privacy concerns about cloud computing. Is the data stored in cyberspace any safer than storing it on your own hard drive? Is the information going to be kept private? Despite these concerns, the technology continues to develop and is becoming increasingly popular.

# Discussion

Are we becoming too dependent on computer technology? Are computers replacing people at work? Do computers make our lives any better? Could we live without them? What is the potential impact of a future that is even more computer dominated than today? What are the advantages and disadvantages of living in the Computer Age?

## Chapter Review

1. List five everyday uses of computers.
2. What are the main components of a computer?
3. What is an e-book and what are its advantages?
4. Explain what cloud computing is and describe its pros and cons.

# Chapter 18
## The Internet

# ▶ Origins

The internet is an international network that links computers and computer networks from all over the world and allows information to travel from one to another. It has been described as the most important technological development for humans since the industrial revolution. It is impossible to be accurate with statistics about internet use, as they are changing all the time, but in 2013 the global figure for internet users stood at 2.7 billion, just over one-third of the global population. In Ireland in 2013 there were 3.6 million users, 76 per cent of the population. Compared to other communications media, the internet has grown far more quickly to become a mainstream medium. Radio took 37 years to reach 50 million listeners. Television took 15 years to reach the same number of viewers. The World Wide Web took just three years to reach the same number of users. The internet gives us access to a vast amount of information that is constantly being updated and expanded to make it faster and more efficient.

Originally developed as a response the Soviet Union's launch of the Sputnik satellite in 1957, the US Advanced Research Projects Agency (ARPA) explored military, space and communications projects. Eventually NASA took over the space programme and DARPA (Defense Advanced Research Projects Agency) took over the military projects.

The ARPANET was born in 1969, when two American universities connected their computer systems via the telephone network, but the first attempt crashed the system. The internet protocol suite, a set of digital rules for communication between computers, was established in 1982 and the idea of the internet was born. The world wide web was set up in 1989 by Sir Tim Berners-Lee. The web is not the same as the internet, but an application of the internet that makes it easy for anybody to navigate their way around it. Essentially it means that there is a common computer language that links all the different documents on the internet, and we can easily jump from one to another without having to learn the language. The web has transformed the internet from a tool for academics and researchers to a global media phenomenon.

The ARPANET was discontinued in 1990 and the internet became commercial in 1995 giving rise to a system that has had an enormous impact on cultural and commercial life ever since.

# ▶ Access

Getting connected to the internet is relatively easy today, since there are so many options available. Internet service providers (ISPs) are companies that connect computers to the internet via their own high-speed computers. Data is transmitted at a speed that depends on the type of connection we use.

Dial-up is literally what it says. Our computer uses the phone line and an inbuilt device called a modem to dial up the ISP. The connection is slow, but it only costs the price of a phone call. Broadband is a faster connection, allowing us to access information much more quickly but at a greater cost. Wireless or WiFi connections use radio technology to connect to the internet using local area networks (LANs). WiFi hotspots are places that offer internet access such as public libraries, stations, airports, cafes and hotels. Smart phones use mobile broadband to connect to the internet.

Due to the enormity of the internet, the task of actually locating the precise information we want can be daunting and frustrating. Some say the internet is like a vast library, but a highly disorganised one without a proper system of classification. There are several ways of retrieving information from the internet.

## The Browser

The software needed to connect to the world wide web is called a browser. The most popular examples are Internet Explorer, Safari, Mozilla Firefox and Google Chrome, and they often include a whole range of facilities and services such as email, search tools and news sites. You can install multiple browsers on your computer to see which one will suit you best.

# ▶ Surfing

When we are set up and ready to go online for the first time, we can click on the browser icon on the desktop, which will open the homepage of our ISP or the browser's homepage. A *homepage* is the first page that appears on the screen and also refers to the first page of any *website*. A *web page* is a page of information that appears on the screen and a *website* is a collection of web pages on a specific subject. When we move the mouse around a page we notice that the arrow becomes a hand on certain words, phrases or images. These are *links* to other web pages and sites and by clicking on the mouse when the hand appears, new pages will appear on the screen. This is what is called *surfing*, jumping around from page to page and site to site, exploring the vast amount of information available to us.

Each web page has an address called a *URL* (Uniform Resource Locator). If we know the precise address we can key this into the address box at the top of the screen and press the return key ⌫ . The browser will locate the page and open it for us.

A URL, like *http://www.ireland.com* usually consists of four parts:

1. The protocol, http (HyperText Transfer Protocol), is the set of rules and standards which enables web pages to be displayed and transferred. When keying in a URL we don't need to include this.
2. www stands for World Wide Web.

3. The host name, in this case, ireland. This is the name of the company or organisation and is called the *domain name*. (*www.ireland.com* is the URL for an Irish tourism site).
4. .com, which tells us that it is a commercial organisation or a company, though this is not always the case.

This ending is called an *extension*, and there are many different types of extension, which give us information about the site. Here are some typical extensions:

◗ .org – originally a non-commercial organisation
◗ .net – originally a company dealing with networks, like *www.eircom.net*
◗ .edu – an American educational establishment
◗ .gov – an American governmental department or institution
◗ .ie – an Irish website
◗ .co.uk – a company in the UK
◗ .de – a German site.

Fig. 18.1 Mozilla Firefox homepage

Each browser comes with a different user interface style but most will have the following buttons to enable easy surfing:

◗ *Back or Forward* buttons or arrows to return to the previous page or go forward again
◗ *Refresh* buttons to reload the current page
◗ *Stop* button to stop loading the page
◗ *Refresh/Reload* buttons are often merged with the *Stop* button

▶ *Home* button to take us to our homepage

▶ *Search Bar* to insert search terms

▶ *Favourites/Bookmarks* buttons are for quick access to our favourite sites

▶ *History* – this shows which sites we've visited

▶ *Full Screen* – enlarges the page to fill up the screen

▶ *Mail* – takes us to our mail server

▶ *Print* – to print pages from the internet

▶ *Edit* – to create and edit web pages.

# ▶ Searching

## Search Engines

If you don't have the exact address of a website, the best way to find what you want on the net is a search engine.

There are many to choose from and here are some of the most popular:

▶ Ask

▶ Bing

▶ Dogpile

▶ DuckDuckGo

▶ Ecosia

▶ Google

▶ Yahoo

Each search engine has its advantages and specific appeal. Some search engines keep track of your searches and use your preferences to build profiles about you to pass on to companies for advertising purposes. Details of your searches may also be saved and passed on to third parties for legal reasons. DuckDuckGo has a privacy policy that keeps your search information secure. Ecosia has an environmental policy and donates 80 per cent of its revenue to planting trees in Brazil.

Go to the search engine's website, type your keywords in the search box, click *Search* or press the return key, and it will almost instantly present you with a list of 'hits'.

The heading is the name of the website. Below that is an extract from the website which you can check to see if it contains the information you need. The bottom line tells you the URL and the size of the website.

The key to successful searching is to make your search terms as specific as possible. For example, if you want to find some song lyrics, you could type in the name of the artist, which will probably get you to his/her website. Then you'd have to search the website for the lyrics page. It is much quicker to type in the song title or, better still, a line from the song. This should take you directly there. Beware of using vague or ambiguous keywords. If you want to find out about the holly tree, if you just key in 'holly' you will get everything from Buddy Holly to Mount Holly, Michigan. If you want to find out the latest football results, don't type in 'sports results' because you will receive hits from all over the world. Be specific. If you are using more than one keyword, try putting them in inverted commas (double seem to work better than single). This means you will find websites in which those two words appear next to each other.

*Fig. 18.2 Google homepage*

## Subject Directories

A *subject directory* provides us with a list of categories to choose from. Two popular ones are Yahoo! (www.yahoo.com) and About.com (www.about.com). Go the website, click on a category and keep clicking on sub-categories until you find what you're looking for.

# Activity

1. Search the internet for national organisations or official bodies related to your area of study.

2. Search the internet for jobs related in your own vocational area.

## Validity of Information

Once you have found the information you need, it is important to question its validity. Is it fact or someone's opinion? Anybody can put up a website and since there is no one checking to see if the information is accurate, we have to check to make sure the information is valid.

Here are some questions to ask each time you read web based material:

1. How relevant is it to your needs?
2. Who is the author?
3. Does the author have credibility?
4. Is it well written?
5. Is it biased?
6. Do you agree with it?
7. Does it have references?
8. Are there contact details?
9. Does it look professional?
10. Is it trying to persuade or convince?
11. Is the information current or out of date?
12. Is the information comprehensive or incomplete?

It is also advisable to check a few websites to see if there is agreement between them on the information you are seeking.

The URL will also tell us about the author's allegiances, for example, if it ends in .com it may be a commercial organisation and may want to sell us something. There can be many different sites for the same organisation so the official website might be more reliable than an unofficial one.

# ▶ Printing, Copying, Pasting

## Printing from the Web

To print a webpage, either click the *Print* button on the toolbar (though this might print everything, images, advertisements and text) or highlight the required section of the page and in the *Print* window click on *Selection* and then *Print*.

## Copy and Paste

Highlight the information required, right click the mouse, click *Copy*, open a document, right click the mouse again and click *Paste*. To copy an image, right click on the image, click *Copy*, and paste in the document as before.

# ▶ Interactivity

World wide web inventor, Sir Tim Berners-Lee, said that he wanted it to be a 'collaborative medium, a place where we could all meet and read and write' (Richardson 2009).

Since the mid-noughties, the internet has evolved to facilitate fully the collaboration of users anywhere in the world in shaping its content. Sometimes referred to as 'Web 2.0', it has developed from an information source to a place of equal participation. Social media refers to online activities in which users share and exchange information, having made the shift from being passive consumers of information to being active producer-consumers.

People now communicate online by blogging, posting news and expressing their opinions, uploading music and videos, meeting and making new friends, sharing files using Peer-to-Peer technology, contributing to online discussions and creating their own websites.

Traditional forms of mass media are one-way and 'top down'. In other words, information is sent from a producer, director, editor etc. 'down' to the public who receive it. The internet is 'bottom up', meaning anyone can send information. This is what the creators of the internet wanted: a system where people can communicate with each other as equals, free from any central authority.

One of the things that makes us equal on the internet is our anonymity. We can hide behind a pseudonym, change our identity and be more confident. This appeal is also one of its drawbacks. Do we really know with whom we are communicating online? The anonymity that allows shy people to come out and freely express themselves has also permitted paedophiles to mislead children in chatrooms. The same exhilarating freedom that permits protesters from oppressive regimes to reach the outside world also gives terrorists the opportunity to plan atrocities.

# ▶ Social Media

Social media has become the most popular form of online communication, allowing people to connect and exchange text, photos, videos and other information over the internet. They are changing the ways in which we communicate, socialise, do business and interact with our communities and the world around us. There are also issues such as privacy and security, bullying, overuse and trolling (posting offensive messages online).

The next section gives an overview of some most popular social networking sites.

### Facebook

Founded in 2004 by Mark Zuckerberg, Facebook has become the most popular social networking site with over 1 billion users worldwide. It is free to register and users can create a personal profile, add friends, share and exchange information by posting updates, 'like' other posts, join common interest groups and create and share events. It is also possible and advisable to change your privacy settings to control who can see specific parts of your profile.

## YouTube

In 2013, around 100 hours of video were being uploaded to YouTube daily. Primarily a video sharing service, users can watch music videos, TV and film clips and a vast number of videos shared by individuals from all over the world on any subject imaginable.

## Google+

Google+ helps users to build new connections as opposed to connect with existing friends. Its 'Communities' feature enables users to connect with others who share the same interests and 'Hangouts' is a feature that enables users to meet and have a group video chat with up to ten users at a time.

## Twitter

On Twitter, users 'tweet' real-time messages that are limited to 140 characters and are often about the latest news and gossip. Users follow others and have their own followers who can 'retweet' their messages. It is a more public form of self-expression that either Facebook and Google+ and useful for keeping up with current events.

## LinkedIn

This is a business and professional networking site where users create a profile containing the equivalent of their CV and can create a list of 'Connections' to find opportunities for work. Employers can advertise jobs and search for potential applicants and potential candidates can view profiles of employers.

## Flickr

Primarily a photo and video hosting site, Flickr lets users edit, organise and share their images and there is a feature for making them into postcards, prints or calendars. Users are encouraged to group images according to subject matter so others can find them using category searches. It is used by skilled photographers.

## Instagram

This is a hugely popular photo and video sharing service with filters for editing and the ability to easily share on other social networking sites. In two years it had attracted 100 million users, lured mainly by its mobile app.

## Tumblr

Tumblr combines microblogging and social networking where users can post small sized content such as short sentences, quotes, images, music, video and other links from anywhere and comment on each other's posts. It is a way to express yourself publicly and its content is more visual than verbal.

*Fig. 18.3 Facebook*

## Internet Telephony

The main advantage of making phone calls over the internet is that it is free to anywhere in the world. Voice over Internet Protocol (VoIP) is the technology that allows the transmission of voice over the internet. The most popular service is currently Skype but a new app, Line, not only offers free VoIP calls but also the ability to exchange text messages, music and video files as well as join groups. With a microphone and webcam on the computer, users can both hear and see each other.

# ▶ Video Conferencing

To save on time, travel costs and carbon emissions, video conferencing allows people to partake in virtual meetings with others across the globe, using computers, monitors, cameras, microphones and speakers. Participants can sit in their own home, office or boardroom and meet and talk with others around the world. Some downsides include poorly displayed eye contact between participants; a time lag in the exchange of messages often leading to interruptions and confusion and self-consciousness about being on camera. Nevertheless, it is a largely successful and popular form of communication particularly for businesses with international offices.

# ◗ Instant Messaging

Instant messaging (IM) is a technology that permits text-based communication over the internet in real time. A list of contacts can be created which will be activated once the user goes on to the relevant website. There are numerous IM services including Google Talk, Windows Live Messenger, AIM, Yahoo! Messenger and it is also a feature offered by Skype and Facebook.

# ◗ Impact on Society

The internet has changed and continues to change the way we live and work. The following section looks at some of the key areas undergoing a transformation.

## Business

E-commerce is the buying and selling of goods on the internet and in 2012 over half of Irish businesses were using the internet for making purchases and 30 per cent of their purchases were being made online. Businesses use the internet in other ways such as for advertising, banking and communicating with customers. Social networking has become an important means of reaching new customers, and word-of-mouth recommendations on social media sites are regarded as a key method of expanding and maintaining a customer base.

## Entertainment

The internet is continuously changing the way we access music, films and television programmes. The sale of CDs and DVDs has declined dramatically in the last decade, and this is being replaced by cheaper and more convenient digital downloads and online streaming. We watch and listen to these forms of entertainment on a variety of devices such as computers, MP3 players, smart phones, TV sets and hifi systems. YouTube, iTunes, Spotify and Soundcloud are some of the numerous sources of music online. Netflix, which began as a video streaming service, is now set to compete with television companies as the prime online TV streaming provider.

## News and Journalism

The internet has become a more popular source of news than traditional newsprint. A BBC survey in 2012 by independent research agency Sponge It, showed that 59.9 per cent of Irish consumers preferred online news and that 57.4 per cent read print newspapers. Online news has many advantages. It has a reduced cost for the reader. The news is more up-to-date, since breaking news is added continuously. Interactivity means readers can control the webpages and instantly send feedback. Also, given the availability of an internet connection, it is more accessible.

'Citizen journalism' or 'participatory journalism' is an alternative to mainstream media and refers to the ways in which information and news is gathered and shared online by amateurs. Armed with a smart phone, a public citizen can take a photo or record a video of a breaking news event and post it online before any mainstream media reporters arrive. The Arab Spring, which began in 2010, is a good example of this, when many participants in the uprisings in Egypt and Tunisia used social media to organise protests and raise awareness of the events. News of Iranians protesting about the election results of 2009 spread to the wider world via blogs and social media as the Iranian government cracked down mainstream TV and newspapers there. A criticism of citizen journalism is that it is not regulated and therefore content may be inaccurate or too subjective.

Blogging (from the words 'web log') is another form of citizen journalism, where people share information and opinions on a range of topics on the web. Some professional journalists also write blogs as part of their job and some blogs are simply individuals keeping online diaries.

Other areas heavily impacted by the internet include the travel industry, with many people booking their transport and accommodation online without the need for a travel agent. The internet provides a wealth of research and educational possibilities, from academic papers to instructional videos. Shopping for almost anything can be done from the comfort of one's home. Housebound users can shop online and get their groceries delivered to their home from the supermarket.

# ▶ Privacy and Security

From the relatively harmless but irritating spam (email advertising) to serious crimes such as identity theft, the internet comes with a number of privacy and security issues. What was once private information is becoming public, whether it involves photos on social media sites or the publicising of confidential documents by whistleblowers.

Even with a firewall protecting your computer from unwanted intrusion, once online, your computer is not 100 per cent protected. Details of online searches may be passed on to third parties for the purpose of advertising. As revealed in 2013, a huge amount of data is being accessed by security and intelligence agencies.

Malware and viruses are transmitted with email attachments or downloads and can cause damage to computers. Email and social networking accounts can be hacked. Children can inadvertently access pornography or violent images. Information exchanged online can travel far on the internet so it is important to take precautions to make surfing as safe as possible.

Fig. 18.4

Here are some tips:

- Make sure your anti-virus software is up-to-date and running.
- Only share personal information on reliable websites.
- Don't share your birthday on social networking sites. It could be used to access bank accounts along with other personal details retrieved from other sources.
- If using public Wifi, such as in a café or hotel, always log out of any email or social networking accounts.
- When asked for credit card details, make sure the page is secure: an 's' will appear after the 'http' in the URL and a padlock icon should also appear in a corner of the browser.
- Use strong passwords with a variety of upper and lower case letters, numbers and symbols such as punctuation marks.
- Change passwords regularly.

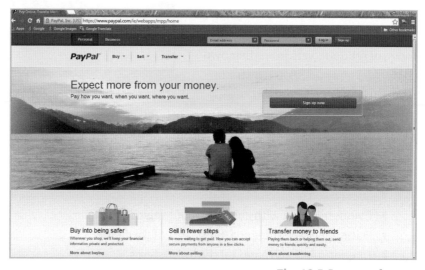

Fig. 18.5 Secure web page

# ▶ Regulation

Regulation is clearly difficult for a medium that crosses all national boundaries. In many countries where freedom of expression is highly valued, any attempt at censorship is seen as contrary to the freedom of expression. Most countries, including Ireland, operate some form of regulation, often for the prevention of child pornography or racism. Some countries have been labelled 'enemies of the internet' by Reporters without Borders, an NGO that advocates press freedom. Amongst these are China, Burma/Myanmar, Iran, North Korea and Egypt, where there is strict internet censorship and control, often to prevent political dissent.

Organisations such as OpenNet Initiative (www.opennet.net) and the Global Internet Liberty Campaign (www.gilc.org) are concerned with internet censorship and work towards improving the situation where it occurs.

Regulation is important for controlling internet content that is dangerous or illegal. Pornography is prevalent on the internet, and in most western countries it is legal to view it in the privacy of one's own home. However, children could inadvertently stumble across a pornographic site with a misplaced full stop in a URL. Child pornography, of course, is illegal, and the internet has provided paedophiles with a new means for them to commit their crimes. They enter chatrooms posing as children, 'talk' to children, arrange to meet them, or set up servers from their own computers and publish and distribute material to other paedophiles. Such activities are difficult to trace, but cyber crime units are having some success in tracing such activities.

Fig. 18.6

Children can be protected from harmful web content by:

▶ Parents understanding how their children use the internet
▶ Supervision of internet activities
▶ Communication with children about their activities
▶ Placing the computer in a 'busy' area of the home
▶ Filtering/blocking/parental control systems.

The Office for Internet Safety (www.internetsafety.ie) was set up by the Department of Justice and Law Reform in 2008 to promote safety online and it oversees the Internet Hotline (www.hotline.ie) where members of the public can report illegal online content.

Illegal internet use that can be reported includes:

- Child pornography
- Child trafficking
- Racism and xenophobia
- Incitement to hatred
- Financial scams.

Fig. 18.7

# ▶ Internet Overuse

Overuse of the internet has been blamed for causing a reduction in some people's attention spans. The average time spent on a website is under 60 seconds, so if this becomes habitual we might lose our ability to concentrate for long periods of time.

Losing our ability to relate to others in the real world may also suffer if we conduct most of our friendships via a computer screen or mobile phone. Face-to-face interaction is a vital part of being human, and millions of people are now forming 'relationships' on social networking sites. This isn't a bad thing in itself, but the more people inhabit virtual worlds, the more their ability to function in the real world might be eroded.

Internet addiction disorder is a theoretical and still debated condition in which users find they cannot live without a regular internet 'fix'. The effects include an increase in the amount of time spent online; restlessness or irritability during times not spent online; loss of significant relationships; loss of job; and reduction in important social, occupational and recreational activities. Specific addictions include online gambling and pornography.

# ▶ Digital Divide

Whether it is based on gender, age, income, ethnic group, level of education or location, this refers to the gap between the information technology haves and have-nots. Globally, at the time of writing, around 34 per cent of the population has access to the internet. The regions with the greatest population penetration are North America (78 per cent), Europe (63 per cent) and Oceania/Australia (67 per cent), while Asia has just 27 per cent and Africa has the lowest at 15 per cent.

In Ireland, 76 per cent of the population use the internet, the majority being students, those in the higher socioeconomic bracket and young people in general, while the over-60s have the lowest percentage of users.

Among the concerns this issue raises are: education, e.g. rich schools provide more computer access than poor ones; the economy (because it widens the global economic gap); and politics, as those without web access may be under-represented in the democratic process. It raises the question of equality and justice and the potential of the internet to improve the quality of life for those living on the margins of society, giving them greater social equity and empowerment.

There are concerns that if this divide is not bridged, it will increase, and the have-nots will be left behind politically, economically and socially in a world that is becoming increasingly dependent on the internet. Others argue that as technology improves and becomes cheaper and easier to use the gap will eventually disappear, and a number of projects, such as Sir Tim Berners-Lee's Alliance for Affordable Internet, are working to bring technology to marginalised communities and the developing world.

# ▶ File Sharing

Peer-to-peer (P2P) file sharing is a technology that allows users to share files across the internet and accounts for up to 70 per cent of all internet traffic. Much of this traffic consists of music, films and TV programmes shared illegally amongst users and is in breach of copyright laws.

Free online music can be a good thing for some artists, such as new bands who want to reach a wider audience, but more established acts complain that they are losing royalties and the music and film companies claim it negatively affects their sales.

Fig. 18.8

# ▶ Online Gaming

Video games played on the internet have become a huge part of the entertainment industry. Highly realistic and sophisticated three-dimensional games involve players taking on roles and participating in multiplayer games with other members of 'guilds' and forming social connections across the globe. One disadvantage is that gamers can increase their activity so that it almost becomes an addiction, replacing more healthy outdoor activities and real-life socialising.

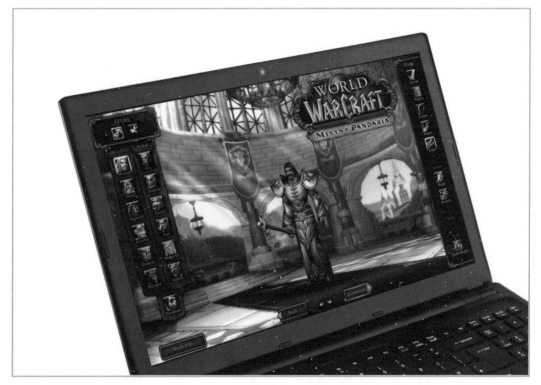

Fig. 18.7

The internet was designed and created in such a way as to invite innovation from anyone who had the know-how. No one sat down and planned it from start to end product. It evolved in a chaotic and haphazard way, open to improvement by computer wizards and amateur geeks as it grew. This openness also means it has been vulnerable to abuse, and the increase in security problems, such as viruses and spyware, may lead to a more regulated web. Some of the best ideas, such as the web itself, Skype, peer-to-peer networking and Wikipedia, came from the margins of the technology world, not the mainstream. Online information itself is also largely free. If we end up with an internet that is more tightly controlled, not only might we lose the creativity and innovation that has made it the exciting revolutionary medium it is today, but we may also have to pay for it.

# Chapter Review

1. How can you verify the information found online?
2. Give an outline the five most common forms of social media.
3. What are the main security and privacy concerns about internet use?
4. How can users maintain their privacy and security online?
5. In what ways are social and working lives being changed by the internet?
6. What is the digital divide?

Some useful websites:

*www.learnthenet.com* – a website to help master the internet

*www.qlinks.net* – links to news items about legal aspects of the internet

*www.internetnews.com* – exactly what it says

*www.amarach.com* – Irish market research, with statistics on technology use

*www.cnet.com* – reviews and price comparisons of all the latest techno gadgetry

*www.globalchange.com* – future trends on anything

*www.internetworldstats.com* – statistics on internet use.

# Chapter 19
## Email

Fig. 19.1

Email, short for electronic mail, is a way of sending messages over an electronic network like the internet. In fact it predates the internet and was actually an important tool in its development. With the growth of the internet, email has become one of the most popular forms of communication.

Today we can send an email message to anyone in the world who has an email address without worrying about handwriting, letterheads, printing, envelopes, stamps or going to the post office, and it will usually arrive within seconds or minutes. We can save it and send it later, and we can check our email box whenever we want. Email has obvious advantages over other forms of distance communication: cheaper than a phone call, faster than the postal service ('snail mail') and more efficient than a fax. This makes it very appealing and essential for any business.

Email is not a secure way of communicating. It is possible for someone to intercept it en route to its destination. It is like sending a postcard and therefore we should treat it similarly.

Email accounts can be hacked, so always use a strong email password and change it regularly. Some email applications offer extra security options to prevent hacking.

# ▶ Using Email

## Checking for new mail

Log on to your email account and check the **Inbox**, **Mail** or **Check Mail** (depending on the email program you use) to read any new emails received.

# ▶ Sending

To write an email to someone click on *Create Mail*, *New Message* or *New Mail* and a mail window will appear.

There are two main sections to an email: header and body. The header consists of the following:

*To:*  Write the recipient's address in here. This must be *exactly* right, otherwise it will not reach its destination.

*Cc:*  This stands for 'carbon copy' for sending the message to more than one person. Separate each address with a comma or semi-colon.

*Bcc:*  Blind carbon copy, for more addresses which will remain invisible to all recipients.

*Subject:*  Type in a subject keyword or phrase here to let the recipients know what the message is about.

The body of the email is where you type your message. When you've finished click *Send*.

# ❱ Replying

It is good to reply to emails as promptly as possible. Since it is such a fast method of communicating, there should be no excuse for not replying quickly. Even one line acknowledging receipt of a mail is enough. When replying, just click on *Reply* and a box with the original message opens and you can type your new message into it. After composing the new message, click on the *Send* button. The *Reply to All* option will send the message to everyone who received the original message, if there was more than one recipient.

# ❱ Forwarding

To forward a message to someone else, click on *Forward*: the message is copied into a new mail and you just fill in the name of the new recipient. One problem with forwards is that you might be exposing someone's private email addresses to others without their consent. To avoid this, delete the original sender's email address.

# ❱ Attachments

The attachment facility enables us to send pictures, word-processed documents, spreadsheets, scanned images and even programs by attaching any of these to an email we are sending. Lengthy documents can take a long time to send. Many computer viruses can be transmitted via attachments, so *never open an attachment from someone you do not trust or know*. If it is infected it could cause serious damage to your computer. We know we have received an attachment when a paper clip appears beside the message in the *Inbox*. If you are unsure, save the attached file to a disk and run a virus check on it.

To send an attachment, click on *Attachment*, *Attach*, or *Browse* next to the attachment box and, from the window, click on the file you want to send. Click *Attach* or *Open* and it will return you to your email with the file attached. You might have to click *OK* to return to your email. Then send the email as normal.

# ❱ Address Book/Contacts

At first email addresses seem to be very long and difficult to remember, but when you get used to them they become easier to recall. As you collect email addresses you can store them in your address book/contacts folder.

# ▶ Email Etiquette

Due to its speed, email is less formal than normal mail, and messages are written, like texts, in a mix of spoken and written communication styles. Keep messages short and concise, avoid writing messages in capital letters (which is the same as shouting) and never use sarcasm. Sending offensive or abusive messages is called *flaming*.

One way of adding tone or expression to emails is by using emoticons (emotional icons) which use a combination of punctuation marks to create sideways-on faces. To some they are cute, to others plain irritating. Here are some examples:

- ▶ :-) smile
- ▶ :-( frown
- ▶ :-D laughter
- ▶ :'-( crying

- ▶ ;-) wink
- ▶ :-o shock
- ▶ o:-) angel
- ▶ }:-> devil

- ▶ :8) pig
- ▶ :-X I'll say nothing
- ▶ X-) I see nothing

# ▶ Business/Formal Email

The normal rules of letter writing do not apply to email. So how do we write a formal email, say as a business communication or as a job application? There are no fixed rules here, and very often the style is still informal and chatty. The sender's address and the date will automatically be sent with the mail and the sender writes the subject in the subject box. However, whereas people seldom start an email with the traditional 'Dear Sir' or finish with 'Yours faithfully', we cannot begin a job application with 'Hi John'. The current standards are 'Dear' or 'Hello' followed by a name (Mr/Ms etc.), or just the name on its own, and the close is 'Regards' or 'Best regards' followed by the sender's full name. You might receive a reply in a far more informal tone than in the mail you sent, but it is better to err on the side of formality at the outset. Let the prospective employer or client set the tone from then on. At present, you shouldn't apply for a job by email unless it has been specifically requested.

# ▶ Email at Work

Because it is fast, efficient and inexpensive, email has become an important method of communication in the business world. Many employees spend up to two hours a day checking their emails, and for many it has resulted in information overload. This is why it is important only to send emails if they are relevant, and to keep them short and to the point.

# ◗ Spam

Spam is junk email. Because email is inexpensive, spammers send out millions of such emails a day. Some email providers use anti-spam techniques, but they are not 100 per cent effective. If you receive emails from people who have included large recipient lists, request that senders use *Bcc* instead of *To* or *Cc* so that your address remains unseen.

# ◗ Phishing

Email pretending to be from your bank, email provider or other organisation asking for your personal details, often on fake websites, is called phishing and if you suspect this, double check the email address with the genuine one on the real website.

## Tips

- ◗ Always re-read emails before sending.
- ◗ Always check attachments for viruses before opening.
- ◗ Think about what information you send – it's as readable as a postcard.
- ◗ Avoid SHOUTING and flaming.

## ✳ Activity

This can be used for the FETAC Level 5 ICT Practical Skills Demonstration assessment.

**Use the internet to find three jobs related to your vocational area.**

1. Log on to the internet.
2. Search for three different jobs related to your own vocational area.
3. Copy and paste the details of the jobs with contact details and the URLs into a Word document.
4. Type '(Your vocational area/course title) Jobs', e.g. 'Childcare Jobs', at the top of the document and your name in full at the bottom.
5. Edit the document to make it as neat and legible as possible.
6. Save the document as '(Your vocational area/course title) Jobs'.

7.  Print one copy of the page.
8.  Log in to your email account.
9.  Write an email to a friend saying that you have found three possible jobs and asking them what they think.
10. Sign your full name at the end of the message.
11. Attach the '(Your vocational area/course title) Jobs' document to your email.
12. Type '(Your vocational area/course title) Jobs' in the subject box.
13. Print one copy of the email.
14. Send the email.
15. When you receive the reply, print one copy.

## Discussion

1.  What advantages and disadvantages have you experienced with email?
2.  What suggestions and recommendations would you give to others using email?

## Chapter Review

1.  What are the key components of email etiquette?
2.  What are the main advantages and disadvantages of email at work?

# Chapter 20
## Legislation

With the increased use of communications technologies, new legislation has been put in place and old laws updated to regulate how they are used. This chapter looks at the key legislation in Ireland that relates to CT.

# ▶ Data Protection

The Data Protection Acts 1988 and 2003 ensure that personal information that is held by any organisation is kept private and secure. An individual has the right to data protection when her details are held on a computer, on paper, on audio, video or photograph. A data controller is an individual or organisation such as a media professional, bank, insurance company or employer that keeps personal data about an individual.

Under the Acts, data controllers are obliged to:
▶ Obtain and process the data fairly
▶ Keep it only for one or more specified purposes
▶ Process it only for the purpose(s) for which it was obtained
▶ Keep it safe and secure
▶ Keep it accurate and up-to-date

- Make sure it is adequate, relevant and not excessive
- Keep it only for as long as is required
- Supply a copy of the data to an individual on his/her request.

Individuals have the following rights regarding their data:
- To have data used in line with the legislation
- To information about their personal details
- To have access to their personal details
- To know if their personal details are being held
- To change or remove their personal details
- To prevent use of their personal details
- To object
- To remove their details from a direct marketing list
- To freedom from automated decision-making
- To refuse direct marketing calls or mail.

For more information visit *www.dataprotection.ie*.

# Electronic Communications Regulations

In 2011, new regulations came in to comply with EU data protection requirements with regard to electronic communications. Under the regulations, telecommunications companies and internet service providers must notify the Data Protection Commissioner of any breach of personal data security as well as notifying the individual concerned if the breach will affect their privacy.

Internet users now have the option to refuse cookies from websites that track their online behaviour. Cookies are small files that are downloaded onto a user's computer or mobile device when accessing certain websites, usually to record the user's online activities for the purpose of marketing. Websites that use cookies must now clearly display this fact to users.

The regulations now make it an offense for companies to make phone calls for marketing purposes without prior consent of the receiver of the call.

# Freedom of Information

Under the Freedom of Information Acts 1998 and 2003, members of the public have a legal right to official information held by certain public bodies and government departments. Public bodies are entitled to charge a fee for the search and retrieval of the information requested. In 2013 a new FOI Bill was published and at the time of writing, it is still to be enacted. For further up-to-date information go to *http://foi.gov.ie*

# ▶ Defamation

The Defamation Act 2009 protects individuals from having their reputation damaged by the publication of false statements. A defamatory statement is defined as a 'statement that tends to injure a person's reputation in the eyes of reasonable members of society'. The law generally affects publications such as newspapers, which may be sued if found in breach of the law. With increased use of social media sites and internet blogs, there has been a rise in the number of online defamation cases. Such defamation can be in the form of text, images, sound recordings or video.

The right to one's good name or reputation is protected by the Irish constitution, and a damaged reputation can lead to difficulties that could negatively affect an individual's family and working life.

Claims for defamation can be made to clear one's good name or to seek damages as compensation. They can be expensive, requiring a solicitor, evidence and proof that damage has actually been caused.

For more information go to *www.defamationireland.com*

# ▶ Copyright

The Copyright and Related Rights Act 2000 protects certain works from being exploited without the permission of the creator of the work. Exploitation refers to copying, distribution, making available to the public, lending, renting, translating, arranging or adapting the work. These restrictions enable the creator to charge a fee to reproduce the work. Works include:

- ▶ Literature, music, art and drama
- ▶ Film, sound recordings and broadcasts
- ▶ Computer software
- ▶ Performances.

*Fig. 20.1*

Exceptions to copyright law can include:

▶ Fair dealing, such as when a small amount of the work is used for purposes of research or review
▶ Education, such as a small passage of text used in an exam or in a school anthology
▶ Libraries, which can have limited rights to copy under certain conditions.

Copyright is automatic and occurs as soon as a work has been created. Proof of creation, which might be needed in an action for infringement, can be achieved by the creator posting the work to himself by registered post and keeping the envelope sealed. This shows that the work was created before the stamp date.

The use of the internet for file sharing has resulted in many users violating copyright laws if they don't have the creator's permission.

For more information, visit the Copyright Association of Ireland website: *http://www.cai.ie.*

# ▶ Health and Safety

Reference to this legislation is required for the FETAC Level 5 Structured Report (see Chapter 14). Under the Safety, Health and Welfare at Work Act 2005, both employers and employees have a responsibility to ensure that the workplace is kept free from hazards and dangers.

## Employer's Duties

▶ Manage and conduct all work activities so as to ensure as reasonably as practicable the safety, health and welfare of people at work.
▶ Design, provide and maintain a safe place of work with safe access and exit and uses safe plant and equipment.
▶ Provide information, instruction, training and supervision regarding safety and health to employees.
▶ Provide and maintain welfare facilities for employees at the workplace.
▶ Prevent risks to others at the workplace such as visitors, customers, suppliers and sales representatives.
▶ Have plans in place for emergencies.

## Employee's Duties

▶ Comply with relevant laws and protect their own safety and health as well the safety and health of anyone who may be affected by their work.
▶ Ensure that they are not under any intoxicant that might endanger themselves or others while at work.
▶ Co-operate with their employer regarding safety, health and welfare at work.
▶ Use correctly any item provided for protection.
▶ Participate in safety and health training offered by their employer.

▶ Report any dangerous situations, practices or defects that might endanger a person's safety, health or welfare.
▶ Refrain from any improper conduct that could endanger their safety or health or that of anyone else.

## Employers are also required to produce:

1. A risk assessment which:
▶ Identifies any hazards in the workplace
▶ Assesses the risks arising from such hazards
▶ Identifies the steps to be taken to deal with any risks at the workplace.

2. A safety statement which:
▶ Is based on the risk assessment
▶ Contains details of people in the workforce who are responsible for safety issues
▶ Is made available to employees
▶ Should be reviewed by employers on a regular basis.

## Visual Display Units

Irish health and safety legislation also makes provisions for the safe use of computers under the regulation 'Display Screen Equipment' or visual display units (VDUs). Under the regulation, employers have a responsibility to:
▶ Ensure the use of the equipment is not a source of risk for the employee.
▶ Evaluate the safety and health conditions of the workstation in particular with regard to eyesight, physical difficulties and mental stress.
▶ Inform the employee about any risks associated with work at VDUs.
▶ Provide any necessary training to employees who are to work at VDUs.
▶ Carry out further analysis of a workstation if any new equipment or technology is introduced.
▶ Inform employees of their entitlement to an eye test before work at a VDU and at regular intervals thereafter.

Employers should plan the activities of the employees to ensure that:
▶ Work at VDUs is periodically interrupted by breaks or changes of activity that reduce work at display screens.
▶ Rest breaks or changes in work patterns should be taken before fatigue sets in.
▶ Employees should not sit in the same position for long periods.
▶ Short frequent breaks are preferable to longer breaks taken occasionally.
▶ Breaks should be taken away from the VDU.
▶ No single continuous period of work at a VDU should, in general, last for more than one hour.

Further information is contained in Schedule 4, Regulation 72, 'Minimum Requirements for all Display Screen Equipment' of the Guide to the Safety, Health and Welfare at Work (General Application) Regulations 2007. These include regulations concerning:

▶ Display screen
▶ Keyboard
▶ Work desk or work surface
▶ Work chair
▶ Space requirements
▶ Lighting
▶ Reflections and glare
▶ Radiation
▶ Noise
▶ Heat
▶ Humidity
▶ Employee/computer interface.

Fig. 20.2

For more information visit the website of the Health and Safety Authority (*www.hsa.ie*). See also the following information on the Citizens Information website: *http://www.citizens information.ie/en/employment/employment_rights_and_conditions/health_and_safety/ health_safety_work.html*

## Chapter Review

1. Outline the main features of each of the following:
   ▶ Data Protection
   ▶ Electronic Communications Regulations
   ▶ Freedom of Information
   ▶ Defamation
   ▶ Copyright
   ▶ Health and Safety.

# Appendix 1

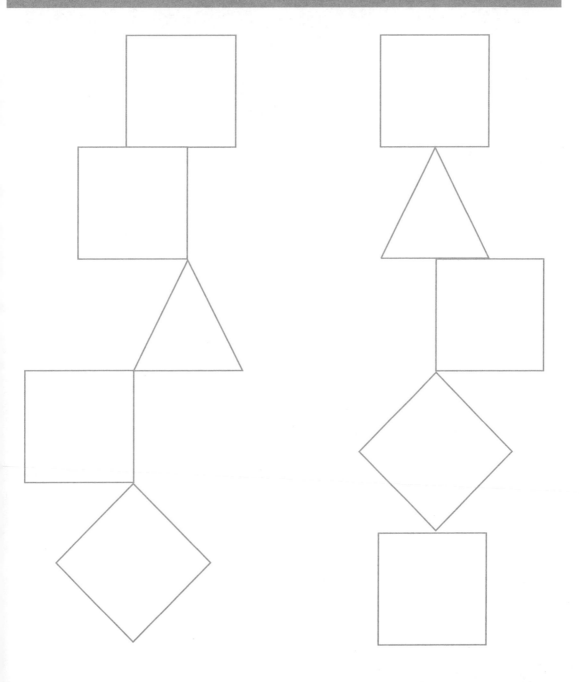

# Appendix 2

| Learning Outcome | Chapter(s) |
|---|---|
| 1. Analyse a range of current issues in communications and information technology | 15, 16, 17, 18, 19, 20 |
| 2. Summarise in practical terms the elements of legislation that must be observed in a personal and/or work context, to include health, safety and welfare at work and communications-related legislation | 20 |
| 3. Use appropriate nonverbal and visual communication in personal- and work-related settings, to include one-to-one, in a group/team, and in formal and informal interaction | 5, 6, 8, 9 |
| 4. Demonstrate verbal skills appropriate to working under general direction, to include making a case and presenting a point of view in group discussion, formal meetings, interviews | 4, 5, 6, 7 |
| 5. Demonstrate listening skills appropriate to working under general direction, to include making eye contact, receiving and interpreting information, control of personal response | 3 |
| 6. Use reading techniques appropriate to a task, to include skimming, obtaining an overview, identifying key points, critical evaluation, in depth analysis | 10 |
| 7. Critique information from a range of complex written material, to include technical/vocational, personal, literary, and written and visual media texts | 10, 11 |
| 8. Research a relevant vocational topic, to include use of primary and secondary sources, acknowledgement of sources, use of enquiry techniques and methods to establish validity and reliability | 14, 18 |
| 9. Demonstrate communications styles and techniques relevant to different situations in work and leisure, to include one-to-one and group contexts in conversation, interview, oral presentation, question and answer session and for the purposes of persuading, advocacy and informing | 4, 5, 6, 7 |
| 10. Choose the appropriate communications technology to give and receive requests, instructions, suggestions, discussion and feedback in both work and leisure, to include a rationale for choosing one technology over another in different contexts and for different messages. | 15, 16, 17, 18, 19 |

# Bibliography

Agostini, Franco, *Visual Games*, London: Macdonald & Co. 1988.

Barry, Anne Marie Seward, *Visual Intelligence. Perception, Image and Manipulation in Visual Communication*, Albany: State University of New York 1997.

Beck, Andrew, Peter Bennett and Peter Wall, *Communication Studies: The Essential Resource*, London and New York: Routledge 2004.

Beddows, Christopher, *Communication Pack*, Maidenhead, Berks: McGraw-Hill 1991.

Briggs, Beatrice, *Introduction to Consensus*, Morelos, Mexico: 2000.

Bryson, Bill, *Mother Tongue: the English Language*, London: Penguin 1990.

Buckley, Peter, and Duncan Clark, *The Rough Guide to the Internet*, London and New York: Rough Guides Ltd 2009.

*The Complete Letter Writer*, Foulsham: Berkshire 1998.

Chalker, Sylvia, and Edmund Weiner, *The Oxford Dictionary of English Grammar*, Oxford: Oxford University Press 1998.

Crystal, David, *Txtng, the gr8 db8*, Oxford: Oxford University Press 2008.

Cuddy, Amy, *Your Body Language Shapes Who You Are* [Online], http://www.ted.com/talks/amy_cuddy_your_body_language_shapes_who_you_are.html, 29 October 2013.

Daunt, Stephen, *Communication Skills*, Dublin: Gill & Macmillan 1996.

Department of Justice, Equality and Law Reform, *Illegal and Harmful Use of the Internet. First Report of the Working Group*, Dublin: The Stationery Office 1998.

Dimbleby, Richard, and Graeme Burton, *More Than Words. An Introduction to Communication*, London: Routledge 2007.

Doherty-Sneddon, Gwyneth, *The Great Baby Signing Debate, The Psychologist,* Volume 21, Part 4, April 2008, [Online], http://www.thepsychologist.org.uk/archive/archive_home.cfm/ volumeID_21-editionID_159-ArticleID_1330-getfile_getPDF/thepsychologist/0408 doherty.pdf, 29 October 2013.

EurekAlert, *Genetically Speaking, Race Doesn't Exist in Humans*, 1998 [Online], *http://www.urekalert.org/pub_releases/1998-10/WUiS-GSRD-071098.php*, 11 September 2009.

Forsyth, Patrick, *30 Minutes Before a Presentation*, London: Kogan Page 1997.

Foy, Geoffrey, *Text Production with Microsoft Word*, Dublin: Gill & Macmillan 2009.

General Assembly of the United Nations, *The Universal Declaration of Human Rights* [Online], *http://www.un.org/en/documents/udhr/*, 11 September 2009.

Harkin, James, *Cyburbia, The Dangerous Idea That's Changing How we Live and Who we Are*, London: Little, Brown 2009.

Hurst, Bernice, *The Handbook of Communication Skills*, London: Kogan Page 1996.

Irish Traveller Movement [Online], *http://www.itmtrav.ie/citizentrav.html*, 11 September 2009.

Janner, Greville, *Janner's Complete Letter Writer*, London: Business Books Ltd 1983.

Lester, Paul Martin, *Visual Communication: Images with Messages*, Belmont, California: Wadsworth/Thomson Learning 2000.

McClave, Henry, *Communication for Business*, Dublin: Gill & Macmillan 2008.

McCroskey, James C., *An Introduction to Rhetorical Communication*, Massachusetts: Allyn and Bacon 2001.

*Microsoft Encarta '98 Encyclopedia*, Microsoft Corporation 1993–1997.

Morgan, John, and Peter Welton, *See What I Mean. An Introduction to Visual Communication*, London: Edward Arnold 1986.

Morris, Desmond, *Manwatching*, London: Triad 1978.

Parkinson, Mike, *The Power of Visual Communication, Billion Dollar Graphics*, [Online], http://www.billiondollargraphics.com/infographics.htm, 29 October 2013.

Pinker, Stephen, *The Language Instinct*, London: Penguin 1994.

PR Web, *BBC Worldwide Survey Reveals Irish People's Appetite for Digital News Consumption*, [Online] http://www.prweb.com/releases/2012/6/prweb9607635.htm, 23 October 2013.

Purves, Bryan, *Information Graphics*, Cheltenham: Stanley Thornes 1987.

Raha, Maria, Angel, 1999 [Online], *http://www.storybytes.com/view-stories/2000/angel.html*, 11 September 2009.

Richards, Jack C., *Teaching Listening and Speaking, From Theory to Practice*, New York: Cambridge University Press 2008.

Richardson, Will, *Blogs, Wikis, Podcasts and Other Powerful Web Tools for Classrooms*, London: Sage 2009.

Rivers, Denis, 1997–2008, *The Seven Challenges Workbook, A Guide to Cooperative Communication Skills for Success at Home and at Work* [Online], *http://www.new conversations.net/w7chal2.htm*, 11 September 2009.

Rosenberg, Marshall B., *Nonviolent Communication, A Language of Life*, Encinitas, California: Puddledancer Press 2005.

Scher, Anna, and Charles Verrall, *100 + Ideas for Drama*, Oxford: Heinemann Educational 1975.

Scott, John F., and Catherine Fox, *English and Communications for Business Studies*, Dublin: Gill & Macmillan 2005.

Seely, John, *Dramakit*, Oxford: Oxford University Press 1977.

Stanton, Nicky, *Mastering Communication*, London: Macmillan 1990.

Swann, Alan, *Communicating with Rough Visuals*, Oxford: Phaidon Press 1989.

Tovey, Hilary, and Perry Share, *A Sociology of Ireland*, Dublin: Gill & Macmillan, 2003.

Truss, Lynn, *Eats, Shoots & Leaves*, London: Profile Books Ltd 2003.

Van Rooij, A. J., *Online Video Game Addiction. Exploring A New Phenomenon*, [PhD Thesis], Rotterdam, The Netherlands: Erasmus University Rotterdam 2011.

Weiner, E. S. C., and Andrew Delahunty, *The Oxford Guide to English Usage*, Oxford: Oxford University Press 1994.

Winser, Jill (Ed.), *Future Talk. BT, Millennium Project. A Special Millennium Initiative*, London: Forward Publishing 2000.

Wood, Julia T., *Communication in our Lives*, Stamford, CT: Wadsworth, Thomson Learning 2000.

# Picture Credits

For permission to reproduce photographs, the author and publisher gratefully acknowledge the following:

© Alamy: 19TL, 19TCL, 19TCR, 19BC, 19BR, 97, 104BL, 241B, 242, 261; © Brick: 9, 129T, 129B, 141, 154; © Facebook: 131 (b), 254; © Firefox: 131 (e); © Getty Images: 104TL, 110L, 110R; © Google: 250; © Kris Wilson/Cyanide and Happiness: 113; Library of Congress Prints and Photographs Division: 15; © McDonalds: 131 (a); © Mercedes-Benz: 131 (c); © Mozilla: 248; © NASA: 125; © PayPal: 257B; © Press Association: 24; © Rex Features: 104TR; © Shutterstock: 3, 18, 19TC, 19TR, 19BL, 48, 61, 72, 87, 104BR, 107TL, 107TC, 107TR, 107BL, 107BCL, 107BCR, 107BR, 108, 111L, 111C, 111R, 115R, 126, 130 (b-d, f-o), 143, 235, 236B, 257T, 258, 259, 260, 271, 274; © Shutterstock/ Frank Gaertner: 241T; © Shutterstock/Laszlo Szirtesi: 115L; © Shutterstock/Tanjala Gica: 236T; ©Tom Mathews: 263; © Twitter: 131 (d); Wikimedia: 130 (a, e, p); Courtesy of Concerto Brussels: 23; Courtesy of the Irish Traveller Movement: 22; Courtesy of Torstar: 237.

The author and publisher have made every effort to trace all copyright holders, but if any has been inadvertently overlooked we would be pleased to make the necessary arrangement at the first opportunity.